Kinnickinnic

Stories of a River and Its Insect Life

Clarke Garry

*A portion of the proceeds from this collection supports
the Kiap-TU-Wish Chapter of Trout Unlimited
and the Kinnickinnic River Land Trust
in their efforts to conserve, restore, and
protect the Kinnickinnic River.*

ISBN-13: 978-1548201562
ISBN-10: 1548201561

Photograph prefacing *Looking and Learning* and author photo © Charles Rader;
photograph prefacing *Postscript* courtesy of University of Wisconsin-River
Falls Archives and Area Research Center; all other photographs and drawings
© Clarke Garry.

Designed, printed, and distributed by Romeii, LLC.
Visit our website at ebooks.romeii.com

For Susan and Dana,
and in memory of Tom Helgeson

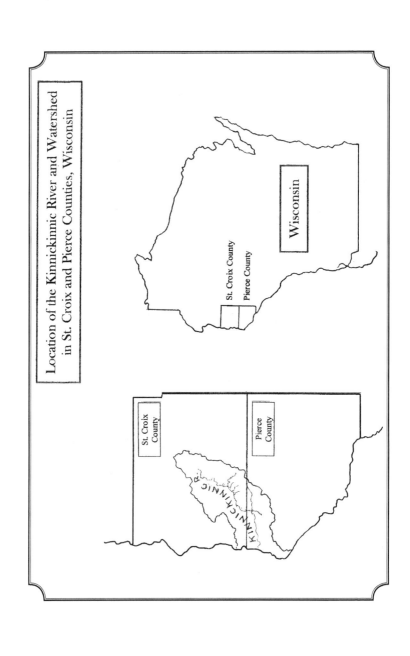

Location of the Kinnickinnic River and Watershed in St. Croix and Pierce Counties, Wisconsin

Wisconsin

St. Croix County

Pierce County

St. Croix County

Pierce County

KINNICKINNIC

CONTENTS

PART III

PART IV

PREFACE

I n the far reaches of western Wisconsin an uncommon river descends through an ancient valley. Its flow begins amid rolling hills where big bluestem prairie once flourished. It passes through a town built on flat terrain, long ago the bottom of an ocean and later a glacial lake. Ultimately it drops into a rocky gorge with steep wooded slopes and weathered dolostone bluffs, a setting with elements of historic oak savanna. This is the Kinnickinnic (kih-NIK-kih-nik) River, the Kinni (KIN-ee) as it's known to locals and admirers. In pre-settlement days, water cascaded over stone ledges where dams now impede the river's natural flow. Indeed, the original nonnative resident, Joel Foster, was attracted to the area in 1848 after hearing a stranger in a bar describing "the damnedest prettiest falls you ever seen."

The Kinnickinnic is a model coldwater river, its thermal regime and mineral content a result of its origins in rocky subterranean spaces. This is a river brought to life by omnipresent seeps and springs. Here surfacing groundwater supports optimal temperature conditions for cold-adapted fish and invertebrate life. One may hike to see the location where Kinni surface water starts to flow, but they should appreciate the fact that the river has countless "headwaters" that contribute to its volume and physical characteristics.

Several named tributaries and many unnamed ones join the twenty-three-mile Kinni main stem before it converges with the St. Croix River. In these waters fish—and the organisms on which they feed—abound. Within the Kinnickinnic watershed fifty river and creek miles are of the highest classification given to Wisconsin trout streams. With considerable attentiveness and action on the part of state agencies, organizations, and the public, this incomparable river runs rich in natural history.

Living and working a short distance from this moving water, I couldn't escape its pull. I took pleasure in hiking and running the trails along its banks, canoeing through its easy rapids, and casting a fly while standing in its current. I enjoyed being near the river, watching water weaving through riffles and slowing to imperceptible movement in quiet pools. The Kinnickinnic valley was a place I could experience the meditative effect of running water, away from the clamor of daily life.

Then I began to focus my attention beneath the surface. While engaging my students at the University of Wisconsin-River Falls in river insect projects, I looked for references to confirm what I was seeing as prevalent Kinni species. I didn't find any prior technical invertebrate records until I read of a series of biotic indices done by the Wisconsin Department of Natural Resources. These detailed insects and crustaceans that live specifically in riffles. This was a good start. Determining the inhabitants of other river habitats would be up to me.

Over time, my intermittent collections evolved into longer-term projects. The broadest in scope, carried out through calendar year 2001, was designed to determine what insects and crustaceans were living in the river by following a multifaceted sampling protocol. The plan incorporated multiple river sites, diverse habitats, and four seasons. Specimens were collected, identified, and ultimately archived at the Department of Biology, UWRF. The resulting list of invertebrates supported my coursework, answered some of my most fundamental questions, and furthered documentation of species inhabiting the river. The essays in this compilation are based primarily on data assembled from field work done in 2001 with additional results from a similar project, involving fewer samples, in 1999.

As projects progressed, I enjoyed sharing my findings at gatherings of interested people, including those in the conservation and fly fishing communities. It was during this time that I first considered writing narrative accounts of my stream experiences. I planned to structure them around the most common Kinnickinnic insect and crustacean species I was encountering through routine sampling. I would attempt to convey their roles and, therefore, their importance in this productive aquatic ecosystem. Because the stories would be written for a general audience and not in the form of a scientific report or publication, I could insert thoughts about my obvious attraction to, and love of studying, the intricacies of this special place.

Earlier versions of some of the included essays appeared in the entomology column of *Midwest Fly Fishing*. The late Tom Helgeson, editor and publisher of the magazine, invited me to contribute stories about insects and crustaceans living in Midwestern waters. When I expressed to Tom my limited background regarding fly fishing, he explained that he was interested in content that would inform readers about aquatic life, particularly the invertebrates with which I was familiar. Tom loved rivers. He was a prominent advocate of environmental stewardship and he respected the science that contributes to that cause. I am forever appreciative of the opportunity Tom gave me to write about river life.

There is inspiration to be found for exploration close to home. Robert Macfarlane, for example, tells of Scottish explorer Martin Martin who wrote in 1698, "… men have travelled far in search of foreign plants and animals, and continued strangers to the productions of their own climate." Macfarlane also shares the wisdom of his mentor and friend Roger Deakin who suggested that wildness is everywhere, that we just need to stop long enough to look around. Macfarlane called Deakin an explorer of the country of the nearby, one who was amazed by what he saw close at hand. Beyond an appreciation of local discovery, these authors, including Robert Macfarlane and others like Barry Lopez, John Muir, and Sigurd Olson demonstrate how place-writing can communicate with descriptive precision on the smallest of scales in the vastness of landscapes.

An intriguing assortment of invertebrate creatures thrives in the cold water of the Kinnickinnic River. Many of these animals never leave this environment, spending their entire existence beneath the surface, out of sight. Others, like midges, caddisflies, and mayflies, take to the air briefly upon emergence, and live the other ninety-nine-plus percent of their lives unseen below the surface.

People may be indifferent or incurious about these organisms for any number of reasons, including not knowing they are there, not readily seeing them, or not being quite sure *how* to see them. For those wanting to learn more there are many ways to address the "invisibility" issue.

Gaining familiarity with river invertebrates and their habitats can be a casual pursuit or the quest of a lifetime. It is my hope that these narratives provide assistance in either approach. If I have answered some questions about life in the Kinnickinnic and stimulated thinking about the exceptionality of the place in which these organisms live, I will have achieved my goal.

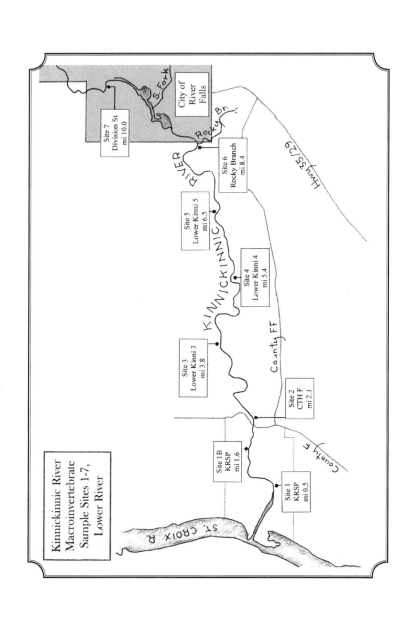

Kinnickinnic River Macroinvertebrate Sample Sites 1-7, Lower River

Site 7 Division St mi 10.0

City of River Falls

S. Fork

Rocky Br.

Site 6 Rocky Branch mi 8.4

RIVER

Hwy 35/29

Site 5 Lower Kinni 5 mi 6.5

KINNICKINNIC

Site 4 Lower Kinni 4 mi 5.4

County FF

Site 3 Lower Kinni 3 mi 3.8

Site 2 CTH F mi 2.1

Site 1B KRSP mi 1.6

County F

Site 1 KRSP mi 0.5

ST. CROIX R.

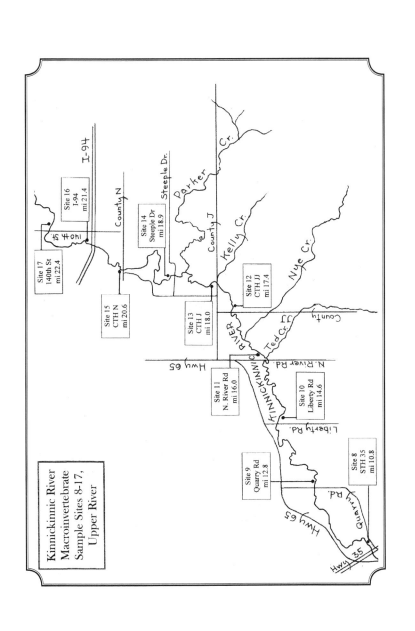

Kinnickinnic River
Macroinvertebrate
Sample Sites 8-17,
Upper River

Site 17
140th St
mi 22.4

Site 16
I-94
mi 21.4

I-94

County N

Steeple Dr.

Site 14
Steeple Dr
mi 18.9

Site 15
CTH N
mi 20.6

Parter Cr.

Site 13
CTH J
mi 18.0

County J

Kelly Cr.

Site 12
CTH JJ
mi 17.4

Nue Cr.

County JJ

RIVER

Hwy 65

Ted Cr.

N. River Rd

Site 11
N. River Rd
mi 16.0

KINNICKINNIC

Site 10
Liberty Rd
mi 14.6

Liberty Rd

Site 9
Quarry Rd
mi 12.8

Site 8
STH 35
mi 10.8

Hwy 65

Quarry Rd

Hwy 35

Part 1

In the middle of every difficulty lies opportunity.

—Albert Einstein

Lower Kinnickinnic River in Kinnickinnic River State Park

DAY ONE

On the first day of the new year, 2001, I stopped by the lab to pick up collecting gear and headed for the river. I was launching a project designed to establish an insect and crustacean species list for the Kinnickinnic River in western Wisconsin. At the same time I hoped to answer a number of questions I had about these creatures. I could work toward both goals by sampling multiple river habitats and locations through a calendar year. After several months of planning and anticipation, I couldn't have been more excited for this first collection and the data set it would initiate. Daylight would be limited, the occasion coming about a week after the winter solstice, and the forecast was for temperatures in the teens, but there wasn't anything that was going to dampen my eagerness to be in the river on this day.

My destination was a site in Kinnickinnic River State Park, about a half mile upstream from the confluence of the Kinnickinnic with the St. Croix River. Driving into the park I saw no other vehicles or visitors. The lot where I parked my van was snow-covered and untracked. Across this open prairie high above the converging rivers the wind crossed unimpeded. I looked forward to the shelter of the valley, to be down in the woods at river level, out of the wind.

Most of my gear was stowed in a trapper-style pack, a basket woven from ash strips with shoulder straps attached, the perfect container for river work because the weave allows sand and water to find a way out. In it I carried river maps, GPS, digital thermometer, specimen jars, clipboard with data recording forms, water in an insulated bottle, a thermos of coffee, and waders. Expecting that some of my access would be off-trail, I bungee-corded snowshoes onto the outside of the basket. I swung the pack onto my back and hand carried an aquatic net and sorting tray. The trail started in grassland, soon entered woods of oak, birch, and pine, and ultimately led to river-bottom lowland. For the last leg of the hike I strapped on the snowshoes to cross a stretch of trackless snow, and arrived at the riverbank.

When I started into the valley, the sun was near its highest point of the day, mid-winter bright, but notably absent of warmth. Its light filled the canyon and flashed off the water surface. I was at first surprised, and then encouraged, to see the river so open, having anticipated more ice this time of year. I had much to learn about river water temperatures and the variables that were preventing ice formation.

At the sample site I leveled a spot in the snow, set down my gear, and donned my waders. I looked around, taking in the serenity and unspoiled nature of the valley. I thought about the living things that are visible here during any other season. I could only imagine green leaves and the sounds of songbirds. So much was now dormant or had migrated away. A few raucous crows and determined woodpeckers communicated their presence. Tracks recorded recent movement of cottontails and fox. And close by, but hidden from view, significant additional animal activity occurred. Short-tailed shrews and deer mice were navigating under the snow while scuds and common stoneflies searched for food in their own versions of unrevealed living spaces.

The first order of business at the site was to look at river structure, distinguishing features such as riffles and pools that would predictably support different types of aquatic insect life. Once I was in the water, moving from place to place, it was possible to check for the variety of materials composing the streambed: rocky, mineral-based features from boulders to silt deposits versus organic substrates, like aquatic vegetation, woody debris, and accumulated leaves. Determining where individual subsamples should be taken, at this stage of the visit, was a strategy to ensure diversity and balance in the habitat types to be sampled.

I was using the standard tool for aquatic insect collecting, the D-net, that catches debris and living things when bottom substrates are disturbed just up current from where it is placed. The entire netted mix is transferred to a sorting tray that allows crawling, swimming, and wriggling organisms to be easily seen and captured. Each netting effort of approximately two minutes comprised a subsample. This was followed by extracting as many specimens as possible from the debris in ten minutes. Ten subsamples would complete a full site sample. In this way, I could obtain representation of up to ten habitats in approximately two hours. I was using a new sampling approach, performing simple procedures that would contribute to a larger objective. To say that I was elated to be in this place, at this season, seeing these living things coming from their respective underwater habitations, would be an understatement.

While I was focused on acquiring specimens, the sun had disappeared over the valley ridge, casting the river in blue shadow. Air temperature reflected the change, falling into the single digits. For something over an hour I was standing in thirty-eight degree water in summer waders. Now, becoming aware of the situation, I realized I was uncomfortably chilled, possibly on the verge of being dangerously cold. The prospect of warming up—by snowshoeing out—became an increasingly welcome thought. I finished gathering the last subsample, exchanged my waders for boots, packed up gear, strapped on snowshoes again, and was glad to be in motion. I reached my van just in time to see the sun disappearing behind the clouds over the western horizon.

Back at the lab, I poured over the catch specimen-by-specimen, counting those I recognized and identifying unfamiliar ones with a neophyte's fervor. Initial observations of nearly two hundred specimens suggested the project was off to a successful start. The sample showed that this section of the river supported a variety of insects and crustaceans, many of which had an established association with high quality water. These included larvae of mayflies, stoneflies, caddisflies, and crane flies. One particularly curious find was the single larva of a distinctive burrowing mayfly, *Hexagenia limbata*. I couldn't have known then that this was a species I would collect only one other time during the upcoming year.

That evening I worked through my notes, thinking about the day's experience, and adding ideas for future sampling. I was satisfied the approach I put in motion on this first day would yield useful results in the different locations and seasonal circumstances I might encounter through the year. Each sample held the promise of capturing a unique moment in time, recording the kinds, life stages, and locations of resident Kinni organisms. I thought of the different scales at which I was working, from the small aquatic creatures to the greater river setting, and how they connected with each other. I recognized my good fortune to experience this extraordinary environment in full winter conditions, quietly nurturing an unseen and, at first look, thriving aquatic community.

Headwaters area, Kinnickinnic River

HEADWATERS

One warm spring day I crossed the bridge over a small version of the Kinnickinnic and pulled off the road to park under the shade of an immense cottonwood. I gathered up sampling gear and found a well-worn path leading down to the water at the near end of the bridge. The first steps revealed a disturbing sight. Just over the railing the slope was desecrated with cans, bottles, tangled clothing, and broken furniture, someone's idea of a dump site. I was annoyed by this display of indifference to an otherwise unspoiled natural setting, but my frame of mind changed when I reached the river and realized what a unique place this was.

Here, less than a mile north of where the river passes under Interstate 94, would be my most upstream sampling location, Site 17 (upper river map). Experiencing this segment of stream would be memorable, not only because of what I would find here, but because this is where the river begins its productive life.

I was returning to a location I had marked on my map, a small pool and braided river section not far from the upstream end of an established Wisconsin DNR habitat evaluation station. For now I was heading in the approximate direction of the site, passing through undergrowth in the lowland woods on the north side of the river. Kicking through dry leaves under box elder trees, I was focused on what I might find living in the water.

On an earlier visit, I followed the dwindling river upstream until it completely lost its identity in surrounding wetland—a spring-fed area of grasses, sedges, and cattails. Until that day, I was under the impression that the river originated at Casey Lake, over eight miles to the northeast, the source I perceived from a topographic map. But in reality, after a brief hike, I was standing where the river starts to visibly flow. I marveled at its small size and thought about what it would become in just a few miles.

Back at the sampling station the small stream ran cold and unimaginably clear. Here the gradient is low and the water moves slowly. A couple of pools hold water that requires a close look to make sure it is not standing still. Bottom substrates are primarily fine, but some gravels and cobble-sized rocks are also present. Out of the trees and onto the grassy stream bank, I reach what will become my regular starting place for sampling. The location has an enclosed feel to it, very different from the openness of lower portions of the river. Where I stand the nascent river flows at a rate less than ten cubic feet per second. Downstream, at the USGS gage near County Road F, it averages ten times this volume.

In spite of the small scale of this part of the river, I know trout are present in abundance. The area has a qualitative habitat rating of Good (second only to Excellent), derived from a standard assessment procedure involving multiple quantitative stream attributes. Electrofishing surveys carried out in 1996 by the Wisconsin DNR estimated the brook and brown trout populations (all ages) here, respectively, at nearly 600 and over 5,000 fish per mile.

Of all the familiar stretches of the Kinnickinnic this one is where I first learned to appreciate the significance of groundwater seepage. This early snapshot of groundwater importance rapidly grew into a full-scale panorama. Springs are the lifeblood of the Kinni. They support the continual flow of water without which its inhabitants could literally not survive. Groundwater provides the constant addition of cold water, making the river a coldwater stream. This means that necessary thermal conditions for trout and cold-adapted insects can be maintained.

We don't often see the seeps and springs that contribute to the important qualities of the Kinnickinnic, but these features occur in multitude throughout the watershed. Some of them are historic moist soil environments, like the Kinnickinnic Wet Prairie State Natural Area, while others contribute directly, and more obviously, to the river. One of the easiest to observe is the spring that creates Kelly Creek, a tributary that joins the Kinni main stem between mile points 17 and 18 near County J. The creek begins rather abruptly, and highly visibly, with an outpouring of water from an opening in exposed limestone bedrock. Kinnickinnic River Land Trust sources report this outflow at more than 700,000 gallons per day (29,000 gallons per hour). Another spring of note, unnamed and considerably less obvious than Kelly, is located just downstream from Interstate 94. From what appears as a slough attached to the river, water is added at 48,000 gallons per hour. For the Kinni, all of these are headwaters in a sense, whether they are large or small, occurring upstream or down, emerging on land or underwater. All contribute physical and chemical qualities that make the river distinctive.

We understand details concerning the survival of cold-adapted aquatic invertebrates, such as sensitive mayflies of the genus *Ephemerella*, from laboratory experiments. Work carried out under controlled conditions has shown that acute lethal temperature for *Ephemerella subvaria*, a common spring-emerging mayfly, is 70.7°F (acute lethal temperature is defined as that in which 50% of the population would die after 96 hours of exposure). By comparison, the warmest water temperature reading I recorded at this site was 55.7°F during the second week of July, when the air above was 81.1°F.

When I first began winter stream visits, I expected to contend with iced-over sampling sites. I carried my ice chisel with me for those early efforts, but almost never needed it. I was spared the work of chopping through ice because groundwater, exiting from underground at about 48°F, warms the stream during the winter and inhibits significant surface ice formation. I did, during a few very cold periods, have to deal with *frazil* (crystals of ice suspended in moving water) and *anchor ice* (cloud-like formations of frazil clinging to bottom substrate materials). Both make using an insect net underwater problematic because the crystals do not pass easily through mesh, but these were uncommon occurrences.

A large scale temperature perspective on the Kinnickinnic may provide clues to unique qualities of the river in supporting aquatic life. We know the river is kept warmer than air in winter by groundwater input and maintained cooler than air in summer by the same mechanism. What if there are subtle changes in groundwater temperature on a yearly pattern where higher groundwater temperatures occur in the winter and colder temperatures occur in the summer, with these patterns benefiting both trout and aquatic invertebrates? This is what Kent Johnson found in year-around temperature monitoring of a large spring on Pine Creek in southeast Minnesota. Johnson speculates that these opposites in temperature between winter and summer could be due to a delayed heating and cooling influence of air temperatures on underground aquifers, with interesting ecological implications.

For spring creeks such as the Kinnickinnic the relationship between water minerals and aquatic life is another important ecological feature. All levels of the food web benefit, directly or indirectly, from water containing certain dissolved minerals. What we call hard water contains calcium and magnesium, in the form of the carbonate minerals calcite and dolomite, leached from the limestone rock through which it passed on its way to the surface. Part of the benefit of the alkaline nature of these materials is the counteraction of acidity.

Fish biologists have understood for some time that a relationship exists between water-borne minerals and trout. In field studies which measured specific conductance of water to indirectly determine total dissolved solids, including calcium and magnesium compounds, the growth rate of brown trout was shown to be significantly and positively correlated with water hardness. Hard water, such as that of the Kinni, is considered to be conceptually synonymous with fertility and biological productivity.

I came to appreciate this site closest to the origin of the river for its physical, chemical, and biological features, including abundant fish populations. To those measures I was adding the names of resident insects and crustaceans. Using a protocol based on larval collections, I documented numerous examples of resident mayflies and caddisflies in my catch, but was generally unsuccessful in finding stoneflies here, with one curious exception. On a visit to this site in January, I recorded a number of well-developed specimens of the winter stonefly, *Taeniopteryx*. These larvae were approaching adult size in preparation for emergence. Because timing of their appearance is late winter or early spring, these adults are typically seen on streamside snow. In the absence of other stoneflies, it's good to find this one, not simply because it is a stonefly, but that it has a documented low tolerance to organic pollution.

I collected many of the same insects in this small river environment that I encountered previously in larger downstream river settings. These included spiny crawler mayflies (*Ephemerella excrucians*), three species of small minnow mayflies (*Baetis*), and humpless case-maker caddisflies (*Brachycentrus occidentalis*). As representatives of the orders Ephemeroptera (mayflies), Plecoptera (stoneflies), and Trichoptera (caddisflies), along with their known intolerance to organically polluted water, species in these orders are considered, with some exceptions, examples of a high quality stream.

Through a year of resampling this site I observed cold, clear, mineral-rich water giving rise to a pristine trout stream. Here, this embryonic river, largely hidden by woodland and riparian shrubs and grasses, out of sight of passers-by, begins its way through the landscape. Few people will ever see this place, imagine it, or think of its importance, choosing to fish, canoe, or hike where the stream is larger and more accessible. But this part of the Kinnickinnic has the attraction of water that is small and fresh and pure, a truly distinctive river location.

Bluffs of Prairie du Chien dolostone
above the lower Kinnickinnic River

ROCK AND WATER

One of the Kinnickinnic access trails has the capacity to shift my mental focus instantly from the surroundings of city and subdivision to the wildness of a wooded valley through which the river runs. I park my van on a neighborhood street and organize sampling gear. Between two houses is a path, a wood chip easement provided by River Falls for public use. Beyond the backyards the footpath enters the woods and begins its descent into the valley. What comes next is a unique world of rock, water, and living things, each formed and integrated with the rest by natural processes only possible with the immensity of geologic time.

Through the canopy on my side of the valley, glints of light from moving water and river noise become evident. The trail descends beside weathered limestone hinting at millions of years of history. In no time at all I am beside the river. With luck a great blue heron will be perched on a streamside snag. When it sees me, it will lift into the air with a few effortless wing beats and land, still in view, a comfortable distance away. This short hike is as much a journey of the mind as it is of the feet. I have traversed farther from the urban edge than actual measurement would suggest.

✦✦✦

No limitations are posed by the dictionary definition of the word *discovery* when stated as the act or process of discovering. It can apply just as well to a personal quest as it can to finding something out for the first time. Nothing I would do in my aquatic insect work had not been done many times before, in other places. But I could explore this system driven by an entomological viewpoint and my own kind of enthusiasm. "The real voyage of discovery consists not in seeking new landscapes, but in having new eyes," was the way French author Marcel Proust expressed it. My specific objective was to determine the insect fauna in this river by exploring its diverse habitats, but I would *see* far more than that as my projects evolved.

While carrying out routine tasks, traveling to and from sites, and collecting river samples, I asked myself questions about the larger setting and history of the river: How did these hills and valleys originate? Why does the river follow the course it does? How do flow rates, stream gradients, and substrates contribute to the nature of the river? What biological changes have occurred in and around the river through time? What impacts have people, both native and immigrant, had on the valley? The more of the river I experienced, the more I wanted to know about it. I hoped to pursue my project goals and, at the same time, begin to understand the character of the landscape in which I was working.

Descending into the Kinnickinnic gorge below River Falls is more than an imaginary journey back through geologic time. The hike down passes through the physical record of millions of years of sedimentary accumulation resulting from a succession of ancient marine environments. We are provided a view of these rock formations today because of an unimaginably large amount of material that was removed as the valley was created by water and wind at the level of individual particles.

The rock layers underlying the entire Kinni valley and composing its bluffs and walls were generated during the Ordovician Period, 490 to 450 million years ago. North America was on the earth's equator and largely covered by a vast shallow tropical sea. This is a world where erosion and deposition are the primary geological processes, give-and-take on an immense scale. Currents, wind, and storms are transporting products of erosion from their areas of origin (higher, uninundated parts of the landscape) to depositional locations in the sea in a predictable sequence: coarser sands are deposited near shore with smaller materials (finer sands, silt, and clay) accumulating further off-shore. Much further out, carbonates are precipitating to the bottom. With time each of these sediment types, through compaction and cementation process-es, produces, respectively, a characteristic type of rock: sandstone, shale, and limestone.

Our local Kinnickinnic bedrock geology is based on two major sedimentary cycles that occurred during the Ordovician. Each depositional cycle represents the classic progression of rock formation, beginning with sandstone and transitioning through shale to limestone. We find evidence of each of these oceanic cycles by close examination of exposed areas of bedrock in the valley.

In the gorge, between River Falls and the St. Croix, the river cuts through Prairie du Chien dolostone (magnesium-enriched limestone), the upper and last rock unit that formed from sedimentary accumulation during the earlier of the two marine cycles. This rock is known for its abundant stromatolites, laminated cabbage-like structures formed by oxygen-generating blue-green algae (cyanobacteria), and indicators of shallow water habitats. These first cycle inundation deposits were significantly eroded before the second cycle began.

Upstream, in the River Falls area, deposits of the second cycle are evident: St. Peter Sandstone is at the base of the bluffs; next, moving up in the sequence, is Glenwood Formation; then Platteville Formation, dolostone noted for its fossils, at the top of the bluffs. This rock holds remnants of corals, cephalopods, bryozoans, clams, snails, and trilobites.

We see quite different Kinnickinnic river qualities developed in these very different geologies. The city of River Falls sets on a fairly flat bench between the St. Peter Sandstone and the underlying Prairie du Chien dolostones. Above the city of River Falls, the softer St. Peter was easier to cut through, so the river created a wider valley there. Below the city, the river cuts through the hard dolostone of the Prairie du Chien.

The sheer depth of erosion, for example from the tops of the surrounding bluffs to the level of the St. Croix, approximately 365 feet lower in elevation, provides perspective on the extent to which the horizontal Ordovician sea bottom was cut, exposing the present-day strata. These rock layers were eroded, notably during the Ice Age (Pleistocene), with lowering sea levels. Forces generated by huge amounts of water during and after glaciation were responsible for the deep valleys we see in the region, including those of the St. Croix and Kinnickinnic Rivers.

Limestone, and its converted form, dolostone, have special biological meaning from the perspective of their origin. This rock was generated in these ancient seas, in part, because of the living things that existed in them. The fossil record in these strata provides evidence of a diverse array of animals that depended on the calcium containing compound calcite ($CaCO_3$) for production of supportive and protective shells. These can include corals, clams and snails, trilobites, and microscopic single-celled organisms called forams, short for foraminifera. Much of the sediment at the bottom of these ancient seas was the result of accumulation of skeletal fragments of these beings. Writer Robert Macfarlane, alluding to limestone deposits in the Burren area of western Ireland, refers to each hill there as a burial ground, holding the remains of more creatures than the number of people who have ever lived on Earth.

In the Upper Midwest, characteristically marked by Ice Age events, we are familiar with landforms and other features related to glacial activity. The Driftless Area of southwestern Wisconsin is known for its absence of glacial evidence. The Kinnickinnic landscape, however, was not driftless. Pre-Wisconsinan deposits have been well documented by Bob Baker (University of Wisconsin-River Falls) and colleagues and are referred to as *older drift*. Reading Baker's papers, I superimpose the images of glaciers I've observed in Alaska and Washington State on western Wisconsin. Ice, estimated to be nearly three-quarters of a mile thick, advances from the northwest before 300,000 years ago, bringing forces beyond our imagination to grind away at existing landforms. With demise of this ice, deposits of gray till (unstratified drift of clay, sand, gravel, and boulders) overlay the eroded Ordovician remains. (Note that till color is an important component of this evidence, potentially visible in the stratigraphy exposed in a roadcut or quarry.) Also, as a consequence of this advance, ice dams the Kinnickinnic valley and forms Glacial Lake River Falls. This results in sediment accumulation responsible in part for the flat valley floors we see today. The cycle of erosion and deposition is repeated as a second advance of ice, between 300,000 and 130,000 years ago, comes from the north out of the Superior lowland and leaves similar evidence, but the till deposited this time is reddish in color.

For many years a mammoth tusk was on display in a glass cabinet at the back of a lecture hall in which I had regular classes. The tusk was found in the lower part of Kinnickinnic valley, exposed as the river bank eroded away. Although the time period in which this animal met its demise was undetermined, it was unquestionably Ice Age in context and capable of eliciting impressions of glaciers and periglacial environments. It doesn't require a great flight of imagination to put oneself on the vantage point of a local bluff, similar to those present today, above Glacial Lake River Falls watching a group of wooly mammoths grazing on wetland sedges below.

The final advance of glacial ice (Wisconsinan glaciation) terminated in St. Croix County north of the Kinnickinnic valley. By 10,000 years ago this lobe and others were gone from Wisconsin. At that time the rugged postglacial landscape of the region began transitioning toward the environment of today. Glacier-proximal vegetation, adapted to cooler and wetter conditions, became established first and then a major warming period 8,000 to 6,000 years ago produced conditions suitable for prairies. By 3,000 years ago, eastern forests were replacing grasslands, ultimately providing the mix of prairie, savanna, and forest encountered by the first Euro-American migrants.

➳⟩⟨➲

When I became interested in the settlement-era vegetation of the Kinnickinnic area, I ordered the *Map of the Original Vegetation Cover of Wisconsin* and hung it in the hallway just outside my office. The map was derived from observations made by government surveyors as they established the original township and section lines in the region. The grid covering the middle and lower Kinnickinnic regions was completed in the fall of 1847. With further research into the archives at UWRF, I found copies of the hand-written notes of Deputy Surveyor James M. Marsh on which the local part of the map was based. I studied the descriptions of landscape features he and his crew recorded that they "entered and exited," following surveying protocol, and detailed records of the tree species they found.

As I traced the course of the Kinnickinnic from its start to the delta, I created a mental image of the plant communities that natives and settlers would have encountered along the river in the 1840s. From the upper reaches north of Interstate 94 to where River Falls is today was grassland, part of a huge prairie that existed in what is now western St. Croix County. The area of the city, and continuing downstream, was primarily oak savanna, also known as oak openings, a mix of trees and prairie. Oak savanna is often called orchard-like or park-like, where oaks (bur, white, or black in this location) and grasses create a characteristic open environment.

Today, extensive prairie and savanna are gone from the Kinnickinnic River watershed; small remnants remain and restorations are in progress. Euro-American settlement, with its cultivation of crops, brought the end of widespread grasslands. Both of the historic plant communities required fire to exist and burned almost annually before white immigration. Without regular fire oak savannas lost their prairie component and grew into the denser woodlands seen today. As we look over the 174 square miles of the Kinnickinnic watershed, land use today reflects the prevalence of historic grasslands. According to Wisconsin Department of Natural Resources records, agriculture occupies 78% of the area, followed by woodland, wetlands, and natural areas at 17%, and an urban use of 5%.

━╱╲━

In addition to developing an understanding of the history of the river and its larger setting, I had much to learn about the twenty-three miles of main stem. I wanted to explore the different geographic areas I had heard about. I was familiar with the campus stretch of one tributary, the South Fork, but there were five additional named tributaries I still needed to experience: Parker Creek, Kelly Creek, Nye Creek, Ted Creek, and Rocky Branch. What was the significance of the designations by local residents and the fishing public that divided the Kinnickinnic into upper and lower regions? Was it simply a demarcation of convenience? Would there be biologically significant distinctions to emerge?

With miles on the van and net in the water, the logic of upper and lower Kinnickinnic region designations based on stream characteristics and biology became increasingly apparent to me, with the qualification that the point of division might differ from the traditional demarcation. That standard characterization was expressed by Humphrey and Shogren, when they referred to the Kinni as two streams, differing from each other on features of substrate and structure. They defined the upper river as a typical *spring creek*, flowing clear, deep, and narrow over silt, sand, and gravel streambeds. In contrast, the lower river was described as a classic *freestone stream* with its rock-strewn riffles, runs, and pools.

Wadable stream habitat evaluation data shared by Wisconsin DNR Fisheries Biologist Marty Engel support the popular characterization of upper Kinni versus lower Kinni. Stream gradients increase noticeably from 3.3 - 8.3 feet per mile above River Falls (Sites 8-17) to 14.3 - 16.6 feet per mile below River Falls (Sites 3-6). In the same general area, between Liberty Road (Site 10) and Quarry Road (Site 9), three to four river miles above town, sand-plus-silt substrate percentages decrease as gravel-plus-cobble percentages increase. Substrate size classes (shown on the example collection data form) can be an extremely important aspect of habitat suitability for insects and crustaceans. Analysis of aquatic invertebrate collections coincides with these substrate changes. (tables 3, 4, and 5 and accompanying maps.) A number of species that are well represented downstream do not extend upstream beyond the Liberty Road and Quarry Road sites.

⚬∕⎪∖⚬

Rock and water are the elemental physical entities of a river ecosystem and a good starting point for understanding its qualities. Rock and water, the most fundamental of environmental components, were the new beginning between 300,000 and 130,000 years ago, when the demise of the last glaciers exposed a raw, uninhabited terrain. On this barren landscape plant and animal life would become established, first in the form of cold-adapted communities and later temperate ones.

Then, as now, rock controlled where the primary channel of water would find its way over the landscape. It determined where groundwater moved through permeable subterranean materials, there defining its chemistry and determining its temperature. It influenced where and to what extent this cryptic water would make its appearance at the surface and add volume to the stream. Ultimately rock and water provided the setting in which a distinctive river ecosystem could develop.

Rock and water were also the foundational elements on which my personal endeavor began. If I could adequately develop *new eyes* in pursuit of a third component, the living things, I might experience and document my own "real voyage of discovery."

Freshwater sponge attached to debris collected from the
Kinnickinnic River near Division Street in River Falls, Wisconsin

RIVER INVERTEBRATES

The summer of 1965 was coming and I looked forward to it as I had no other. I was registered for Invertebrate Zoology at the University of Missouri, a course required for my major and one that would put me four credits closer to my degree. I was, and had been for as long as I could remember, a biology geek. My interest in living things made all my previous biology classes attractive, but this course held a special appeal for me.

From that summer long ago I have a lasting impression of working over formalin-preserved invertebrate specimens from intestinal worms to sea stars, lab windows open in the Missouri heat, examining the details of external and internal morphology with my lab partner, Jim. I earned money for school by waiting tables in the evening at a local pizzeria. There was no way I could have known at that time how much an individual college class might influence my future.

The course followed a classic approach. It started with protozoans, single-celled animals as we called them then, and progressed through the major and minor groups of invertebrates. The instructor was well versed in his craft and extremely intense in his presentation. He would describe the anatomy, physiology, and ecology of each new group of organisms while generating an image of each in colored chalk on the blackboard. The drawings were then hastily erased in preparation for illustration and discussion of the next group. Wanting to savor each kind of new organism as I first heard about it, it took me a while to get used to this whirlwind approach. But there was a lot to cover and it's typical to have courses compressed to fit the shorter summer term. I realize now that I learned not only the minutia of invertebrate life, but also a great respect for the organisms that are commonly characterized as "lacking a backbone." I carried away a fundamental understanding of the kind of living things I would study and teach about the rest of my life.

I've had a long time love for everything animal-related as far back as I can remember. My passion for collecting living things led to an assortment of terraria and aquaria I assembled to contain the personal zoo I maintained in my early teens. The pale green two-story stucco house my parents rented from the neighborhood church seemed large enough for a family of five. But unusual odors emanating from my room became issues. My mother eventually reached her breaking point with my menagerie. "As far as I am concerned you can keep your animals," she said, "as long as they're not in the house. Maybe your father will let you have them in the garage."

The move to the unattached garage made everyone happy and I was back in the business of teenage zoological inquiry. I remained inquisitive about all animals that I encountered. And while the fish, snakes, and turtles were always of interest to me, I could most easily find and maintain various worms, crustaceans, and insects.

There was much to be learned by having these animals close at hand. After bringing several crayfish home from a local pond to live in an aquarium, I was drawn into their underwater world. Peering through the glass, and then referring to books on the subject, I began to understand how they were adapted for aquatic life. I admired their complex anatomy, including their numerous and diverse extremities. I was aware of the lore surrounding their oversized pincers (modifications of the first pair of walking legs) and carelessly discovered how well they worked. With time I learned about the other pairs of appendages and their specific functions in crayfish life, from swimming and mating to food handling and egg transport. As a naturalist practicing on the smallest scale, these animals challenged my imagination and gave me a chance to become engaged with what made them unique. When the opportunity came to enroll in college level invertebrate zoology and entomology classes, I entered with fascination and curiosity.

My first formal experiences with insect life came in an entomology course during my sophomore year of college. It featured insect anatomy and metamorphosis, classification principles on which the twenty-six major insect groups (orders) were organized, and insects of human importance. Lab sessions involved hands-on study of a wide variety of pinned and pickled specimens. A gifted instructor opened my eyes to the insect world through active engagement and a challenging atmosphere. These qualities made me want to learn. He also had a direct, practical instructional style that made me think about a life in teaching. He was quick to supply a number of reasons for the unparalleled biological success of insects, in one example averring, "In the animal world, six is the perfect number of legs." I knew then that I had found my academic Eden.

‑⁄⁀⁕‑

I realize that many people view invertebrate life as a bewildering array of strange and unconnected life forms. But as we endeavor to understand them, they can help us comprehend ourselves. Our own multicellularity, bilateralism (having a body with left and right sides), paired appendages, cephalization (development of a head), and organ systems (*e.g.*, nervous, circulatory, digestive) originated in these early creatures. When we observe stream invertebrates, we are viewing descendents of organisms that lived long before vertebrates arrived on the planet.

During the Cambrian Period, which began 570 million years ago, most of the major groups of animals alive today became established. This was an extraordinary time for life on Earth. The concentration of oxygen was rising in the atmosphere, the result of millions of years of generation by evolving O_2-producing organisms. More complex life forms, those capable of oxygen metabolism, were capitalizing on this efficiency. This was also when hard exoskeletons were originating, which protected previously soft-bodied organisms from predation, and coincidentally promoted fossilization. The proliferative event which led to unprecedented biodiversity came to be known as the Cambrian explosion. Fossil remains from this period record the origin of many marine groups, including sponges, brachiopods, molluscs, annelids, arthropods, and echinoderms. The extinct trilobites, ancient arthropods, were especially abundant during this time.

The French naturalist Jean-Baptiste de Lamarck is credited with the first use of the term *invertebrate*. Lamarck occupied the "insects and worms" position at the French Natural History Museum in Paris in the early 1800s. There he carried out the first formal systematic study of invertebrate biology. His extensive early work on these organisms, including a classification system for them which persists to this day, was published in his multiple volume *Natural History of Invertebrates* (1815-1822).

A more recent icon associated with the study of invertebrate life, and one who contributed to the lore surrounding my invertebrate zoology classes, was Libbie Henrietta Hyman, a research associate with the American Museum of Natural History. "Libbie," as we called her, not in disrespect but in endearment, was in the process at that time of completing the last volume of her comprehensive six-volume treatise, *The Invertebrates* (1940–1967). This twenty-seven year effort grew to be the definitive work on invertebrate life. It was referred to often in classes and consulted regularly as a resource for library research projects. This multivolume set became for me far more than a reference. It was the portal to an exotic and mysterious world for a committed invertebrate biology student.

❧

We have a fascinating diversity of microscopic and macroscopic multicellular invertebrate life forms in our Midwestern freshwater environments. With little in the way of specialized equipment we can gain perspective on these organisms. One can use an aquatic net to obtain substrate materials and catch organisms disrupted from the streambed, or simply pick up and examine submerged rocks or woody debris for attached or clinging creatures. Perhaps the most extraordinary and rewarding part of using any type of sampling method is that one can never predict what curious life forms might be found.

Using a net in the Kinnickinnic to collect from different habitats, I have come across many macroscopic invertebrates beyond the insects and crustaceans I was targeting. These included *freshwater sponges* (prefacing photograph), amorphous porous masses encrusted on submerged tree branches; *planarians* (free-living flatworms) gliding through the film of water on the underside of extracted rocks; numerous free-living aquatic *roundworms* (also known as *nematodes*), common ones being less than one centimeter long; and their relatives, the surprisingly long and thin (Kinni specimens are commonly over ten inches) *horsehair worms* from open water or mixed substrates; various small molluscs including *fingernail clams* and *snails*; small, almost microscopic *aquatic earthworms* in silt deposits; and tiny free-living *water mites* in all river habitats.

❧

An extremely common word in the lexicon of aquatic biology is *macroinvertebrate*, commonly abbreviated as *macro* (plural *macros*). It might be easiest to think of the word as a simple combination of the root *macro-* (meaning long or large) and the base *invertebrate*. However, in everyday usage the word carries far more meaning to biologists than simply "large invertebrate."

The working concept of macroinvertebrates is based on practicality and convenience. Kent Johnson reminded me that the sampling gear we use, including mesh size of nets and other equipment, is the "first determiner of what macroinvertebrates we collect for identification." When sampling is carried out for purposes such as population studies, diversity assessment, and biomonitoring, correct identification to the lowest taxonomic level is of primary importance. Most insects and crustaceans that are under, for example, one-eighth inch (three millimeters) are too small to be identified to genus or species or both (as pointed out by Hilsenhoff in his 1982 and 1987 biotic index papers). This is because keys used for larval identification are written for larvae with full character development. (These are often called *mature* larvae, maturity here defined as developmental, not sexual, which is an adult characteristic). The ultimate issue is not absolute size, but the acquirement of diagnostic features that accompany larval growth.

It might seem the word macroinvertebrate could be used in a broader context, but it most commonly refers to *aquatic macroinvertebrates* or *benthic macroinvertebrates*, which are, for all practical purposes, the same things. This is because they are everyday words of aquatic biologists, especially aquatic entomologists and ecologists who are encountering these organisms in sampling and other research efforts. *Aquatic* obviously involves water in running or standing situations. *Benthic*, derived from *benthos*, refers to bottom dwelling, but in practice is used to define anything living beneath the surface, including things clinging to submerged debris and plant materials.

➤╱╲◄

For stream aficionados knowledge of invertebrates fits well into our understanding of the intricacy of river ecosystems. The physical environment, represented by inorganic substrates, water chemistry, temperatures, and flow rate, provides the non-living infrastructure of the system. A large and diverse population of microscopic organisms, including bacteria, algae, and protozoans largely go unseen, but carry out valuable ecological roles. Aquatic macroinvertebrates depend on this base of the community when performing the roles of carnivore, herbivore, or omnivore. They, in turn, as prey, provide the energy and nutrient resources for predators—fish, frogs, birds, and bats.

The term *invertebrate* is a mainstay of the biological lexicon. It is a valid and descriptive designation. It readily clusters everything from sponges to insects to sea stars into one gigantic pot, and there is practicality in that. However, it bundles these many different living things in unfortunate negative terms, emphatically proclaiming them *not vertebrate*. It would be refreshing to have a positive replacement. In the absence of this highly unlikely probability, we should recognize the biological success of this 97% of the world's species of animal life and understand that it paved the way for our own existence.

Sampling equipment in use on the Kinnickinnic River
near its confluence with Rocky Branch

OPPORTUNITY, SERENDIPITY, STRATEGY

The idea sounded simple enough. I would assemble a list of insect species of the Kinnickinnic River to serve as a reference for future classes and research projects. From various visits to the river I had gathered an informal personal reference collection consisting primarily of aquatic larvae. From years of student projects on the South Fork I had archived specimens that I could readily revisit. The summary of these collection materials would be followed by a search of published literature for data on Kinnickinnic species. Using resources obtained from different perspectives—both personal and acquired by way of the aquatic biology community—should make for a robust synopsis. How hard could it be?

It was time to get started on a review of pertinent entomological literature. I hoped to find a comprehensive Kinnickinnic insect summary, like DuBois's insects of the Brule River of northern Wisconsin or Hilsenhoff's insects of the Pine-Popple River system, also of northern Wisconsin. It seemed logical to me and others that similar faunal work had been done on insects of the Kinnickinnic, considering its status as a high quality trout stream. Would studies have been conducted by someone at the Department of Entomology, University of Wisconsin-Madison, or a similar lab at the University of Minnesota, just thirty-six miles away? I supplemented my literature review by contacting colleagues across the aquatic insect community. Occasionally, researchers will have unpublished data they are willing to share. But this approach was, like the paper chase, unsuccessful. As time passed, the reality of there being no technical fauna record for the Kinni became increasingly apparent.

During my search, I found a useful resource on the distribution of mayflies of the Upper Midwest assembled by Randolph and McCafferty of Purdue University. This publication documented five mayfly species collected as larvae from the Kinnickinnic. Most of these records originated with William Hilsenhoff, aquatic entomologist at the University of Wisconsin-Madison, and his students who collected stream insects throughout Wisconsin. Some were specified only as "[UW]," indicating the records originated from the insect collection at UW-Madison.

Eventually, a key resource brought to my attention a series of Hilsenhoff Biotic Index (HBI) samples completed for the Kinnickinnic watershed in 1995 and 1997. This document was the 1998 *Kinnickinnic River Priority Watershed, Surface Water Resource Appraisal Report*, prepared by Ken Schreiber, Watershed Monitoring Coordinator (West Central Region, Wisconsin DNR). Upon request, Ken provided me with detailed summaries of the HBI results, documenting insect and crustacean species and their numbers collected at Kinni main stem and tributary sites. These were very useful data sets, keeping in mind that HBI samples are restricted to: 1) riffle habitats and 2) collection dates occurring before 1 June and after 1 September. Following recommended protocol, there were no summer records. The data remained valuable, beyond their monitoring importance, as a record of species—independent of my own—with which I could make comparisons.

I also benefited from discussions with members of the area fly fishing community. The majority of anglers with whom I interacted were curious about the kinds of insects my students and I were encountering. It was always a pleasure to share information about what we were finding. I, in turn, was kept aware of what they were seeing. Members of the Kiap-TU-Wish Chapter of Trout Unlimited served as a valuable resource for me and ultimately provided financial support for my projects in the way of supplies and student assistance.

With time, the unexpected nature of the situation turned into a realization of extraordinary opportunity. The circumstances called for a comprehensive study to document insect inhabitants of the river. The work would gain value if it involved the river in its entirety, and included all seasons and a diversity of habitats. To see the river and its surrounding landscape from this larger perspective of time and space was more than I had previously contemplated. I started to think about what might be within my means to accomplish.

Considering the complexity of a river, it's obvious that a total assessment of even a few meters of river length for its insect population would be nearly impossible. This kind of problem is resolved by *sampling*, that is, obtaining a small part of the population that would be representative of all inhabitants.

Given that strategy, many possible approaches, tools, and techniques could be used. Decisions needed to be made to assure that the methodology chosen was consistent with the project objectives.

—⁊⟨∿—

Serendipity is the phenomenon of finding valuable things not sought. Such was the nature of an encounter I had when speaking with David Lenat of the North Carolina Division of Environmental Management. By chance, I attended a talk he delivered at the North American Benthological Society annual meeting in Duluth, Minnesota, and was able to speak with him informally after the session. Lenat was testing a technique to assess water quality using aquatic invertebrates while avoiding the time requirements and costs of formalized quantitative or semiquantitative sampling. My objectives did not include assessment, but I learned that his sampling protocol contained key methods appropriate for the time and resources I had available.

Lenat's approach was based on these components: 1) it was multihabitat; it explored all possible habitat types in a sample area, 2) it was based on ten subsamples per site, enough to represent the variety of prevalent habitats, and 3) it utilized sorting of organisms from substrate materials in the field. Specimens were collected and preserved in proportion to their numbers in the habitats available. No attempt was made to preserve all specimens netted. With the goal of making a comprehensive list of species for the Kinnickinnic, I decided to adopt a similar sampling strategy for my study.

Sampling Larvae vs. Sampling Adults

Most river watchers see aquatic insects after they have become aerial, or terrestrial, and are no longer residing in subsurface habitats. So the question arises, "Why focus on larvae and not on the obvious emerging adults?" The reasons for collecting larvae are practical ones.

A major advantage of sampling the larval stages of most aquatic insects is their continuing presence in the water once they have hatched from the egg. Aquatic larval stages of what will become flying insects persist beneath the surface as long as it takes them to reach full larval size. This requires from several weeks to several years. The biologist can take advantage of this extended larval availability by repeated and regular sampling. Patterns of location and seasonal change for each taxon can then be derived from collection records.

It is also important to consider the idea that some aquatic insects and crustaceans lack a flying adult in their life cycle. The scud, a crustacean, and most aquatic beetles and true bugs do not emerge at the surface into a flying stage, as do mayflies, caddisflies, stoneflies, and true flies like midges. So an additional benefit of larval-based sampling is that these aquatic adults are collected along with larvae and contribute to the diversity discovered.

The utility of this approach contrasts, for example, with trying to sample a mayfly population on the exact day or days the flying stages are active. Seasonal variation and unpredictable weather can make subimago and adult emergences difficult to anticipate, a quandary with which fly fishers are well aware. There is simply no way to adequately assess emerging insects without being at all sites at all times through the season. Larval sampling eliminates many of the problems associated with these timing issues.

When adult aquatic insects are used in species accounts, they bring one more critical element into consideration. Let's use mayflies again as an example. All keys written for technical adult mayfly identification require microscopic examination of male genitalia to confidently assign a species name. This is not a difficult procedure to carry out, but it does negate the determination of all female adult specimens that might be caught and returned to the lab, in spite of a well-timed emergence encounter.

The aquatic net, also called the D-net or kick net, is a versatile tool for sampling many different stream habitats. It can be applied to a variety of submerged substrates from pure silt deposits to sands, gravels, and cobble, masses of underwater plants, leaf packs, woody debris, and overhanging banks. Standard net collecting begins by resting the flat side of the D-shaped net hoop on the stream bottom while disrupting the up-current substrate with one's foot. It utilizes water movement to sweep insects into the mesh, so any substrate or mixture of materials can be sampled where a current exists. In non-current situations, for example where aquatic vegetation is present, the net can be moved through the leaves and stems with a shoveling motion, scooping up specimens as they are dislodged. We take a tool of such apparent simplicity for granted, but its power in the assessment of the underwater fauna cannot be overemphasized. Eminent ecologist E. O. Wilson pointed out this potential in his book, *The Diversity of Life*, when he wrote that much biodiversity is yet to be found the old-fashioned way, including by net.

SAMPLING MULTIPLE HABITATS VS. USING BIOTIC INDEX TECHNIQUES

In the larger scheme of things it was tempting to skip over the planned presence-absence assessment phase and proceed directly to biotic index techniques. This alternative would have the benefit of direct analysis of river conditions while accounting for some of the common species. The key word here is *some*. A monitoring protocol such as the HBI, the one of choice in Wisconsin, requires that samples are collected in riffle habitats (some substrate alternatives are allowed) with a swift current (minimum flow of 0.30 meters/second). This precludes the opportunity to sample lower energy, slow-water environments such as eddies, pools, and undercut banks. Added to this limitation is the expense of HBI sample processing and taxonomic analysis. After consideration of the alternatives, a simple qualitative multihabitat approach became the method of choice.

A PROJECT MATERIALIZES

With project planning underway, Marty Engel, Wisconsin DNR Fisheries Biologist, provided me with particularly useful data his agency collected on the Kinnickinnic River main stem and its tributaries in 1996. This work was carried out to establish a baseline of objective, quantifiable stream information using standardized field protocols. Employing these procedures on the Kinni, seventeen stream assessment stations, or reaches, were set up for habitat evaluation. The details on these stations would be invaluable in my insect project planning and organization. The materials included station-specific maps locating stream features (runs, riffles, pools), transect data, and habitat rating summaries for the entire Kinnickinnic system.

As an example of their utility, the compiled field notes contained detailed bottom substrate analyses for each of the seventeen reaches. Twelve evenly distributed transects (linear sample lines perpendicular to the stream channel) are required per station, each with four equally spaced examination squares (0.3m x 0.3m), to determine substrate (bedrock, boulder, rubble/cobble, gravel, sand,

silt, clay, detritus) percentages across the channel. This gave a quantified an-
alytical perspective on station streambeds as they existed in 1996. Obviously,
stream features and substrate locations change with time, but the summaries
would be an excellent resource for understanding the basic nature of each station. In the end it was not a difficult decision to utilize pre-determined Wisconsin DNR habitat stations as study locations for multihabitat insect sampling.

A primary objective of my project was to survey aquatic invertebrate
populations as broadly as possible in time and space. With sampling time
limited, I divided the habitat evaluation stations into two groups: the eight
even-numbered sites would be sampled in even-numbered months and the
nine odd-numbered sites would be sampled in odd-numbered months. During
the visit to each site, ten D-net subsamples were taken with the goal of exem-
plifying the range of river structure, habitats, and substrates available. Each
subsample was netted and transferred to a sorting tray for extraction. Specimens were removed from the tray with an emphasis on obtaining proportional
representation of types present. Removal was limited to ten minutes. In this
way the visit to a stream site, which included multiple subsamples and the time
required to move from one to another, could be completed in about two hours.

Standing on the verge of a new project, I thought about the places that insects
had taken me in the past: to landscapes as varied as the foothills of the Colom-
bian Andes, mountains and valleys of the Yukon Territory and North Slope of
Alaska, and subarctic zones of the Hudson Bay region. Now I was preparing
for a new challenge, one as mysterious and motivating as any I embarked upon
before. Opportunity set the stage for a project and a serendipitous encounter
led to development of a strategy that would contribute to realization of its
objectives.

Ahead was the river in all its dimensions, physical surroundings, and
weather conditions. Stretches of water I hadn't sampled before were on the
schedule and familiar ones were to be seen from a fresh perspective. Exploring
new and different river habitats would increase my breadth of experience both
in terms of collection diversity and in appreciation of the broader river environment. Elapsing time and changing seasons added parameters of interest
to the project that were not unknowns, but were unsupported by larval data.

Anticipation was the operative word at this stage. And there was one thing of which I could be sure, even before the initial samples were taken—that the greatest reward of these efforts would be the extraordinary procession of insects and crustaceans I would encounter along the way.

Fly fishing group viewing Kinnickinnic River
macroinvertebrate specimens in sorting tray
(Photo courtesy of Charlie Rader)

LOOKING AND LEARNING

Putting our solo canoes into the water below Glen Park in River Falls, we were on our way, paddling to a sample site on the lower Kinnickinnic River. There were trail approaches to this location, but going by water was direct and admittedly more enjoyable than walking. This access had the added benefits of renewing familiarity with the river and its surroundings, including finding riffles and sand bars changed by the pushy water of spring. So, paddling *and* sampling on a beautiful day? Could it be any better? Surprisingly, it would become so, but that was later, at the site.

My friend, paddling partner, and colleague, Charlie Rader, joined me. As he had on several occasions, he was more than willing to assist with the sampling protocol. It was early June, sunny and warmer than usual for this time of year at eighty-six degrees. We would canoe a little over three miles downstream to the location, carry out the sampling plan, and then paddle to the take-out, another three or so miles, where we had a vehicle parked. All-in-all it would be something over a four hour venture evenly split between sampling and paddling.

We arrived at the site and settled our canoes onto the gravel bank, unpacked equipment, assessed aquatic habitats, and got to work netting specimens. Well into the procedure we heard the elevated pitch of youthful voices carrying upriver to our position. Seasoned fly fisher Dave Norling was leading a very keen group of young fly fishers our way. Our most recent catch of insects was still in the sorting tray and we invited the group to take a look. Before long all eyes were on the swimming, crawling, and wriggling bodies in the shallow water of the tray. Amid the mix were larvae of mayflies, caddisflies, stoneflies, crane flies, and midges. There were adult and larval beetles. And, as in all Kinni collections, scuds of all sizes were present. A flurry of exchanges buzzed through the huddled group. Various organisms were pointed out and talked about. Names were attached. The enthusiasm of the boys was especially gratifying.

I don't know if the encounter impacted these youngsters beyond the short term. Certainly, there was a palpable excitement and eagerness generated in them, a sheer joy of living things, an unhidden display of appreciation of the natural world. The day was a memorable one for me, paddling, sampling, and the unanticipated opportunity to share the wonder of these incredible aquatic invertebrates.

➤ ⁄ ⁌ ⬸

Looking is the first step in learning about river insects. Whether we are neophyte or skilled in this endeavor, we process the sizes, shapes, behaviors, and other special qualities of these creatures and integrate the mental images into the framework, weak or robust, that we already have. With each of these experiences we build a greater understanding.

One of the highlights of looking is that we look where we enjoy being, in or near water. We can glean much by taking time to focus on the water surface and watching for activity. Is an emergence (a hatch) occurring? Is there more than one kind of insect taking flight? We learn to see and detect differences in body sizes, colors, and flight patterns. We hone this skill as we do in other endeavors—with repetition.

If we want to remember what we observed this day, it helps to keep personal records. A journal of insect observations made at the river detailing what we saw and noting locations, dates, times, and water and weather conditions soon becomes an invaluable resource. Measurements of air and water temperature with a handy pocket thermometer can be helpful for explaining insect activity.

Now, to the noted aerial activity, add what is living below the surface. Hand collection of aquatic specimens is an extremely valuable learning exercise. This is done as simply as picking up a rock from the bottom of the stream or lake edge and seeing what insects are present on it. A net, aquarium size or larger, may be employed to find free-swimming, floating, and drifting insects. A piece of ordinary window screening rolled onto two dowels is very handy for catching aquatic arthropods after disrupting bottom debris. These tools can also be used to catch and determine naturally drifting and surface floating insects that might otherwise go unnoticed.

A valuable practice that takes one beyond simply looking is *observing*. I think of this as a longer and more studied look. One practice, which greatly enhances the view of aquatic insects, is placing the catch into a tray of water. A small white styrofoam tray from the supermarket or a light-colored plastic shoebox lid is handy for this. The process not only spreads insects and debris out but, more importantly, allows for the observation of insects in their aquatic mode. One can see body movement, such as crawling and swimming, and finer anatomical details like tail length and gill activity. If the stream visitor hopes to gain an understanding of what fish might be preying on as insects swim or are dislodged from their habitats, this quick version of sampling provides important clues.

The observations that we make in the field are made more effective by creating a foundation of insect anatomy, classification, and development—on your own or with assistance of an instructor or knowledgeable mentor. In the beginning it is helpful to understand some very basic things: that insects in general have three body regions (head, thorax, and abdomen), three pairs of legs, and one or two pairs of wings.

Not to be confused with legs is the pair of antennae on the head and the multiple, one to three, posterior appendages, often referred to as tails, on the back end. Larvae may exhibit early wing development in their immature forms with abbreviated structures called wing pads. Once you start looking for anatomical details, it's helpful to carry a small, inexpensive hand lens, one that enlarges 10-15X (times).

I can still recall, as if it were yesterday, sitting in a musty, antiquated lecture hall hanging on the words of my most admired zoology professor, Dr. John Farmer. This memory from my first semester at college is especially vivid because Dr. Farmer, always enthusiastic and humorous, presented the same lecture at two o'clock in the afternoon as he did at ten o'clock in the morning. I attended both. In the afternoon I added to the notes I had taken earlier, checking off the witticisms he repeated at exactly the same points in both lectures. The only difference I can remember between morning and afternoon was through which windows sunlight came as it entered the hall.

Here I had my first lessons on the basics of animal classification and naming. The value of tradition and rules associated with their origin took on meaning for me as they were reinforced time and again through years of studying biology. But two and a half centuries of practical usage have not made the modern-day teaching of these ideas any easier, and anguish on the faces of students when they first encounter scientific naming gives away the level of anxiety caused by its discussion.

Biologists use *taxonomy*, roughly the equivalent of classification, and *taxonomic principles* to organize living things in a meaningful way. Taxonomic levels are categories that group similar organisms together; the higher a level, the larger and more inclusive it is. The lower a level, the smaller and more specific it is. These precepts generate a hierarchal system, traditionally starting with kingdom and progressively subdividing into phylum (pl. phyla), class, order, family, genus (pl. genera), and species. Each level has a name based on Latin or ancient Greek.

Here is an example taken from a common insect of the Kinnickinnic, the small minnow mayfly, *Baetis brunneicolor*. The genus name *Baetis*, as I understand it, originated in European geography. The species name is based on the Latin word *brunneus*. *Brunneus* refers to the rich brown abdominal color of this larva, a feature which distinguishes the species from other *Baetis* living in the Kinni. "But why Latin?" students ask with apprehension. "Why the obscure terms that sound so foreign to us?"

Consider the idea that words and languages evolve with usage. What if organisms could be named using descriptive terms with meanings that do not change because their root language is no longer spoken? Latin and ancient Greek are obvious choices. The idea of a brown hue denoted by *brunneicolor* does not vary. The meaning of *brunneus* is frozen in time with no pressures of modern usage that might change its connotation.

The hierarchal system and grouping organisms based on their similarity were the contributions of Swedish botanist Carolus Linnaeus in the mid-eighteenth century. Linnaeus also restructured the scientific name, joining genus and species names to form a binomial (*bi* - two, *nom* - a name). He simplified the technical names of organisms from unwieldy, paragraph-long Latin descriptions of plants and animals to two descriptive words. Today all known living things have a singular scientific name established in the scientific literature. Most people know *Homo sapiens*, the technical name for humans, and may be familiar with *Zea mays* for the corn plant and *Canis lupus familiaris* for the domestic dog (*familiaris* is a subspecies name; the dog is a subspecies of the wolf *Canis lupus*). More details on technical naming can be found online at *What's in a name? Scientific names for animals in popular writing*. An organism may also have a non-technical common name that is useful in everyday communication, such as human, corn, dog, and wolf. Unlike scientific names, common names of a species often differ by region. They can be a source of considerable confusion when multiple species have the same name or when multiple names are applied to the same species.

A primary tool for placing an unknown insect or crustacean into its correct order, family, genus, or species is the *dichotomous key*, or simply, *key*. The process of using a key is called *keying*. Dichotomous keys, as the name implies, are written in couplets, or paired lines, requiring the user to make a choice between a character or characters visible in the unknown. Each decision leads to additional couplets, all written to further separate different organisms, eventually, to a target taxonomic level. The challenge of the keyer is to progress through the key character-by-character until the endpoint is reached.

The choice of a key or keys to use for identification depends on the level of taxonomic specificity required for your purposes. Is it environmental monitoring or fly fishing goals that you pursue? For students, citizen volunteers, and resource professionals determination of organisms to the family level is appropriate. This is also a practical level to know for fly fishing purposes. If the final required taxonomic level is genus and species, as for government agencies and scientific study, highly specialized keys must be used.

We might fantasize that we live in a perfect world where all of our river insects can be identified to species. However, this can happen only if: 1) a pertinent key has been written and published, and 2) the person using it has the necessary training and experience to use it. People working in aquatic disciplines assemble the taxonomic keys they need from the scientific literature or obtain them directly from colleagues working on specific groups.

—╱╲—

While technical and avid amateur river watchers depend on keying, considerable identification can be built on simple, less formal, streamside experiences.

Based on examination of elementary parts, one can learn to separate major insect groups such as mayflies, caddisflies, stoneflies, beetles, and flies (midges and crane flies). This is basic insect classification to the order level. The process doesn't change much, but requires examination of greater detail, to get to the family level. Closer scrutiny will separate, for example, mayflies into baetids, flatheads, ephemerellids, hexes, and others. This is not a difficult skill to acquire, but does require motivation and practice.

For putting a name on a specific organism one can do no better than having the right guide or other resource readily at hand. Like any good tool, it will be the one that is reached for over and over again, and that assists in getting the job done. And, following the tool analogy, it's the one that the user gets more and more proficient in using. My bias is toward books that are strongly based in the science of aquatic entomology and contain carefully worded keys and clear illustrations.

For starters, and in the category of general use, the following are those I've found most useful: *Naturals: A Guide to Food Organisms of the Trout* by Gary Borger, *Guide to Aquatic Invertebrates of the Upper Midwest* by R. William Bouchard Jr., *An Angler's Guide to Aquatic Insects and Their Imitations* by Rick Hafele and Scott Roederer, and *Aquatic Entomology: The Fishermen's and Ecologists' Illustrated Guide to Insects and Their Relatives* by W. Patrick McCafferty. Each of these offers a somewhat different perspective, so it is worthwhile to do some exploring, including finding what others recommend for the user's particular pursuit.

Identification of specimens to species for technical purposes often requires the use of keys found in the published entomological literature. A great help in locating these papers is a publication such as *Aquatic insects of Wisconsin, keys to Wisconsin genera and notes on biology, habitat, distribution and species* by William Hilsenhoff. This guide contains keys to orders, families, and genera, and lists recommended keys for species determinations.

The Appendix of McCafferty's *Aquatic Entomology* book contains an extensive summary of fly fishers' common names matched with scientific names of eastern/central and western North American mayflies. Application of names to life stages (adult, subimago, and larva) are clearly denoted. McCafferty writes of inevitable problems in this naming practice, including using multiple common names for a single species, using a single common name for multiple species, and the effect of ongoing taxonomic revision on established technical names. Also, common names may be different for the subimago and adult of the same species and there is variability in naming that comes with geography.

In the practical application of common names to river macroinvertebrates, fly fishers communicate at all taxonomic levels, starting with standard order equivalents (mayfly, stonefly, caddisfly) all the way to species, as in McCafferty's mayfly list. The genus level is often used to describe an emergence of mayfly subimagos, as in the examples: Blue-Winged Olive for *Baetis*, Trico for *Tricorythodes*, Sulphur for *Ephemerella*, and Hex for *Hexagenia*.

Next to having active, living insect specimens to view, readily accessible example images can serve as valuable tools in the learning process. Several on-line resources display reference photos of immature and adult aquatic insects. An especially useful web site for larval identification to the family level is Rufer and Ferrington's *Volunteer Stream Monitoring Interactive Verification Program* (VSM-IVP). Images on these pages are designed to complement Bouchard's *Guide to Aquatic Invertebrates of the Upper Midwest*, previously mentioned. A display of clear photos with which identified specimens can be compared allows a user to efficiently move specimens from order to family level. The visual aspects of this kind of resource provide the opportunity, when away from the stream, to make progress in the practice of *looking*, and learning what to *observe* for continuing and future identifications.

Many other tools and techniques are available for continued learning. An aerial net, also called an insect net or butterfly net, is extremely useful for catching emerging adults in flight and getting a closer look at them. Collecting full-grown immatures from a stream and maintaining them in an aquarium until they emerge and escape into a catch net suspended above it is instructive. Examination of fish stomach contents yields information about what the fish has recently ingested. These additional techniques are detailed in various resources and are limited only by one's interest and imagination.

━╱╲━

Each person can decide the level of involvement they want to pursue for their own comprehension and appreciation of aquatic insects. This applies to anyone interested in understanding the river environment, including the weekend naturalist, fly fisher, river watcher, and conservation-minded citizen. One need not spend an inordinate amount of time and effort to develop a basic understanding of aquatic insects. Of course, this pursuit can be a life-long endeavor and for many folks it is. Simply knowing what major groups exist in your home waters, along with their life cycles and seasons, can yield great rewards, both pure and applied.

Follow your instincts in the direction, and at a speed, that you want to go. Take time to make personal observations and to integrate them into the larger scheme of things. Keep a journal and compare observations with other interested stream watchers. Appreciate the larger world these experiences open for you, as it did for the young lads and their mentor hovered over our sorting tray on that fine June afternoon.

Ephemerella excrucians subimago reared from a larva collected in the South Fork of the Kinnickinnic River

PUTTING A NAME ON A MAYFLY

Sometimes it's useful to retrace a journey, and it helps if there is still evidence of the route one followed before. This was true the time I reached for my notebook bearing the label *Aquatic Insect Identification Correspondence* and leafed through the pages. Before long I was caught up in the back-and-forth of e-mail messages I exchanged with aquatic insect taxonomists at various institutions around the country. My binder was divided into sections, each dedicated to a particular species or group of aquatic invertebrates. Most recorded a complete, or nearly so, chronology of communication on identification or confirmation of shared specimens. The pages told stories that intertwined aquatic insects, devoted people, and biogeography.

A typical sequence of events surrounding these exchanges went like this: 1) River specimens were collected and preserved. 2) An appropriate key or series of keys was used to advance specimens from unknown status to those with names. 3) If an insect was new to me or varied from a description provided, or if it fell outside of the stated geographical range, my tendency was to contact a specialist for identification confirmation. 4) With permission granted to send specimens they were mailed to the authority for examination. 5) The person receiving the specimens may recognize them on sight, run them through a key or keys, compare them with reference materials, or carry out some combination of these approaches, and then communicate their determination(s) to the sender. 6) The specialist often keeps some specimens for their reference collection and returns representative individuals to the sender, identified and labeled.

The sender benefits greatly, not only by receiving expert verification, but also by having confirmed examples that contribute to a reliable personal or institutional reference collection. After a number of years, I accumulated an abundance of Kinnickinnic insects, including larval mayflies, stoneflies, caddisflies, true flies, isopods, and crayfish, that were examined by an authority for the specific group, often someone of national reputation.

Little did I know, when I collected the larger of two *Ephemerella* larvae from the Kinni in the spring of 1997, where the path would lead. My first step in identification was to take specimens through the "Key to Genera of Ephemeroptera Larvae in Wisconsin" in William Hilsenhoff's 1995 *Aquatic Insects of Wisconsin*. This process substantiated the fact that my examples were members of the family Ephemerellidae and genus *Ephemerella*. This key does not allow identification more specific than genus, but Hilsenhoff suggests which key to use for species determination. The go-to key for *Ephemerella* was in a journal article written by Allen and Edmunds in 1965, *A revision of the genus Ephemerella*. My pursuit continued with a trip to the Entomology, Fisheries, and Wildlife Library (since 2012 part of the Natural Resources Library) at the University of Minnesota to make a copy. Back at my lab the first couplet in the key for mature larvae presented a choice between western North American species and eastern North American species. When I chose eastern, I struggled to make progress. But, when I hesitantly chose western, the key identified the specimen as *E. inermis*. Interesting!

The time had come to ask Professor Hilsenhoff if he would be willing to look at some of the Kinnickinnic materials. He said he would be happy to, suggesting I send mature, late instar larvae. I put them in the mail and in a week received his answer. He said he called these *Ephemerella* species A in earlier publications, but recently concluded that it was *E. inermis*, a western species. This was an important and revealing response for me, considering this was one of the two species of Kinni *Ephemerella* I was finding in greatest numbers (*Ephemerella needhami* was the second species). He also sent me a copy of the *Ephemerella* key he published, with his handwritten notes and updates in the margins. At one point I asked him if he would look at male adults that I raised from similar larvae. He declined, citing lack of experience with the adults. I learned a lot about the practicality of working with larvae from his reply.

In 1999, I began corresponding with Pat Randolph, author, with Pat McCafferty, of *Diversity and Distribution of the Mayflies (Ephemeroptera) of Illinois, Indiana, Kentucky, Michigan, Ohio, and Wisconsin*. Both were specialists in the mayfly lab at Purdue University. By that time I had examined penes (male genitalia) of aquarium-raised specimens, compared them with characters described in the

Allen and Edmunds adult key, and determined them to be *E. inermis*. I inquired about sending adult specimens for confirmation and received a positive reply. Pat (R.) added in one of his notes that mayfly guru George Edmunds himself suggested there might be a sister species of *E. inermis* extending into Wisconsin.

Resolution of many *Ephemerella* issues came in 2003 with publication of the paper, *Revisionary contributions to North American Ephemerella and Serratella (Ephemeroptera: Ephemerellidae)*, by Luke Jacobus and Pat McCafferty. Work of this type is no small task. It requires extensive review of pertinent specimens, including: 1) type material (specimens originally examined and named by the discoverer of the species), 2) museum specimens on loan from institutions across the United States and Canada, 3) specimens acquired by the researchers on their own field excursions, and 4) samples sent from various locations by collaborators and other investigators for evaluation.

Adult male and larval *Ephemerella* from a variety of locations across North America were brought together for the Purdue project. Many long series of specimens—each series representing a different population—assured that a range of individual variability was present. New descriptive data derived from comparison of study specimens with reexamined type materials supported revision of existing *Ephemerella* species. This included establishing synonyms—a process of determining where names were incorrectly applied to variants as separate species and reorganizing them under the name of the valid type. The journal article detailed observations made in the study, providing descriptions and comparisons of the species included and updated geographic distributions.

Jacobus and McCafferty emphasized the importance of recognizing structural and color variability within species. They also suggested the need to view a combination of characters when making identifications. Species differences in *Ephemerella* larvae were based on abdominal segment and tarsal claw characteristics with features such as body and caudal filament colors noted. Species differences in adults were based primarily on characters associated with the male genitalia, including the shape of the penes and location and number of spines on the penes.

Beyond identifications, it was rewarding to have Kinnickinnic specimens among the many considered in the revision study. I had submitted *Ephemerella* samples to the Purdue lab on several occasions. In one e-mail reply to a confirmation request I made, Pat (R.) opened his response with "The more the merrier." All larvae I sent were ultimately identified as *Ephemerella excrucians*. The specimens referred to in the paper were adults I raised from larvae. They were collected from mixed sand and gravel substrate where clear, fast moving water passed through a shallow riffle in the lower valley at Site 2.

Ephemerella excrucians was named in 1862 by Benjamin D. Walsh in his paper, *List of the Pseudoneuroptera of Illinois contained in the cabinet of the writer, with descriptions of over forty new species, and notes on their structural affinities.* He described the species based on male adults from Illinois. The larva was not described until 1949 when J. W. Leonard in Michigan associated two Au Sable River adult males with their immature forms. As a result of the Jacobus-McCafferty paper, we now know that *E. excrucians* exists from Washington, Nevada, and Arizona in the west to Ontario, Virginia, and North Carolina in the east. The species emerged from the study not as western (the equivalent of an unsynonymized *E. inermis*) and not as eastern (as *E. excrucians* was represented in previous analyses), but widely occurring across the United States.

I learned to appreciate the omnipresence of this species in the Kinnickinnic. Early-on larvae were recognizable in the sorting tray, and I was finding them at all of my sampling sites. The species carried additional significance, too, because of its documented intolerance to organic pollution. It is truly a living symbol of water quality.

I came to know this Kinnickinnic mayfly first by a practical letter designation, then with a useful but tentative western epithet, and ultimately the name *Ephemerella excrucians*. Correspondence in the notebook I took from the shelf that day reminded me of the evolution of my many *Ephemerella* questions, starting with species A. And it further demonstrated the expertise and commitment made by a capable group of mayfly researchers to give a noteworthy species an elegant and well-deserved name.

PART 11

In all things of nature there is something of the marvelous.

—Aristotle

Spiny crawler larva, *Ephemerella excrucians*

A UBIQUITOUS PRESENCE

On one of my earliest invertebrate sampling excursions to the lower Kinnickinnic I had a thought-provoking encounter with a middle-aged gentleman fly fisher. It was an April afternoon, one of the first truly warm days following the end of winter. As enjoyable as it was to walk through the lowland woods, seeing green leaves and sensing the long absent smell of damp earth and decaying organic matter, I was there for the moving water and what I might find living in it. This was a scouting mission that came with lessons well beyond any I might have anticipated.

It is said that we remember the moment rather than the day. I met the fisherman on a dirt path in a wooded segment of the valley above the bridge on the county highway. He was walking downstream, I was walking upstream. I recognized him as a fly fisher by his rod, waders, and vest. I assume that he likewise identified me as an aquatic insect collector by my net, waders, and equipment pack.

It's not unusual for fly fishers to ask in passing "How's it going?" (meaning: "Have you caught anything?" and, if so, "What fly are you using?"). Our exchange was comparable. He was politely inquisitive about my pursuit and what I might be finding in the water. I shared with him the specimens I had found. At that point my experience in stream insects was limited to a level of identification that might best be called general. With my background in entomology I could point out major insect types to the order level fairly easily, recognizing midges, mayflies, stoneflies, and caddisflies. I could also distinguish the common families of mayflies. However, I was totally unprepared for the next question he asked, "Have you seen any Hendricksons?"

One of my standard operating principles, begun around the time of oral exams in graduate school and continuing through many years of college teaching, was to admit up front when I did not have the answer to a question. Before

I had a chance to display my ignorance of the fly fisherman's name for this particular early season mayfly, he unknowingly let me off the hook by suggesting his interest was in what was hatching. I could say to him in all honesty that I had not observed any mayflies emerging that day.

By the time of that experience I had started to assemble a list of insect species for the Kinnickinnic in the only way I knew how, using formal scientific naming. The occasion prompted me to start learning the fly fishers' traditional insect names and this, in turn, made further discussion about insects easier with members of the fly fishing community.

The fly fisher's Hendrickson question that day by the stream eventually played out in a curious way. Although this species of mayfly, known in the entomological literature as *Ephemerella subvaria*, occurs in most trout waters in Wisconsin, it never appeared among the thousands of specimens I collected over the years from the Kinnickinnic. There is no absence, however, of members of the family Ephemerellidae (eh-FEM-er-el-ih-dee) or the genus *Ephemerella* (eh-FEM-er-el-ah) in the Kinnickinnic River. Numerous adult observations point toward two *Ephemerella* species, one larger and one smaller. These are light-colored yellow to yellow-green *Ephemerella* mayfly adults, often referred to as sulphurs. Data based on larval collections (larvae are called spiny crawlers) provide the most solid evidence. Over the years of guiding student collecting and biomonitoring projects, and my own personal sampling studies, I encountered these distinctive and extremely common larvae on a regular basis.

The smaller *Ephemerella* that I found keyed reliably to *E. needhami*, a species common throughout eastern North America. The larger one had been called *Ephemerella* species A, then *E. inermis*, and now *E. excrucians*, the changes reflecting not so much an update in identification as one of taxonomic clarification and revision. This mayfly occurs broadly from East to West, including the Midwest. In a convincing case of widespread presence, from the headwaters to Kinnickinnic River State Park, I found *E. excrucians* at every Kinni location I sampled (table 3). *E. needhami* was present in most of the same locations, but was not collected at the four most upstream sites, the upper three and a half miles of the river (table 3). One or both of these species can be easily obtained from bottom gravel, sand-gravel mixes, and submerged vegetation in moderate to fast flowing water.

The two *Ephemerella* species are different in many ways and, with practice, larvae can be easily distinguished from each other and other mayflies. Size is highly variable. Larger *E. excrucians* larvae are one-quarter to three-eighths inch long (excluding tails), and *E. needhami* one-quarter to five-sixteenths inch. *E. excrucians* has a blocky or rectangular body compared to that of *E. needhami* which is more elongate. Both larvae have three tails, and plate-like gills that lie on top of the abdominal segments, with the exception of the first and second segments where gills are missing.

Color is never a definitive identification tool for any insect, because of genetic variability and dependence on factors such as food resources, but knowing the range of variation in color for a species can provide some assistance in the process. *E. excrucians* larvae can appear as exotic as a tropical bird, having a body color of dark brown or black highlighted with numerous cream-to-tan-to-yellow spots and alternating dark and light bands on the tails and legs (prefacing photograph). Other specimens are almost uniformly dark brown or brownish black with reduced light colored areas or spots. *E. needhami* is often dark brown, black, or green with a pale yellowish-to-greenish dorsal midline stripe running from the middle of its head to the end of its abdomen.

With only two *Ephemerella* species recorded I wondered if I was finding the actual number in the Kinnickinnic. Nine species had been documented for the state of Wisconsin in 1995. Did I have diversity expectations entangled with productivity? These early questions prompted me to ask river sage Tom Waters for a consultation.

Tom was particularly familiar with Valley Creek in Washington County, Minnesota, which has summercool parameters similar to the Kinnickinnic. Opening his response with the caveat that my inquiry called for some interesting speculation, he described the high diversity and low productivity of multiple North Shore, Minnesota, streams compared to the lower diversity and high productivity of Valley Creek (which he said had one or two species of mayflies). He set my mind at ease when he posited that an inverse relationship exists between productivity and diversity, indicating that my observation of low mayfly diversity in the highly productive Kinni would fit this model.

━╱╲━

Although few river observers get the opportunity to experience the frequency of *Ephemerella* larvae in underwater substrates, one might be fortunate to see their impressive emergence as small subimagos (duns) taking flight over the river on a memorable summer day. My friend and trusted fishing advisor, Mike Alwin, said what seems to work for most people is understanding the emergence of two Kinni species, a larger daytime-emerging sulphur and a smaller evening-emerging sulphur. The well-observed two-part pattern of *Ephemerella* emergence as subimagos is consistent with larval records of a similar size relationship: the larger *E. excrucians* and smaller *E. needhami* of my data set.

All species of *Ephemerella* are univoltine, that is they have one complete generation per year. Hilsenhoff describes the spiny crawlers as abundant in unpolluted, fast streams during fall and early spring. Monthly Kinnickinnic records show *E. excrucians* larvae collected October through July and *E. needhami* found March through June. This suggests that both species exhibit a diapausing stage, presumably the egg, longer in *E. needhami* (eight months) and shorter in *E. excrucians* (two months), followed by a fast seasonal life cycle. Edmunds and Waltz point out that diapause is a likely adaptation in many temperate zone mayflies species, a physiological feature that impedes egg hatching by three to nine months. Looking to the river bottom for mayfly life cycle chronology data may initially appear counterintuitive. The approach, however, can help provide useful answers related to the larger curiosities of mayfly life.

Data derived from Kinnickinnic larval samples, combined with revisions detailed in the 2003 Jacobus-McCafferty paper, answered a number of questions I and others had asked regarding which spiny crawlers reside in the river. *Ephemerella excrucians* and *E. needhami* are, as demonstrated, common residents. The classic sulphur, *Ephemerella dorothea*, doesn't occur in the Midwest. It is now understood that *E. dorothea* is a mayfly restricted to the hilly or mountainous regions of the East (*E. dorothea dorothea*) and West (*E. dorothea infrequens*). Its previous Midwestern representation is a case of mistaken identity. Additionally, *Ephemerella rotunda* has now become one in the same with *E. invaria*, after being synonymized. This species does range across the Midwest and East, but larvae were not found in the Kinnickinnic during the 2001 survey or in other sampling efforts.

━╱╷╲━

Starting with a clean slate on knowledge of Kinnickinnic insects, I had no preconceived notions on what species should or should not be found. Questions, such as that about *Ephemerella subvaria*, the Hendrickson, had value and would eventually get answered with data. An array of hatch charts of various degrees of specificity and technicality posed similar questions: Are these insects really there? Are they prevalent enough to be seen in routine aquatic collecting?

It's a good day when one can be at the river. It's even better when a flight of mayflies is on. The sensation of countless, virtually weightless bodies gathered cloud-like above the stream makes an impression likely to settle permanently into one's brain. The details may go well beyond visual imagery to include sounds of moving water, scents of fresh vegetation, and the feel of a warm breeze.

Doesn't each of us hang on to memories of these natural events for the pure elation of reviewing them? One of my lasting recollections arises from an experience on the lower Kinni during one of my early fishing trips. On that steamy June afternoon mayflies filled the air above the stream, a protean mass of hundreds if not thousands of diminutive, fluttering, ethereal beings. A scene of sky, water, and woods made to last by a complementary horde of flying insects.

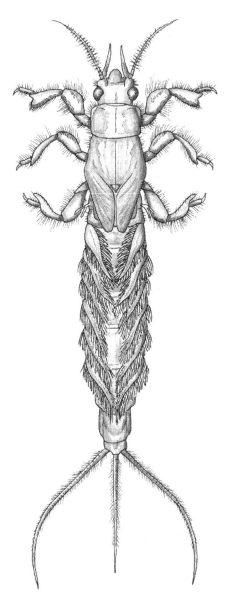

Burrowing mayfly larva, *Hexagenia*

WONDERFUL MYSTERY

People living in towns along the Mississippi River in Wisconsin and Minnesota know all about the midsummer emergence of mayflies. Many have witnessed this mostly June and July phenomenon, remembering how untold numbers of *Hexagenia* (hex-uh-GEEN-ee-uh), the hexes, take to the air. These subimagos fly instinctively to rest on terrestrial objects and, after molting into the adult stage, mate and return to the river to deposit their eggs. As the cycle unfolds, lights projecting from storefronts, service stations, and parking lots attract them *en masse*. They cling to every available surface obscuring signs and windows. Tree limbs and bushes droop as if snow-laden under their weight. On nearby lighted roads and bridges vehicles skid on accumulated bodies and snowplows are called out to clear a path. An acquaintance told me of seeing mayflies plowed into piles along the edges of a gas station parking lot near the Mississippi and how a unique smell emanated from the heaps of decaying insects.

For some Midwestern localities anecdotal emergence evidence suggests a continuous abundant presence of hexes; for others, similar observations support the idea of diminishing populations. In a conversation I had with angler and writer Jim Humphrey on the topic of *Hexagenia* of the Kinnickinnic River, he called the ups and downs of this mayfly through recent time "a wonderful mystery." This was a story that I definitely wanted to pursue.

When I initiated my aquatic insect work in the mid-1990s, I anticipated collecting specimens of common burrowing mayflies, especially the hex. A retired colleague who had taken biology classes to the upper Kinni in the early 1970s recalled finding mature burrower larvae. He shared their length with his thumb and forefinger spread about an inch and a half apart. Of course I wanted to experience these specimens firsthand. I targeted collections in suggested reaches of the stream and looked over the shoulders of students as they extracted specimens from samples in the same areas. In river length multihabitat sampling I made a point to include the silt and clay mixtures the larvae prefer for burrowing. There was something strangely exotic about working in the low energy parts of the stream and running my net through the muddy, oozy bottom into which my waders sank. Midge larvae and aquatic earthworms, however, were what I was catching. Only a few hex larvae appeared from these prime habitats. Questions continued. This was before I understood that an insect in decline can be an indication of improving water quality.

In our discussion, Jim referred to large and consistent *Hexagenia* emergences on the Kinnickinnic as far back as the mid-1940s. His account of the river, and considerable experience fishing during these events, including the prelude to a "spectral hatch," are eloquently described in a July 1989 article in *Fly Fisherman Magazine*. Follow-up discussion with Marty Engel and Roger Fairbanks further piqued my interest in the subject. Jim and Bill Shogren in their book, *Trout Streams of Wisconsin and Minnesota*, added ideas regarding the subsequent decline of the hex, and suggested possible reasons, all of which were related to improved water quality: decreasing water temperatures, reduced siltation, increasing flow, or other factors beyond our perception.

Over the years my Kinni insect data set remained nearly hex-free. There is little question regarding the nearly complete absence of *Hexagenia* in the Kinnickinnic River today. During a year long pilot study, I collected 6500 mayfly larvae; two of these specimens were *Hexagenia*. Later, in a year of comprehensive, multihabitat sampling, I collected 9700 mayfly larvae. Of these, five were *Hexagenia*. All seven of these specimens were collected from one sampling location, in a variety of silt deposits appearing no different from those in other parts of the river. This site was approximately one-half mile above the confluence of the Kinnickinnic with the St. Croix River (table 3).

Mayfly specialist George Edmunds and his coauthors published a relevant analysis of *Hexagenia* and related mayflies in the mid-1970s:

> No doubt there have been spectacular mayfly emergences for centuries, but it is almost certain that the great masses of mayflies ...are a symptom of man's unknowing influence with the environment. Modern man has enriched streams and lakes with sewage from cities, manure and fertilizers from farms, and nat-

ural nutrients from eroding soils. While such overenrichment makes conditions unsuited for most mayfly species, a few forms that strain their food from the water, such as *Hexagenia ...*, *Ephoron*, and certain caddisflies, thrive on it and greatly increase in numbers.

Aquatic ecologists, like other scientists, view the world as much as possible in numerical terms. The ability of aquatic insects to tolerate organic and nutrient pollution can be quantified in what is known as a *tolerance value*. These values are determined through previous observations and are designed to be used in calculations supporting a biological monitoring process. A quantitative indication of the capacity of *Hexagenia* species to tolerate organic and nutrient pollution can be seen, for example, in the Hilsenhoff Biotic Index. All four species of the genus *Hexagenia* found in Wisconsin have an assigned tolerance value of 6. Based on a ten point scale, 0 is excellent (non-tolerant species) and 10 is very poor (tolerant species). If we were to generate a hypothetical biotic index sample composed entirely of *Hexagenia*, it would rate the source water quality as Fair, the middle of seven water quality categories. This is in striking contrast to the most commonly found Kinnickinnic mayflies today, such as *Ephemerella excrucians*, *Baetis tricaudatus*, and *Stenonema vicarium*, which have low tolerance values, respectively, of 1, 2, and 2. All of these indicate water quality in the Excellent category.

Looking through historic materials one day in the UWRF archives, I found a photo taken around 1900 depicting an "idyllic" riverine scene. It showed the Kinnickinnic River with cattle wading in the water. The image is a classic "What's wrong with this picture?" as it portends bank erosion, sediment loading, and improper manure management. Today we are the fortunate beneficiaries of stream protection work started in the 1950s by the Wisconsin Department of Natural Resources. These efforts included installing in-stream habitat structures, cattle crossings, and miles of fencing. The state worked with landowners to establish perpetual easements on the upper river. These protections collectively helped reduce the negative impacts of sedimentation and the kinds of direct and indirect nutrient enrichment expressed in the Edmunds document. By the 1970s water temperatures upstream of River Falls had dropped 10°F during the warm season.

These days we are uniquely positioned to observe a river as it moves toward a healthier state. The apparent decline of *Hexagenia* is serving as a marker of that success. Can we know which of the management practices has had the greatest influence on *Hexagenia* populations? Or if there is more than one variable responsible for improved biological conditions?

Here is what we know: 1) Ample silt deposits exist in the Kinni in which larvae could develop, particularly in the upper river and the far lower river, based on 1996 WDNR habitat analysis, 2) Fencing and cattle restrictions, stream bank stabilization, and improved wastewater treatment by the city of River Falls have helped to reduce the organic enrichment of stream water and sediment from direct manure deposition, nutrient runoff, and inadequately treated wastewater, 3) Improved water clarity and less-organic sediment mean less filterable food for mayfly larvae such as *Hexagenia*, and 4) There has been a significant decrease in Kinnickinnic water temperatures since the 1950s. Limited available data suggest that the cumulative daily temperature requirements (degree days) are insufficient for development of *Hexagenia limbata*, the putative Kinni *Hexagenia* species.

Multiple Kinnickinnic River habitat variables have significantly adjusted with the realization of improved watershed management practices in the last half of the twentieth century and into the twenty-first. It would be ideal if monitoring studies were in place that would document additional insect community modifications, should they occur. In the meantime it is likely that the mystery element of declining *Hexagenia* populations will remain in place, with decreased water temperatures and reduced organic enrichment suspected as the primary contributors.

─╱╲─

Hexagenia limbata, order Ephemeroptera (eh-fem-er-OP-ter-uh), family Ephemeridae (eh-fem-ER-eh-dee), is very possibly the most studied and written about species of mayfly. Its public reputation is based on abundant emergences and large size (the larval and adult length of one and a half inch is without tails). Larvae inhabit U-shaped burrows they create in muddy deposits outside of the main channel. In these excavations they move their gills in a continuous wave-like pattern to propel water and extract oxygen from it. The forelegs are used to gather in food: detritus, algae, and bacteria from surrounding mud. Studies show that the main food source is the sediments (not the seston brought in with the respiratory currents) and that larvae selectively obtain organic matter with a high caloric content.

These delicate and fragile-looking larvae, with gills in rhythmic motion, serve as a reminder of the natural beauty that can exist, largely unseen, hidden in silty deposits at the bottom of a stream. Placing one or more of these larvae in a tray of water allows the observer to easily see key features of their anatomy. While a good starting characteristic for confirming *Hexagenia* larvae (as well as subimagos and adults) is size, more accurate larval determination can be made by finding: 1) tusks (forward-oriented mouthparts) that curve up and out, 2) a rounded frontal process between the antennae and above the mouthparts, 3) feathery gills along the sides of the abdomen, 4) large legs, especially the forelegs, adapted for digging, and 5) three fringed tails.

In the Upper Midwest eggs deposited in the summer by common burrower females, such as *H. limbata*, require one or two years and as many as thirty molts to reach full size larvae. The late larval and post-larval life of *Hexagenia* then unfolds as a series of critical and, as might be intuited for insects classified under the name Ephemeroptera, surprisingly brief events.

Last stage *Hexagenia* larvae leave their burrows and swim toward the surface of the lake or stream. This emergence can occur as a highly synchronized event on an evening between late June and early August. In spite of the large number of larvae moving simultaneously, and seeming safety in numbers, it is a migration filled with danger. Active prey of this size are easy for predatory fish to detect.

On reaching the surface, subimagos (duns) exit the last larval skin and take flight. Now free of the water, they fly to the shelter of vegetation and other streamside objects. Life for successfully emerging *Hexagenia* then becomes a short terrestrial existence incorporating many essential aspects of insect life: predator avoidance, mate finding, copulation, and egg release. Within twenty-four hours, or longer in cool weather, they molt again, this time to the mature adult stage. Shortly after this last transformation, adults are ready for the mating flight, an event that various authors have referred to as blizzard-like and a sight never to be forgotten.

In the dimming light of a warm July evening *Hexagenia* males take to the air generating an aerial swarm reaching the tops of streamside trees. Individual males instinctively fly upward within the flurry and then drift down, in a stereotypic vertical dance, while the visible mass grows and mutates through nebulous forms. Females take flight and enter the horde on horizontal paths. As flight trajectories intersect, females are grasped by awaiting males and inseminated during a brief tandem flight. Through the duration of swarming activity it is said that the soft crackling of mayfly wing beats can be heard.

Once mated, the female drops to the surface of the water, exuding several thousand fertilized eggs as she wriggles with the last movements of her life. The momentous event marks the beginning of a new generation of *Hexagenia*, the death of untold numbers of the present cohort, and a bountiful feeding opportunity for fish watching the surface for food.

— ⁓⟩⟨⁓ —

I think about what an 1850, pre-Euro-American settlement, macroinvertebrate sample might have revealed. What a resource it would be if we had insect data starting then and at fifty-year intervals thereafter? And into the future? I can envision a sequence that would show with entomological support how human activity and decision-making have affected the natural landscape. It would document the consequences of those times when exploitation superceded protection. It would also, in no uncertain terms, shout out the successes that follow careful, methodical, and effective watershed policies. I am confident that *Hexagenia* would be a major character in this story, going through its ups and downs and shedding light on the details of its wonderful mystery.

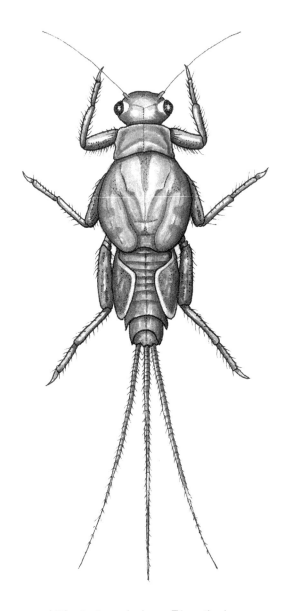

Little stout crawler larva, *Tricorythodes*

LIFE AFTER THE SOLSTICE

I admit to feeling a certain dread with arrival of the summer solstice. This is because a good part of summer is already gone and I'm just realizing that fact. It is said that our distant ancestors were anxious about this astronomical event because it suggested the hardships of winter were yet to come. I sense some of that, in a minor way, of course, and consider it a reminder of things needing to be done. River watchers, especially canoeists and anglers, may believe that the best of their year is behind them by now, thinking stream levels are down and exciting insect emergences are over. But, there *is* life after this day, with meaningful biological events yet to come, some obvious and others obscure.

I recall a July day in 2001, two weeks after the solstice. In the warmth of an afternoon sun, collecting gear packed and ready, I started my hike to the river, destined for a sampling site. Prairie soon gave way to woodland and I was relieved to be in the welcome shade of hardwood forest. I made my way on well-traveled paths nearly to the valley floor and then began bushwhacking through mixed vegetation. Beneath the canopy of cottonwoods, elms, and box elders were dense stands of nettles. I held my arms up as I passed through, hoping not to make contact.

Evidence of spring flooding was obvious in the bottomland. Piles of jumbled woody debris were stranded in place, likely to remain there until the return of high water in some future spring. I tried to imagine how much force it would take to move masses of wood the size of tree trunks down river. Silt covered much of the accumulated flotsam and marked the height to which water had risen before it returned to control of its banks. Thoughts of the power of this moving energy, and the way the river and its surroundings respond to it, were in my head when I arrived at the site. Deep within the valley, bordered by steep wooded hillsides, this setting was a natural retreat: remote, secluded, and quiet. It would become a place where something tiny and unforeseen would have meaning, even on the scale of a watershed.

My field notes for the day showed an afternoon air temperature of 87.3°F. I had written "Sunny and hot!" next to the entry, exclamation point included. When I placed my thermometer a few inches below the surface of the water at midstream, it read 69.4°F, a value above the high end of the optimal range for growth and survival of brown trout (66.2°F), and much above that point for brook trout (60.8°F).

At this location, the river gradient has noticeably decreased compared to reaches just a few miles upstream. With the accompanying slower flow, silt and sand make up a large part of the bottom sediment. There are also riffles of mixed cobble, gravel, and sand, and snags laden with trapped wood and leaves. I began recording the diversity of substrates I found so I could coordinate net collections as closely as possible with the proportion of habitat types present.

As I spread the contents of one collection in the shallow water of my sorting tray, I discover something as yet uncollected to this point in the season: small crawling larvae of the genus *Tricorythodes* (tri-cor-ee-THO-dees). On that day and many others, for reasons I found later, these insects appeared as moving accumulations of miscellaneous river bottom particles and fragments. This seasonal first deserved acknowledgment and I celebrated with a spoken "Interesting!" to myself as I attempted to discern the uncertain larva's true form through its attached clutter.

This was the first of what became a steady series of little stout crawler collections continuing into the fall and dwindling to zero by January. A year of sampling also indicated an affinity of this insect for the lower Kinnickinnic. Ninety-eight percent of collected specimens were from five locations in the lower Kinni, starting in the Glen Park area and ending in the state park (table 3). Eight remaining specimens were found above the city of River Falls, most at a site just upstream from the city bypass.

Little stout crawlers are members of the mayfly family Leptohyphidae (lep-toe-HYPH-ih-dee). The name little stout crawler expresses not only larval size and shape characteristics, but also their propensity to crawl through benthic substrates rather than swim, similar to the spiny crawlers, *Ephemerella*. The frequently used common name *tricos* is an abbreviation of the genus name

Tricorythodes. Trico can also refer to the now superceded family name Trico-rythidae (try-cor-ITH-ih-dee) found in earlier literature.

There may be as many as three species of *Tricorythodes* occurring in Wisconsin. *T. allectus* (previously *T. atratus*), however, was the only one confirmed by Hilsenhoff after decades of larval sampling throughout the state. Larvae are found in permanent streams of various sizes and most commonly in gravel, vegetation, and debris-based substrates, where they function as herbivores and detritivores.

With a little practice these larvae are readily distinguished from other aquatic insects. For example, when finding them on a rock removed from the stream bottom or emptied from a collecting net into a tray, a close look will suffice to confirm their identity. They are little, mostly in the one-eighth to one-quarter inch range, smaller on average than other mature mayfly larvae encountered. Second, gills occur on top of abdominal segments two through six. Those on segment two are roughly triangular in shape and operculate, meaning that they are adapted to cover and protect the remaining gills (prefacing illustration). Larvae have a distinctive stout thorax and three long tails of equal length.

One way to spot them in a sorting tray is to look for tiny accumulations of slowly moving debris. Long slender hairs covering the body and legs gather habitat *trash*, as Leonard and Leonard expressed it. Most of the Kinni *Tricorythodes* I've examined have been covered to some extent with this mix of particles and debris. Having fresh specimens in a tray with sufficient water allows these well-camouflaged insects to give themselves away with movement.

Subimagos have many of the characteristics of adults, although the wings look whitish rather than clear. Adult tricos are small, blackish-bodied insects with distinctly large wings and, as with the larvae, have three especially long tails. The wings are widest at their base and there is no second pair. This last characteristic must be checked for carefully, but, seeing other features is normally adequate.

In the Upper Midwest *Tricorythodes* emergence usually starts in the third week of June, the time of the summer solstice, and beyond. R. J. Hall and his colleagues studying *Tricorythodes allectus* (when it was called *T. atratus*) in Minnesota observed subimago emergence only during periods of low light intensity. Watching in decreasing light until no longer viewable, they documented these larvae transforming to subimagos underwater. After sunset, male emergence began and continued until the following morning. They completed the molt to adults an hour before dawn. Females started emerging primarily near dawn and soon molted to adults, showing an immediate or very short two-hour transformation. Hall watched thousands of males assemble, flying in unison in an up-and-down pattern to treetop height. Females in groups of three or four flew continually into the swarm, increasing their presence. They then left the mass, dropping to the stream surface, using the last of their living energy to oviposit. Soon the males fell spent onto the surface. Adult life lasted between nine and ten hours, starting at dusk and ending after sunrise. It isn't hard to imagine how easy it becomes for predators to take advantage of this abundance of energy and nutrients.

A common misconception about little stout crawlers is that they undergo an extended July through September single generation emergence. This is how it appears above the water and for some observers that is all that is important. Further observation indicates greater complexity. *Tricorythodes* overwinter as eggs. My data set shows no larvae collected from January through May. So the eggs hatch in the spring and tiny larvae begin feeding and growing, becoming large enough to collect by net in June. This is generation one, members of which develop at different rates, as Borger suggests in *Naturals*. While the first generation is displaying a staggered emergence, the second generation is developing, and the two emergence peaks blend into one surface-apparent long emergence.

Tricorythodes hold a special fascination for anglers, entomologists, and other river observers. This is shown, in part, by the imaginative names and descriptions applied to them. J. G. Needham, early twentieth-century aquatic entomologist, suggested the name *snowflake mayflies* for *Tricorythodes* in reference to the whitish wings of the adults and the flurry of their mass flights. Others, seemingly frustrated anglers, have applied designations such as White-Winged Curse, Tiny Black Curse, and Fisherman's Curse to them, as trout are said to feed especially selectively when an emergence of these insects is on.

The newly discovered macroinvertebrates that enlivened me on that mid-summer day, and on many occasions to follow, were destined to become participants in the frenzy of ensuing emergence—and the possible consternation of a fly fisher. Little stout crawlers remain in my thoughts as diminutive camouflaged mayfly larvae carrying not only a sample of habitat litter but the promise of growth, transformation, and continuation of the species. With timing refined by eons of natural selection, they would become the transcendent bodies gathering into a flurry-like mass above the stream and, for reasons beyond our perception, at a time of the season when general emergence activity is low. And in the end that is the best of timing, not only for them, but for the stream observer as well.

Flathead mayfly larva, *Stenonema*

FLATHEADS IN PARADISE

I t's easy to be inspired by the natural beauty of the lower Kinnickinnic valley: the slopes forested with oak, maple, birch, and pine; the rugged gorge topography and weathered dolostone bluffs; the weeping cliffs, goat prairies, and oak savanna; the timeless motion of the river below. The valley is all this, and much more. For the ecologist, fly fisher, birder—anyone interested in living things—appreciation of the natural setting is just the beginning, a compelling invitation to further understand how the pieces fit together, and a chance to encounter its individual players up close.

In these reaches lives a six-legged metaphor for such a pristine place, the flatheaded or flathead mayfly, *Stenonema* (sten-oh-NEE-ma), an elegantly colorful and patterned insect—an eyeful to match its surroundings. This creature is one of the simplest macroinvertebrate larvae to put a name on: first, as a mayfly, because of the three tails and single plate-like gills on its first six abdominal segments, and second, as a flathead mayfly, with its uniquely broad head, flattened body, and laterally extending legs (prefacing photograph). With a larva resting on, or partially in, natural substrates the dark brown and gray-brown markings, light gray-to-cream spots, and hints of orange-red on the legs and tails can make the creature disappear.

Fortunately, this icon of river health is common enough in the Kinni that we can wade in and find larvae any time of year. All we need to do is reach into the water, pick a rock from the bottom, and look carefully for one of the large flatheads clinging to it. With this approach the finder may also notice how tightly the larva holds to the wet rock (family members are called *clingers* in a categorization system of mayfly larvae based on behavior) and, when they do move, how close they stay to the surface of the object they are on. The low profile body and superior grasping ability are both adaptations for living in moving water. Larvae tend to occupy crevices among the rocks or within accumulated leaves in pools and backwaters. They are not normally seen actively moving through open water, but do swim, when necessary, with an undulating motion.

Of the ten genera and twenty-three species of the family Heptageniidae (hep-tah-gen-EE-ih-dee) mentioned by Hilsenhoff in his *Aquatic Insects of Wisconsin*, I documented two genera and three species from the Kinnickinnic River. These are *Stenonema vicarium* (the fly fisher's March Brown, also known as the American March Brown), *Stenonema mediopunctatum*, and *Stenacron interpunctatum* (the Light Cahill).

These species are true lower Kinnickinnic inhabitants (table 3). Ninety-five percent of the specimens collected from this family were found at sites between River Falls and Kinnickinnic River State Park. The remaining catches were made at locations just upstream from the city. This distribution puts these populations where rocky substrates are prevalent and the current is moderate to fast. All three of the noted flatheads are regularly encountered in those locations, with *Stenonema vicarium* appearing to be the most abundant.

Larvae of the three putative Kinni species can be distinguished from each other on the basis of a few additional characteristics. First, *Stenacron* has flat gills which are distinctly pointed; the two *Stenonema* species have flat gills which are truncated (somewhat squared) at the ends. *S. vicarium* is the larger of the two *Stenonema* at about three-quarters of an inch long (not including tails) and in ventral (belly) view has a dark band on the posterior (back) edge of each abdominal segment. *S. mediopunctatum* is smaller, under one-half inch, and the dark bands on the ventral side of the abdomen are on the anterior (front) edge of each abdominal segment. Additionally, in *S. mediopunctatum,* the last visible abdominal segment has, on its ventral side, an inverted, dark U-shaped mark that contrasts with the lighter body color.

As far as confirming that subimagos (duns) and adults are heptageniids, the distinctive size is a start. *S. vicarium* adult males are about five-eighths inch long (without tails); *S. mediopunctatum* and *Stenacron interpunctatum* are about one-half inch. Then a closer look is required. All three of these species have two tails and five tarsal segments in the hind leg. The latter are small segments of the foot that require magnification to discern.

-⁄↓↖-

One of the more engaging aspects of flathead life, and mayfly life in general, is the mating behavior of adults. This plays out as an impressive collective event a day or so after the subimagos have left the water. Imagine it's late afternoon or early evening on a warm summer day in late May or June. The ritual is just beginning. Small numbers of males are starting to take flight above the stream. We can see the activity of individuals as they a repeat a stereotypic cycle of up-and-down movements: they are reaching tens of feet above the stream and then dropping close to the surface. More and more males join in and a hovering swarm is formed. Numbers increase into the hundreds. Females take flight and enter the horde. Each is promptly seized by a male. Mating is completed in flight or after the pair falls to the ground. Males die quickly after coupling. And in one last act before death the females fly to the water and release fertilized eggs as they repeatedly touch their abdomens to the surface.

After a year of growth and development as larvae, and as suggested by their order name Ephemeroptera (*ephemero* - living but a day), these new adults live no more than a few days. For many the end is a scene of dead and dying adults, especially females, lying scattered over the water surface, floating downstream with the current. Hungry trout efficiently exploit this last appearance. As a vulnerable stage, it is also one imitated by hopeful fly fishers.

The cycle of life starts anew as tiny flathead larvae hatch from deposited eggs. Larvae feed and grow, becoming noticeable in October as they develop large enough to be seen. They can be found throughout the winter months moving slowly in the cold water. As water temperatures moderate in the spring, larvae become more active and grow to full size. This is a classic univoltine life cycle with one complete generation per year. By the time late spring arrives, larvae are ready to swim to the surface and transform themselves into flying organisms. Emerging subimagos (duns) and adults (imagos, spinners) of *Stenonema vicarium* are sporadically seen on the Kinnickinnic between mid-May and mid-June, according to Humphrey and Shogren, although it is not unusual for some hatches to come later. Larval collections drop off noticeably from July through September. By then most larvae have metamorphosed from aquatic creatures to aerial terrestrial forms.

꒛

Insects were the first organisms to take to the air and the ability to fly is one of the more important factors contributing to their successful evolution. Mayflies hold key evidence regarding the history of this development. To understand their role we need to follow the fossil evidence back to tropical continents of the Carboniferous Period, 360 to 299 million years ago. Landmasses were converging to form the single supercontinent Pangea. Extensive swamp forests existed across much of the landscape. These forests were very different from those of today. The dominant "trees" were giant lycopods (clubmosses) up to 40 meters tall, horsetails, and tree ferns. Diverse and abundant invertebrates lived in this tropical environment: land snails, insects, spiders, scorpions, and millipedes. It was in this setting that the primitive wing-joint mechanisms of mayflies and dragonflies originated.

Insect wing attachments are based on thoracic exoskeletal processes and small integrated plates (axillary sclerites), something like the primate wrist joint with its multiple parts. Details of mayfly and dragonfly wing articulation anatomy, both fossil and modern, reveal a sclerite pattern arranged differently from other flying insects. This ancient connection, without the means for flexing, or folding back, is responsible for upright positioning of the wings of subimago (dun) and adult mayflies when they are seen on the water or clinging to an object. This contrasts with the ability that most insects have to fold the wings flat over the body when at rest, something that was yet to be derived.

━╱╲━

Wing pads of a fully developed flathead larva appear dark and swollen, a sign that emergence will occur in the not-too-distant future. As the metamorphic process plays out, wings that were incrementally enlarged in each larval instar are extracted from their exoskeletal covers and unfurled to take full form.

In spite of the absence of sophisticated flexion, mayfly wings provide the means to accomplish important biological objectives: Subimagos leave the aquatic environment of their previous life and become terrestrial beings—by flying. Intermingling of individuals within the population (with potential genetic benefits), as well as local or more distant dispersal—begin with flight. And the crowning achievement in the lives of these ephemeral living things is the creation of the next generation of flatheads, continuation of the kind into the future. This process is profoundly dependent on flight, first in terms of mate-finding in the dance-like swarm above the water and, within a short period of time, on habitat-specific on-the-fly deposition of eggs.

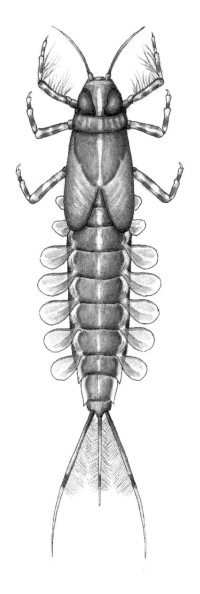

Brushlegged mayfly larva, *Isonychia*

IN SEARCH OF LARGE SWIMMERS

I admire the ability of anglers I know who can hike to a trout stream with confidence. They look for insect emergence and signs of feeding fish, make methodical decisions about an approach, and get to work casting and catching. I appreciate the fact that they have acquired such skills through years of practice and persistence. I have also observed that these folks are especially focused once they tie on a fly and start casting. I mention the idea of attentiveness because that seems to be something on which my own fishing efforts could use some work.

In addition to scheduled insect sampling trips to the Kinnickinnic, I visited the river on many occasions with the primary purpose of fooling a fish. I have not always been skunked, but some might say I have experienced that feeling on more than my fair share of efforts. I am also aware of my tendency to set down my rod and spend an undue percentage of my fishing time extracting rocks from the river to see what insects might be found on them. I am not admitting to lacking focus, just to pointing it in a different direction.

Many years ago, on a Saturday in mid-May, I took part in an instructional fly fishing field trip to a trout stream in southeastern Minnesota. In two prior meetings, instructor Mike Alwin taught the fundamentals of the craft. The day of the outing came and everyone was excited to test their newly acquired skills. Catching a fish was a possibility. The day was perfect for the occasion. Spring was giving way to summer; skies were clear and temperatures warm. We spent the morning going over basics: assembling equipment, casting, reviewing knots, and identifying live insects. The afternoon was devoted to fishing the river under the watchful eyes of Mike and his friend and associate Jonathan Jacobs. In spite of their expert guidance and, as per my usual personal fishing outcome, not a single fish was I fortunate enough to catch.

I do vividly remember, however—in the way of a personal highlight for the day—turning my attention to discovering insects in this new setting. I lifted random cobbles from underwater and examined them for invertebrate life. Clinging to one rock, bold and beautiful, was a larva of the mayfly genus *Isonychia* (eye-so-NIK-ee-ah). It would be hard to measure my elation in finding this specimen compared to, say, that of landing a trout, but my memory of that day remains bright in part because of that specimen. It is likely, too, that this collection remained novel and notable for me because the genus continued to be a rarity through years of sampling in the Kinnickinnic.

Isonychia larvae, once identified, are not easily forgotten. This is an insect that stands out prominently in a net or sorting tray. They are darkly colored, elongate larvae with a vertically oriented head, three tails, and single plate-like gills positioned laterally on each segment along the abdomen (as in accompanying illustration). They have a double row of long hairs on the inner surface of the forelegs, which they hold in front of the mouth to filter food from the current. The rows of hairs, which may require a hand lens to see, are a particularly good identification character, and are responsible for one of their common names, brushlegged mayflies.

Color and markings require caution when they are used to assist in insect identification, but in this example they can supplement other observations. Much of the distinctive appearance of larval *Isonychia* is the dark brown body color interspersed with reddish-brown and light brown-to-tan striping and mottling patterns. Also, it's not uncommon to see a pale mid-dorsal stripe starting on the head and continuing down the abdomen, although it is not always present.

The opportunity to observe behavior of *Isonychia* larvae can complement visible body features for identification. Here is where setting up a tray with enough water to allow larval movement is particularly worthwhile. We conveniently and nontechnically classify *Isonychia* larvae as swimmers, based on an ability in which they excel. They propel themselves efficiently with an up-and-down motion of the abdomen and tails. Observing this behavior considerably narrows down identification possibilities. It can also suggest how fish may perceive active prey as these larvae dart through the water, including through the strong currents of habitats in which they live. The characteristic swimming behavior of *Isonychia* is a hard trait to miss, even in casual collecting.

Be aware that the described swimming movement in larval mayflies is not unique to *Isonychia*. Small minnow mayflies, members of family Baetidae, move in a similar way and are also known as swimmers. Baetids are smaller (one-eighth to one-half inch long) than *Isonychia* (three-eighths to five-eighths inch, excluding tails). Because of the greater average size of *Isonychia* and other members of the family Isonychiidae, they are sometimes categorized as *large* swimmers.

Larvae of *Isonychia* are usually found in fast flowing water, in riffles, living on and among rocks, branches, vegetation, leaf packs, and other debris. In their Pine-Popple River study, William Hilsenhoff and coauthors also mention commonly netting them from vegetation in slow-moving water along the banks. While the most prevalent factor in *Isonychia* larval habitat descriptions, as reported by mayfly workers, is the presence of fast water, this does not appear to be an absolute requirement.

Where *Isonychia* occur in Minnesota and Wisconsin they are typically seen emerging July through September. This occurs in part because they overwinter in the egg stage. It also means that larvae must grow quickly as they prey on immature midges, black flies, and other mayflies and feed herbivorously on microscopic diatoms and algae. Something I find curious is that isonychiid larvae are also known to crawl out of the water onto a rock or stick before the subimago appears, similar to the emergence behavior of stoneflies, while others are said to make the transformation directly at the water surface in classic mayfly style.

Subimagos and adults of *Isonychia* are one-half inch to five-eighths inch long, excluding tails. Both have dark, reddish-brown bodies, two pale yellow-to-whitish tails, and a second pair of wings about half the length of the first pair. In the classic Midwestern form, *Isonychia bicolor*, adults project their dark front legs forward showing the white feet, or tarsi, a characteristic responsible for the catchy imitation name, White-Gloved Howdy.

Subimagos emerge late in the day and require twenty-four hours to mature. The flights by adults of most species occur at dusk. Adults do their mating swarm well above the water, females dropping eggs or dipping their abdomens to release eggs. All become potential fish food as the spent adults fall to the surface in this generation's last contribution to the food chain.

‑⁄ι∖‑

Isonychia are scarce in the Kinnickinnic River. I obtained very few specimens in project collections, including from habitats that appeared to be suitable. For example, during Kinnickinnic faunal studies in 1999 and 2001, I collected just over 16,000 mayfly larvae. Nine of these were *Isonychia*. All of these specimens were derived from three sites in the lower river (table 3). Finding *Isonychia* in the Kinni was a rarity, and I realized later this result was not entirely unprecedented.

Hilsenhoff collected aquatics extensively from the rivers of Wisconsin. In his comprehensive 1995 publication, *Aquatic Insects of Wisconsin*, he characterized *Isonychia* larvae as "…fairly common, being found throughout the year among rocks and debris in rapid currents of a variety of streams." However, *Isonychia* numbers can vary widely in Wisconsin rivers, as shown by two earlier faunal studies. Both of these used conventional sampling techniques, but it needs to be noted they did not necessarily use matching sampling strategies. In the study of the Pine-Popple River system of Florence and Forest Counties in northeastern Wisconsin using multiple methods and 20 sites, Hilsenhoff and his crew found *Isonychia* larvae to be abundant. By contrast, in a study of the Brule River of northwestern Wisconsin using multiple methods and 35 sites, DuBois collected just one *Isonychia* larva.

‑⁄ι∖‑

There is much we don't understand about river organisms. Nature does not readily provide answers for some of the questions we ask. Yet we continue to utilize the inquiry process because it is our most powerful tool. We observe, we formulate problems, we gather data and, based on what they tell us, we go forward. Then we endeavor to learn more. Through years of persistence and practice, continued investigation opens doors into new worlds.

Writer and conservationist Nancy Wynne Newhall said that we have not yet learned to ask many of the questions for which the wilderness holds answers. This applies to the natural world at all scales, including on issues related to river creatures and the lives they lead. There is no shortage of curiosities, like those of *Isonychia* and *Hexagenia* that are close by, poised to prompt the next meaningful inquiry.

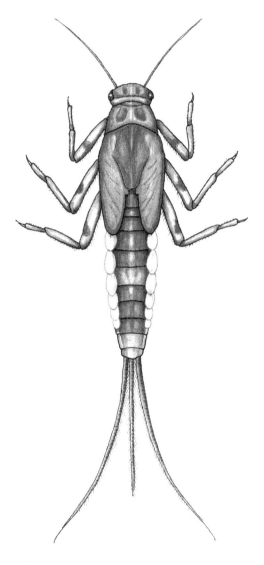

Small minnow mayfly larva, *Baetis tricaudatus*

THINKING SMALL

We were a few weeks into fall semester when I had a field trip scheduled for my Friday afternoon entomology class. We would take the short walk from our building to the South Fork, a tributary of the Kinnickinnic River, so my students could gain experience in collecting aquatic specimens. After previous collecting hikes in grasslands and woods, one of the lessons to be learned this day was that that visiting new habitats would yield another array of insects. This would include several new orders and families.

This was the first time most class members would have an opportunity to look closely at the stream flowing through their campus. While still in the lab room, I provided a brief background on the nature of the South Fork, stressed the idea of collecting diversely within the aquatic environment, and suggested an approach that would accomplish our goal. There were no complaints when we abandoned the classroom and carried our gear outside on that glorious October afternoon. It didn't hurt that this was a hands-on field experience. Active engagement was welcomed, even in these closing hours of the academic week.

The South Fork is a clear, coldwater creek largely hidden from view by virtue of setting and concealing vegetation. The portion that flows through campus is impacted by, among other things, the absence of adequate fish habitat. But the brook trout move swiftly and appear to eat well. On our field trip we should see numerous examples of insect and crustacean species that serve as food for those fish. When we arrived at the stream, we looked for the kinds of places in which invertebrates might live.

Teams of two to three people were equipped with an aquatic net, a cafeteria tray for sorting, forceps, and a specimen container. At the water we practiced the most effective ways to use the net and tray. Following that, teams spread out to assigned locations, mainly shallow riffles, to begin sampling. I gave them a chance to get started and then made rounds, visiting with each team to see what was turning up. It must have been a curious sight from the nearby walkway, seeing people on their hands and knees on the banks of the stream pointing out and talking about something interesting in cafeteria trays.

Over the years I learned that beginning collectors favor certain kinds of specimens during their river sampling experiences. Larger insects, and those more active or more colorful, attract the greatest attention, and are the most likely to be picked from the net or tray. I came to appreciate the idea that we, as humans, have an innate, unconscious bias, an initial inability to notice smaller species in the stream community. (Noted ecologist E. O. Wilson says that most people "don't give a hoot" about anything that's smaller than a hummingbird.) When I pointed out small minnow mayfly larvae to my students as an example of an important food item of trout, their perspective started to change. Valuable teaching moments emerge when you least expect them.

~/١\~

Recognition of size can be helpful when looking at mayfly larvae that are holding fast to a rock removed from the stream. Then, considered along with a few additional key features such as body shape and gill characteristics, an approach is in place for practical streamside recognition of members of the family Baetidae (BAY-tih-dee). Their one-eighth to one-half inch length is characteristic enough that it can be used as an aid in distinguishing an emergence of subimagos as they take to the air above the stream.

The common name baetid (BAY-tid) is derived from the family name Baetidae. Baetids belong to the mayfly suborder Pisciforma, a name that refers to their tapered, fish-like body form. The descriptive common name, small minnow mayflies, makes reference to the exceptional swimming ability of these larvae (they are often grouped as *swimmers* for convenience). The larvae propel themselves forward with an up-and-down movement of the abdomen and tails, the effectiveness of the latter greatly aided by the presence of many fine hairs. Fly fishers have many common names for baetid subimagos and adults because of their diversity and frequency in trout streams, often colorful and exotic designations, like the classic Bluewinged Olive.

So why might these particular mayflies be of special interest to aquatic biologists, fly fishers, or other inquisitive stream observers? The answer can be found in their abundance, diversity, and extended seasonal emergence sequence.

Small minnow mayflies are among the most common mayflies in the stream. The ubiquity of baetids in the Kinnickinnic River main stem and tributaries cannot be overemphasized. Out of one hundred and two aquatic collections made from the river over a one-year period there was never a sample which did not include some variety of immature baetids. In fact, two species were present in every sample taken at all seventeen river locations (table 3) in every month of the year.

Over two dozen species of baetids are found in the running and standing waters of Wisconsin. In practicality, if one spends the time to figure out which ones are present in their local water, they will likely be able to tease out a relatively small number of prevalent species. In a stream such as the Kinnickinnic, known for productivity over diversity, a limited number of species make up the baetid complex.

Here is an argument for basing river occurrence data on larval collections. The seasonal appearance and disappearance of larval populations is not only informative from a species determination and documentation perspective, it greatly assists in sorting out what can appear on the surface as undecipherable chaos. Add this to the unpredictable nature of the timing of emergences and whether or not they happen to occur when someone is present to see them, and larval monitoring, paradoxically, helps answer some of the questions about what is going on above the stream.

The following seasonal chronology of baetid hatches for the Kinnickinnic was determined, in part, from larval observations. Knowing this sequence, one can anticipate and, hopefully, experience the waves of emergence as they unfold through a typical season.

The small minnow mayfly, *Baetis tricaudatus* (*B. vagans* of earlier references) shown in larval stage in the prefacing illustration, is the first mayfly species to emerge in the spring. What is interesting about this insect is that it not only begins to emerge before all other mayflies at this time, but that it continues to hatch into the fall. Its continued prevalence is due, in part, to the fact that it is *bivoltine*; that is, it passes through two generations per year. The first emergence lasts from April to May; the second typically begins in June and continues to mid-October.

Another common baetid in the stream is *Baetis brunneicolor*. This species may be univoltine with a single long emergence period or bivoltine with two generations that overlap. Larvae of this species are found from May through December. Subimagos emerge from June through November, significantly overlapping the summer and fall emergence of *B. tricaudatus*. So now the small mayfly picture is not so simple. Two species of similar size (body length is approximately one-quarter inch) with subtle color differences are emerging more or less together through the late season. Because of the apparent numbers of these two species, they can be thought of as the primary small sized mayfly inhabitants of this stream.

However, the description so far is an oversimplification. Two additional members of the family Baetidae are present as larvae in the summer that adds another level of complexity to the fall hatch. These are *Baetis flavistriga* and *Plauditis punctiventris*. Both are univoltine with eggs diapausing (dormant) through winter until early summer. Although subimagos of these species are not particularly distinguishable in flight, they are smaller than the two described previously with a body length of approximately three-sixteenths of an inch. Considering that these two species begin emerging in mid-summer and continue into October, overlapping the emergences of both *B. tricaudatus* and *B. brunneicolor*, we have an interesting but potentially confusing flying assortment above the water. Now I remember why I chose to study mayflies from the orderly, underwater, larval perspective!

Baetids are known widely for large population numbers. Fred Arbona Jr., author of *Mayflies, the Angler, and the Trout*, comments generally about numbers and abundance of the family in trout streams. Leonard and Leonard in *Mayflies of Michigan Trout Streams*, discussing *B. brunneicolor*, write of numerically impressive hatches. It is clear, too, that baetids are among the most common of aquatic insects in the Kinnickinnic River. Humphrey and Shogren, describing the upper Kinni, mention the omnipresence of *Baetis* in those reaches. I would add that larval studies confirm their presence at all Kinni locations sampled, including all sites in the lower river as well (table 3).

〜ノ|〵〜

Baetids live out their lives on a small scale, that is, until you consider their widespread occurrence and numbers. In spite of their diminutive size they are a significant component of the stream community where they function as collector-gatherers and scrapers. They fit perfectly into the category E. O. Wilson calls the *important little things*. Their constant presence in the stream, in bottom substrates, vegetation, and drift, and periodic to continual appearances at the surface, make them especially valuable as food for insects, fish, birds, and other predators.

It was rewarding to see members of my entomology classes expand their observational perspective on aquatic insects by visiting a new and distinct ecological setting. Additionally, all that was needed was a heads-up for a few new orders and families and key features to look for, ideas that any interested person could incorporate into their routine. And *thinking small*, as always, was an important part of that lesson.

Dragonfly larva, family Aeshnidae

Damselfly larva, family Calopterygidae

FLYING DRAGONS AND DAMSELS

We were helping a neighbor with some outdoor work one midsummer morning when someone called attention to the number of dragonflies whirring overhead. A virtual squadron of the ancient-looking insects was on the wing, each individual clearly visible against the blue sky and all flying in the same direction. I later learned that in addition to the typical reasons for dragonfly flight—to eat, to mate, to position eggs—that take place around water, adults venture far and wide, including away from their ponds, lakes, and streams of origin, following emergence. In our open location with no water nearby the mass appeared to be engaged in this post-emergence behavior. People who spend time outside see these distinctive insects regularly and recognize their special flying habits. I wonder how many of them are familiar with the underwater development leading up to these noteworthy flights.

"They're good!" our neighbor proclaimed matter-of-factly, making implied reference to the idea that these flying eating machines consume mosquitos. From a human standpoint it *is* good that mosquitoes are among the many aerial insects preyed upon by dragonflies and damselflies, with the caution that the activity regimes of the presumed predators and their prey do not exactly align. The term "mosquito hawk" has been used in conjunction with dragonfly adults, as well as with adult crane flies, in the latter case totally inaccurately. Dragonflies also play an important biological role when they themselves are eaten and constituent nutrients and energy are passed on to birds, frogs, and fish.

Dragonflies and damselflies, known as odonates from the order name Odonata (oh-doe-NOT-ah), give us a glimpse of insect life after wings evolved but before sophisticated mechanisms of wing folding appeared. Adults of two major aquatic insect groups, Odonata and Ephemeroptera (mayflies), lack the ability to fold their wings flat over the abdomen. These two orders share other characteristics including aquatic development of immature stages and incomplete metamorphosis. They differ, in a general way, in the types of water they inhabit. Most odonate larvae are found in ponds, wetlands, and other standing waters, with a third of the species inhabiting streams. Mayfly larvae, in contrast, are primarily stream dwellers with fewer species living in ponds and lakes.

In a review of Paleozoic arthropod fossils William Shear and Jarmila Kukalova-Peck hypothesized that the abundant and diverse dragonfly-like protodonates (*protos* - first, original) were the top aerial predators of late Carboniferous and Permian skies 300 million years ago. No wonder, considering the size of these prehistoric insects. Fossil remains of *Meganeura monyi* found in France had a wingspan of just under twenty-five inches. Another, *Meganeuropsis permiana*, had wings almost twenty-eight inches across. Both are among the largest insects that ever lived. As one who focuses on aquatic insects, especially larvae, I can only fantasize about the immatures that must have given rise to these enormous adults and the excitement, not to mention the challenge, of netting one as a reference specimen!

Adult dragonflies and damselflies have a number of morphological features in common, including two pairs of elongate, many-veined membranous wings, large compound eyes, and a long, slender abdomen. Dragonflies are known as extremely strong and agile fliers. Their legs are adapted for catching prey, allowing them to ingest what they catch in flight. Although I have not experienced it personally, I've heard on more than one occasion about a dragonfly grabbing onto the artificial fly of an angler in the middle of a cast. Dragonflies tend to be large and robust insects that rest with their wings held out to the sides. Damselflies are not considered strong fliers like their dragonfly relatives, but they are very efficient predators. Damselflies hold their wings together above the back, lacking the mechanism to fold them flat.

Dragonfly and damselfly larvae have distinctively large eyes, short, thin antennae, and well-developed legs. Both have two pairs of wing pads originating on the thorax. The primary differences in appearance of the larvae are the stout abdomen of the dragonfly (accompanying photos) with no apparent tails, except for several small pointed terminal structures, compared to the slender abdomen of the damselfly terminating with three tail-like or leaf-like caudal gills. Dragonfly and damselfly larvae make their way over and through organic debris and substrate materials by crawling. When a quick escape is needed, dragonfly larvae can expel water explosively from the rectum to move with a jet-like action. Damselfly larvae swim using side-to-side undulating movements of the abdomen and caudal gills.

Habitats suitable for odonates do not appear to be limited in the Kinnickinnic, but repeated aquatic collections produced few representatives. This occurred even when samples were taken from slow and moderate current areas and in substrates where they would be expected to reside.

The single kind of dragonfly larva found was *Aeshna*, the common darner genus known for its large size and powerful flight. Larvae of the only two Wisconsin genera of broad-winged damsels, *Calopteryx* and *Hetaerina* were also recorded. Adults of *Calopteryx maculata*, the black-winged damselfly or ebony jewelwing, can be seen fluttering along the vegetated banks of the river in midsummer. They are strikingly colored, males having black wings and females with wings that are gray to brown with a white dot, called a stigma, at the tip. The elongate bodies of both are metallic green. Larvae of two narrow-winged damselflies, also known as pond damselflies, *Enallagma* and *Nehalennia*, live in the Kinni as well. Certain adults of *Enallagma* known as bluets are small with clear wings and a slender light blue body with black markings. They are often seen hovering low over stream banks or perched on bank vegetation.

Odonates develop via incomplete metamorphosis, similar to mayflies and stoneflies, reaching maturity without a pupal stage. In most dragonfly families eggs are deposited directly onto or under the water surface. Some dragonflies, specifically the darners, and all damselflies oviposit into the tissues of aquatic plants above or below the water. Eggs hatch into tiny first instar larvae after one to three weeks. As they feed, each of the ten to twelve larval instars, or stages, reaches the maximum size allowed by that exoskeleton. Then molting occurs and growth continues.

Odonate larvae use one of two predatory strategies to obtain food. Some lie in wait for food organisms and ambush moving prey. Others actively work through vegetation and debris seeking organisms to attack, itself a behavior with potential risk. At the point of encounter, larval odonates project a modified mouthpart, the impressive and formidable hinged *labium*, or lower lip, armed with opposing claw-like hooks for grasping. When thrust, it strikes the prey with extreme speed and power, rendering the victim incapable of escape.

When the last larval instars reach full size, they migrate to shore, drag-onflies crawling and damselflies swimming, to vegetation or other structures on which to exit the water. This shoreward migration is another window of susceptibility of these organisms to fish predation and is the most significant. Both dragonfly and damselfly species emerge during all non-winter months, dragonflies after one to three years of larval development, damselflies after a year. They emerge from the last larval skin above the water, leaving a per-fect—but hollow—representation of themselves attached to a plant stem, tree trunk, or vertical face of a boulder. During this process they may be subject to predation by another insect, a frog, or a bird. Fertilized adult females returning to the water to deposit eggs create the last chance fish have to ingest individuals of this generation.

Predators take advantage of freshly emerged odonate adults because they are an easy target and readily digestible. A number of hours are required for the biochemical processes of hardening and darkening of the new exoskeleton to occur and, until sufficient time has passed, individuals remain soft and pale. In this state they are known as *tenerals* (TEN-er-als), from the Latin *tener* mean-ing soft, tender, delicate.

Assisting on a research project with colleague Mark Bergland, I witnessed firsthand the preferences of parent red-winged blackbirds as they selected in-dividual insects to feed their young. Mark was studying foraging behavior of red wings that were nesting in a cattail marsh in St. Croix County, Wisconsin. His equipment consisted of an elevated platform from which numerous nests could be seen, a spotting scope for a clear view of nests and bird activity, and a camera positioned adjacent to a nest in which young were being repeatedly fed. When an adult returned from foraging, he could capture (using a remote shutter release) an image of food items the adult bird held in its beak. From these photos he determined which parent had foraged and calculated the food biomass delivered. Photographic records showed that tenerals, including many freshly emerged marsh odonates, were frequently chosen to be transported to the nest for consumption by the hungry young.

In addition to impressions of mass flights, I have a persistent mental im-age of adult dragonflies patrolling up and down sections of streams, veering instantly off of a straight course as they maneuver to catch prey. Sometimes they hover in place and occasionally they stop abruptly in mid-air and dart off in a totally new direction. They are known to have sensory mechanisms that allow them to track a target organism, determine an interception trajectory, and capture accordingly. *Selective attention* has also been detected in dragonflies, an ability by which they focus on a single quarry among a cluster of similar insects. Some observations suggest they ambush prey in flight from a direction imperceptible to the prey, as in approaching from behind and below. The flight paths and predatory proficiencies that we observe routinely are based on sophisticated sensory, behavioral, and anatomical adaptations.

By watching adult dragonflies in flight and imagining the aquatic stages that led to these nimble aerial insects, what may appear superficially as disconnected parts of the living world have more meaning. One gains further appreciation by thinking of the adaptations and successful strategies of the predatory larvae that acquired the nutrients on which the adult bodies were built. Connecting this generation with those that came previously, tens of millions of generations back to the Permian, adds the perspective of geologic time. When we are fortunate enough to be at our home stream or in our backyard seeing dragonflies and damselflies flying, we have a perfect opportunity to better understand a well-adapted modern day insect and, at the same time, capture a view of life as it occurred on Earth many millions of years ago.

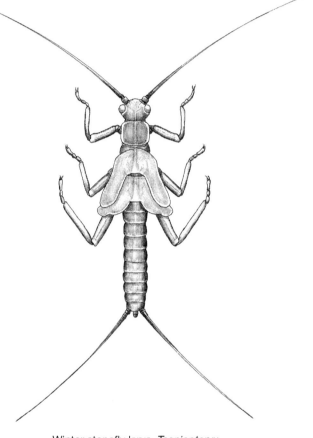

Winter stonefly larva, *Taeniopteryx*

A CASE OF COOL TIMING

One aspect of field biology, particularly field entomology, that normally comes to a halt with the onset of winter, is specimen collection. Fortunately, this is not the case when working with river insects, as the pursuit may not only continue, valuable information can be obtained. After a year or more of records acquisition, data points can be assembled into a yearly cycle for the species in question. Sampling also keeps the river biologist active and happy through the winter.

Late winter has a special feel to it as the sun arches higher and days lengthen. With trees bare and the ground snow covered, terrestrial insect life is understandably quiescent. It might seem in these surroundings that the potential for seeing adult insects would be remote. But near the riverbank at this time of year, it's good to keep an eye on the surface of the crusted snow. This is when and where you may find adult winter stoneflies—that have just made the transition from life in water to life on land—the classic aquatic insect life cycle adapted to a less-than-common schedule.

Entomologists and fly fishers use the term *winter stonefly* to designate stonefly species in which adult emergence happens at this unusual time of year. These stoneflies exit the water, depending on species and conditions, from late January to early April. Various common names exist for these creatures: early browns, little or small browns, little blacks, winter blacks, and others. The names suggest several characteristics they have in common, along with their seasonal emergence behavior. These include a distinctive dark brown-to-black color that contrasts sharply with riverbank snow, the background against which adults are commonly seen, and size roughly one-half inch long. Further help in field recognition comes with observing the narrow body profile of both larvae and adults.

Winter stoneflies encountered in Wisconsin are primarily members of two families: Capniidae (slender or small winter stoneflies) and Taeniopterygidae (winter stoneflies or taeniopterygid broadbacks). The genus *Taeniopteryx* (tee-nee-OP-ter-iks) has been well documented in the Kinnickinnic by larval collections along the length of the river (table 4). They are netted primarily from submerged leaves and other debris found outside of the main current. No documentation exists for capniid winter stoneflies in the Kinni.

Two related stonefly families (in the same suborder as Capniidae and Taeniopterygidae) occur in Wisconsin, albeit with later seasonal emergences than capniids and taeniopterygids. The Nemouridae, known as nemourid broadbacks or brown stoneflies, emerge in spring and early summer. Very small numbers of two nemourid genera, *Nemoura* and *Amphinemura*, were collected in the Kinni. The Leuctridae, roll-winged or rolledwinged stoneflies, emerge May through September in Wisconsin. Leuctrids are not readily collected because of their propensity to stay burrowed in substrate, and none have been found to date in the Kinni.

~/\~

The curious display of late winter stonefly adult emergence takes place on a day, or series of days, for which the exact condition or combination of triggers is unknown. Factors often suggested are moderating water temperature or increasing hours of daylight or both. The timing of the event is only roughly predictable. The latest I've seen overwintering *Taeniopteryx* larvae in spring samples is early in the second week of March, their absence indicating complete emergence by that date. They do this in the typical stonefly manner, with larvae migrating to shallow areas and crawling onto rocks or woody debris at the stream bank. There the adult splits out of the last larval skin, emerges, and crawls to a higher position. Well clear of the water, male *Taeniopteryx* attract the attention of females by thumping their abdomen on whatever surface they are resting. Females sense these species-specific tapping patterns and drum in return. Reciprocal communication brings males and females together for copulation. After mating, females crawl or fly to water and there release their egg masses.

Eggs deposited in late winter or early spring quickly hatch, producing tiny larvae. These progeny then disappear, burrowing into substrate where they spend the rest of spring and all of summer. It's inferred they have entered a state of suspended growth and development known as *diapause*. When diapause breaks—an event considered to be dependent again on temperature or day length or both—feeding and growth resume. Only then, in September in the Kinnickinnic, do larvae become large enough to find in net collections. Development continues rapidly through the fall, winter, and spring months, as part of a *fast seasonal* life cycle. Diatoms and organic detritus are the primary larval food sources, so larvae serve as both herbivores and detritivores in the food web.

━╱╲━

Stoneflies, like other invertebrates, are *ectothermic*. This means, as for fish and reptiles, insect bodies reflect the temperature of their surroundings. Stonefly emergence during this cool time of year presents the possibility, even likelihood, of air temperature being below the freezing point. So how can these insects possibly function in the chilly late winter air of western Wisconsin?

Winter stonefly adults rely on a variety of adaptations to survive and reproduce in less than optimal thermal conditions. This involves behavior, coloration, and internal biochemicals. Adults tend to emerge with optimal diurnal timing, as in the afternoon when days have become longer and the warmth of the sun is available. In the absence of ideal conditions they seek protected areas: under natural overhangs or suspended bank ice and on human-made structures such as bridge supports. Their dark brown or black body pigmentation is particularly advantageous from the standpoint of absorbing solar radiation. Though much study remains to be done on *cryoprotectants* in stoneflies, it is likely the presence of antifreeze materials complements behavioral freeze-avoidance strategies. In a process known as supercooling, the hemolymph, or blood, of the insect and its tissues are allowed to cool below their freezing point without solidification or crystallization. Some materials known to prevent freezing are familiar biochemicals such as sugars and proteins, and the syrupy alcohol known as glycerol.

━╱╲━

When I try to imagine what trout are eating in late winter and early spring, winter stonefly larvae inevitably enter the picture as potential prey. Accidental dislodgement or purposeful nudging of substrate by fish can put these larvae adrift and make them vulnerable to predation. Also, as they migrate to the edge of the river to find an object on which to crawl out of the water, they fall prey to fish in significant numbers.

There were days in late winter when I went to the valley to walk and explore, and found signs of life that enhanced the experience. On one occasion I followed the tracks of a fox paralleling the edge of the river. Along its path I could see where it stopped to dig in the snow, in some places reaching leaves buried since the previous fall. Like the fox, I was attracted by things of interest, paused to satisfy my curiosity, and moved on.

When one is attentive to the possibility of novel experiences, nature responds with corresponding revelations. It is these times along the stream, when we stay aware of the potential of seeing new things, that we discover. On late winter days, when the sun reaches deep into the gorge and its rays warm our skin, we sense the first traces of spring. On those same days we may be rewarded with another sign: richly dark brown or black insects—winter stoneflies— resting on, and in stark contrast with, the bright surface of the lingering snow.

Common stonefly larva, *Paragnetina*

MACROINVERTEBRATE CANARIES

One Saturday morning I was setting up to speak at a suburban Twin Cities (Minnesota) fly shop about insect life of the Kinnickinnic River. As the time approached for the program to start, the crowd grew beyond the sixty chairs provided. I was excited to see this level of interest. I viewed these talks as chances to share my thoughts on a favorite subject with interested people, along the lines of my experiences in biology teaching. Enthusiasm was palpable. Questions from the audience were as perceptive as any teacher could hope for.

I remember it well because upon my arrival at the shop, my former student and accomplished fly fisher, fly tier, and guide, Andy Roth, showed me a larval stonefly imitation he tied. The fly was a perfect match for the common stonefly, *Paragnetina media*, an insect I intended to talk about. It was easy to imagine this artificial fly mimicking a natural larva dislodged from the bottom rubble, dead-drifting in the current, and coming into view of a hungry trout. I began my talk with this verbal picture, a totally unplanned opening.

The common stonefly stands out for me as an especially desirable aquatic organism to encounter. This insect has special appeal because of a combination of features. First, it's found in cold, clear running water, just the kind of environment I like to work in. Second, it inhabits rocky, cobble-strewn bottoms, again, an attraction for me. Third, it lives in water that is clean and free of organic pollution. And, finally, it has a distinctive appearance: a rich mahogany-brown body color inscribed with creamy yellow tortoiseshell-like markings, making it one of the more colorful creatures in the river.

This common stonefly, also known as the embossed stonefly, is a member of the family Perlidae. I found a single species, *Paragnetina media*, year around in the lower Kinnickinnic in moderate numbers (Sites 1-8, table 4). Larvae can be found in the river at any time because development from egg to adult requires two or three years. Observers, from casual to astute, may miss seeing emerging or streamside adults as their activity is primarily nocturnal.

Another common stonefly of the Kinni, *Perlesta*, is smaller, appearing color-wise more like the unrelated little yellows of the family Perlodidae. Magnification may be needed to distinguish *Perlesta* from the perlodids. (*Perlesta* have finely branched gills on all three thoracic segments; perlodids lack gills on thoracic segments.) *Perlesta*, such as *P. decipiens*, require one year to develop. Larvae are present in the water only during the summer and appear to be confined to the lower Kinni (table 4). No larvae appear until June, following a relatively late egg hatch. Adults emerge through August.

Some streams in the Midwest have notable common stoneflies not found in the Kinnickinnic River. One of these is the great brown stonefly, *Acroneuria lycorias*. This is an impressive insect, not soon forgotten. It is particularly remarkable in appearance because its dark brown color is sharply contrasted with yellow to orange-tinged cream-tan markings. It varies in size from one-half inch to one and one-quarter inch depending on age and larval stage. Great brown stoneflies can be found in a variety of stream habitats and seem to be especially numerous in rocky riffles. Adults emerge through the summer.

Immature stoneflies are recognized by having two pairs of developing wings called wing pads, two thin tails, and two tarsal claws. Perlids, family Perlidae, the group to which the commons belong, have finely branched gills near the bases of their legs on all thoracic segments and gills totally absent from abdominal segments. The latter character is an important one to check for to rule out identification as a giant stonefly.

Paragnetina is known as a formidable predator in the stream ecosystem. They feed on mayfly (*Baetis*), caddisfly (*Ceratopsyche, Cheumatopsyche*), and midge larvae, as well as on other small arthropods, actively searching out prey among substrate rocks and debris. They, in turn, become vulnerable to feeding by fish because their exploratory movement makes them more likely to be seen and to become part of stream drift. Additionally, larvae are exposed to predation during their pre-emergence migration to streamside rocks and bank structures, a typical stonefly behavior.

Stoneflies, in general, are regarded as indicators of high water quality. They are an integral part of the EPT metric, a generic richness calculation based on the percentage of Ephemeroptera (mayflies), Plecoptera (stoneflies), and Trichoptera (caddisflies) present in a standardized stream sample. The higher the EPT value, the higher the water quality. Stoneflies, like mayflies and caddisflies, are clustered in this metric because they are generally intolerant of organic stream pollution and resultant poorly oxygenated water.

One is fortunate to have common stoneflies living in their favorite stream. They flourish in the same kinds of environments that promote healthy, self-sustaining populations of trout. Following a talk I gave on river macroinvertebrates (different from the presentation at the fly shop), I was asked which, in my opinion, would be the first insects to disappear if the water quality of a given river were to decline. I responded with the answer *stoneflies*, because they are notoriously absent from degraded river systems. Stoneflies require clean, cold, fast-moving, highly oxygenated water. Unfavorable changes in pollution levels, current rates, and temperatures appear to impact these organisms inordinately.

This discussion reminds me of an experience I had at a meeting of the North American Benthological Society (now the Society for Freshwater Science). I was sharing a selection of Kinnickinnic specimens with an aquatics specialist from a state I assumed to have a poor representation of healthy streams. When I handed the rack of preserved insects to him, including a dozen clearly visible mayfly, stonefly, and caddisfly larvae, he scanned across the series and said with unhidden dismay, "I'd kill to work in a stream that had insects like this." He recognized the quality of the Kinni with one glance of its common creatures. Then we got busy—taking a closer look at the stoneflies.

A single species of stonefly and a well-tied imitation of its larva got me started on a presentation of common species I was finding in the Kinni. It provided a chance, as well, to stress the importance of a healthy stream environment for the future of this species in the river. It would be the most unfortunate of times if conditions under our collective control would lead to the demise of this emblematic insect, or any of its stonefly relatives. Is it healthy for anyone if the canary dies?

Perlodid stonefly larva, *Isoperla*

LITTLE YELLOW
PATTERNED STONEFLIES

By spring, following a new project start-up in January, I was making regular visits to the river. I was working these trips in among teaching and family commitments, with weekends providing the chance to maintain the planned schedule. I kept up on post-collection sorting, preservation of specimens, and identifications at home in the evening. Upcoming visits needed attention, too, so after looking for available blocks of time in my schedule, I would contact landowners for access permission when needed, make sure the equipment pack was restocked with collecting supplies, and check the weather forecast. Once the schedule opened up and preliminaries were completed, I was on my way to spending quality time in the stream.

Finding the characteristic insect inhabitants of a river is its own reward. Following up on what is observed brings meaning. The river *per se* provides a distinctive environment and by simply being there one can start to see its physical and biotic qualities. But, what do different habitats actually offer in the way of shelter and resources? How do resident organisms acquire energy and nutrients? What preys on *them*? Questions may originate while sampling, but most answers come later. They arrive after identification is completed, or well in progress, and literature sources are explored. New perspectives on the aquatic community are realized both in and out of the stream.

April brings many good things in the way of river insects. This is the time of year to look for small versions of stonefly larvae that were maturing, albeit slowly, in the chilled water of winter. They would be reaching full size and nearing their transition to flying insects. I anticipated seeing them in the gravel and cobble deposits, places with fast current and all-important sheltering spaces. Only in habitats of this quality, with substrates of mixed rocky materials, organic debris, and cold, clean, oxygenated water, can one expect to find such exemplary residents.

So, approaching the river, I imagine these exquisite stoneflies. I can visualize their yellow body color, intricate brownish markings, and a seemingly delicate makeup. They remain permanently stored among my larval stonefly memories. Several of these in the genus *Isoperla*, family Perlodidae (per-LOD-ih-dee), are predictable at this time and in this location. They are unique among the benthic fauna and easy to recognize. Two common group names, little yellow stoneflies and patterned stoneflies, are appropriate, considering the size, color, and markings of full grown larvae, and size and color of adults. Both larvae and adults are one-quarter to over one-half of an inch long. Larvae are yellow-to-orange-to-tan in color with brown markings on the head, thorax, and abdomen (prefacing photo). Adults can be different shades of yellow, from pale to bright; some have tinges of green and tan.

Hilsenhoff lists eleven species of *Isoperla* from rivers across Wisconsin. Four of these have been found to date in the Kinnickinnic: *Isoperla slossonae*, *I. transmarina*, *I. dicala*, and *I. bilineata*. Of these *I. slossonae* is collected most often and occurs in apparent highest numbers throughout the Kinnickinnic, with the exception of the far upper reaches of the river (table 4). *I. transmarina* and *I. dicala* appear to have slightly more restricted distributions, living in reaches from Kinnickinnic River State Park to the Quarry Road-Liberty Road areas. *I. bilineata* is known as an insect of larger rivers and was collected in small numbers in far downstream regions of the lower Kinni. Most species of *Isoperla* are carnivorous as larvae, but some studies suggest that *I. bilineata* is an herbivore.

While size and color, along with recognition of general stonefly features, are particularly helpful for initial streamside identification of these Kinni insects, additional characters are necessary for confirmation of this family. Some of these may require magnification. On these larvae look for the pronotum (first thoracic segment) to be wider than the abdomen and wing pads that diverge from the body. It is also important to confirm the absence of branching gills behind the bases of the legs and that the body of the labium (lower lip) is divided into only two parts.

Isoperla larvae are relatively easy to find in the Kinnickinnic (table 4), depending on species, through the fall, winter, and spring months. The developmental process that brings the larvae to full size over these months is a *fast seasonal* life cycle. Emergence of adult *Isoperla* in the Kinni occurs primarily in April and May. By the end of the first week in June, no traces of larvae remain in the river. Their future is now based on an extended period of time in the egg stage. *Isoperla* eggs are programmed for two months or more of suspended development known as *diapause*. Diapause is controlled by physiological mechanisms within an individual stage. Resumption of development can be entirely under intrinsic control or may require, or be subject to, external stimuli such as a change in photoperiod (day length) or temperature or both. When the eggs hatch in late summer and larvae grow large enough to be seen in September, they can be observed as common residents of the river once again. They are now in the *fast* part of the *fast seasonal* growth cycle. What might be the purpose of such a delay? Wallace and Anderson suggest that it may be related to evasion of fish predation or avoidance of the elevated temperatures of summer.

Isoperla emergence is an event that may go undetected. Stoneflies in general tend to be less visible in the vicinity of the stream than many other emerging insects. Reasons for this include: the lower density of stoneflies relative to other macroinvertebrates, the behavior of larvae migrating to the stream bank and crawling from the water before exiting their last larval skin, and the nocturnal emergence of some species. Once adults have emerged, they tend to disperse on the ground and through vegetation as they complete maturation and terrestrial adaptation. Mating is also a cryptic activity, occurring on the ground. There is no aerial swarming. Fish take advantage of larvae when they are migrating underwater to reach the sides of the stream, and prey to a lesser extent on females as they return to the water surface to deposit eggs.

When little yellow patterned stoneflies appear by the stream on a late spring day, they attract attention and create wonder. They add to our appreciation of the landscape from the minute living spaces under river rocks and debris in which they live to the scale of the entire watershed. They inhabit places that represent the highest measures of water quality, from clarity to temperature, oxygen availability, and lack of pollution. As individuals whose lives span a complete year, they show us a less than common temporal strategy, the purpose or purposes of which invite our speculation. Albert Einstein captured the essence of curiosities such as these when he said: "We still do not know one thousandth of one percent of what nature has revealed to us." All the more reason to be amazed by the turns in the life cycle of a stonefly, valuing how each adaptation has been selected for and uniquely refined for a myriad of habitat and seasonal variables.

Giant stonefly larva, *Pteronarcys*

A SHEEP IN WOLF'S CLOTHING

Things are not always what they seem in the underwater world. Take, for example, the insect named for its uncommonly large size, the giant stonefly. In addition to impressive dimensions and overall robust form, these creatures have an exoskeleton that resembles a suit of battle armor, including sharply angular body projections, pointed wing pads, and stout legs (visible in accompanying photo). With these features is camouflaging coloration of grays or browns, and sometimes a greenish or orangish cast. Based on their appearance, it would be natural to assume giant stoneflies are predators, ingesting anything they please, large or small, they might encounter in the river.

Could this be a sheep-in-wolf's-clothing adaptation in which defensive anatomy provides protection against would-be attackers? Certainly the niche these stoneflies occupy is far from that of a predator. Giant stoneflies are *shredders*. Shredding, by definition, is a degradative process whereby something is cut, torn, grated, sliced, or chopped into smaller fragments. These larvae shred proficiently, breaking down what is known technically as Course Particulate Organic Matter (CPOM). CPOM consists of organic pieces larger than 1 mm (one twenty-fifth of an inch) in size. Much of what is degraded is bits of hardwood leaves, an abundant energy source in streams surrounded by trees and shrubs. Giant stonefly larvae render leaves skeletonized, a condition where most of the leaf is gone and only the veins remain intact. In simple and convincing laboratory experimentation Minnesota stonefly researcher Phillip Harden maintained *Pteronarcys* larvae in rearing jars for many months, feeding them on elm leaves.

Inefficient digestion of these materials means that much of it becomes available downstream for microbial colonization and acquisition by collectors. Gut content analyses show that the major food sources of *Pteronarcys* are detritus and algae, specifically diatoms. In other words, these larvae are at the same time detritivores and herbivores. Larvae are collected primarily in fast or moderate current where leaves and woody debris have accumulated, as in leaf packs trapped in the branches of submerged limbs.

One of my early experiences observing an adult giant stonefly in the wild was on a solo paddling trip in the Boundary Waters Canoe Area of northern Minnesota. I just arrived at a new campsite and was unloading my gear when the insect appeared on top of one of my packs. I didn't see it land, but it immediately caught my attention. The winged invertebrate was nearly two inches long and impressive beyond its size. Numerous dark wing veins contrasted with a lighter grayish-tan wing and body color. If the insect settled on the branch of a tree or shrub, or on a rock or the ground, it might have been mistaken for a curled-up dead leaf. But there it rested, standing out against the blue nylon, clearly visible to a predator, mate, or curious human. I found my camera and crept toward it. I fully expected it to take flight, but it remained perfectly still. Close up I could see its long narrow front wings positioned flat on top of one another, over its back in classic stonefly manner. The legs and antennae were slender and dark, and the ends of two tails just showed from under the tips of its wings. A photograph would be all that was needed to confirm its identity once I returned home. After considerable passage of time, I realize that I acquired images in two forms that afternoon: There was the one captured on film and another living in the recollection of the day.

Giant stoneflies, genus *Pteronarcys* (tare-oh-NAR-sees), are members of the family Pteronarcyidae (tare-oh-nar-SEE-ih-dee). For both names the P is silent, as in pronunciation of pterosaur (TARE-oh-sore), the flying reptile of the Jurassic Period. The giant stonefly of greatest renown is the celebrated giant salmonfly, *Pteronarcys californica*, of the western United States. Emergence of large numbers of these adults creates a feeding frenzy for trout and an equally strong response by anglers who attempt to entice the fish with imitations. A trip to fish a hatch of these large stoneflies on the Yellowstone, Madison, and other big western rivers is one of the pilgrimages that enthusiastic anglers make to pay homage at a fly fishing mecca.

In the Midwest we have two species of *Pteronarcys*, *P. dorsata* and *P. pictetii*. These do not emerge in large numbers nor do they attract anglers in the way salmonflies do out West, but they are considered important prey, especially for fish during pre-emergence underwater migration of larvae. Hilsenhoff reported that both species are widely distributed in Wisconsin. Harden and Mickel found a *definite* geographic separation of the two species in Minnesota, with *P. dorsata* only northeastern and *P. pictetii* occurring centrally and to the southern and eastern parts of the state.

Identification of giant stonefly larvae to the family level can be established by finding light colored filamentous branching gills on the first two abdominal segments, as well as at the bases of legs on the thorax. These are features that can be observed streamside on this conspicuously large insect, often without magnification. Family and genus determinations coincide because only one genus, *Pteronarcys*, is known to occur in Minnesota and Wisconsin. When species identification is needed for larvae, as in faunal studies, the shape of the ninth abdominal sternite (the ventral plate of abdominal segment nine) in males is a key feature. In general, larvae and adults of both species look very much alike and have similar life cycles.

Giant stonefly larvae develop primarily in moderate to fast current on rocky stream bottoms where their food sources collect. Larvae molt many times—in a Massachusetts study *Pteronarcys proteus* was reported to have twelve instars—as they grow to maturity. In the Upper Midwest larval development requires two to four years, a life cycle feature that translates into larval collection during any month of the year. When growth is completed, mature larvae migrate underwater to the edges of the stream. They crawl out of the water onto the bank, clinging to a rock or log in preparation for adult departure from the last larval skin. Adults are sometimes seen in early morning after emergence, or in the evening when females return to the stream to oviposit, but they often go undetected because of their nocturnal activity. In the Midwest adults emerge in April and May.

Pteronarcys are best known from medium to large streams, although there is evidence that *P. pictetii* occurs in small streams as well. In the Kinnickinnic River I have found *P. pictetii* exclusively, with the caveat that only male larvae could be determined morphologically using the Harden and Mickel key. All were from the downstream two-thirds of my river sampling sites; none were found above Liberty Road (table 4). Samples rarely yielded more than a few specimens. To influence the population at a site with the least possible impact I limited my collection to one or two individuals for the reference collection. Any others in the sorting tray were counted, recorded on the spot as *Pteronarcys*, and returned to the river, along the lines of a giant stonefly *catch-and-release* procedure.

Stoneflies offer their own perspective on water quality and are relied upon as telltale species in determining certain river metrics. Stoneflies in general bode well for stream quality, as do mayflies and caddisflies. In the Hilsenhoff Biotic Index (HBI), a standard procedure used by the Wisconsin Department of Natural Resources for determining water conditions, both Midwestern *Pteronarcys* species have a tolerance value of zero. This number is derived from a ten point scale where zero is excellent and ten is very poor. Because of their extreme intolerance of organic pollution, these species are dependable biological indicators of high quality water and are absent in the presence of detrimental conditions.

The role that *Pteronarcys* plays in the river food web provides us with an opportunity to understand the elegant nature of ecological relationships. We start with riparian trees and shrubs converting solar energy to carbohydrates via photosynthesis. A portion of the acquired energy is used for production of plant structure, including stems, branches, and leaves. The proximity of plants to the stream and forces of gravity, wind, and rain naturally result in the introduction of these organic materials into the water. Thus we have the beginning of a *detrital food web*. Physical and biological degradation, carried out in part by feeding activity of giant stonefly larvae, reduces these coarse organics to fine particles. In doing so the larvae, with other detritivores, extract and utilize leaf resources to sustain their lives. Downstream, all nature of organisms from microbes to filterers and gatherers derive remaining energy and nutrients as they collect and exploit the products of shredding.

╼╱╎╲╾

Interconnectedness among elements of the natural world has been a theme in scientific thinking for over two hundred years. German explorer, naturalist, and scientist Alexander von Humboldt expressed this idea in the early 1800s. One of Humboldt's colleagues commented that he was the first person to recognize that all in nature was woven together as with 'a thousand threads.'

My own perceptions regarding the giant stonefly took on this concept of connecting threads as I got to know it. First I thought simply and naively of the insect—it was impressively large and daunting. Then, I learned the larva was a shredder and not a predator. Somewhat later, I recognized its significance as a symbol of high water quality. And, finally, it became for me a regular reminder of how diverse river species are linked by energy relationships. In its upstream association with riverside vegetation and countless connections to downstream organisms, *Pteronarcys* demonstrates how important a seemingly basic act like shredding can be in sustaining the threads that connect organisms of an aquatic community.

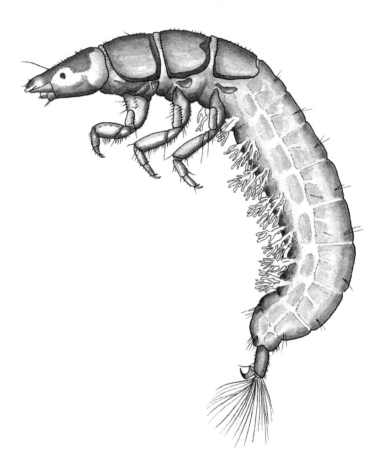

Common net-spinner larva, *Ceratopsyche*

NAKED CADDISFLIES

There is hardly a more remarkable sight at twilight on a calm summer evening than caddisflies lifting from the river in numbers beyond description. Who doesn't think of this display as an escape, a sense of freedom gained by an organism by simply moving from one medium to another? But is it so straightforward and uncomplicated? Unseen below the surface are voracious fish, their focus drawn to the cloaked adults swimming up from the streambed as they are swept along by the current. At the surface the caddisflies act intently to become airborne, to free themselves from both the water and their pupal covering. At this point they must emerge with all possible speed to avoid becoming food items for surface-feeding fish. Some make the transition successfully, the power of numbers and rules of probability working in their favor. For survivors the ultimate reward is the opportunity to pass their genes on to the next generation.

After a day at the river, cold beverages are enjoyed on the deck at home. In growing darkness moths are attracted to the outside light. Someone observes the similarity of flight behavior to that of caddisflies earlier in the day. Recognition of this kind of order in the natural world happens because we intuitively see an evolutionary relationship. The two kinds of insects we observed do in fact belong to two closely related groups. Caddisflies are members of the order Trichoptera, and moths and butterflies of the order Lepidoptera. These groups correspond to two branches of the superorder Amphiesmenoptera (am-fees-men-OP-ter-ah), a name which translates as *dressed-up wings*. Biologists recognize Trichoptera and Lepidoptera as *sister groups*, indicating they share critical characteristics and have an immediate common ancestor.

Of many qualities that caddisflies and moths have in common, two are particularly useful for understanding their relationship. Familiarity with the first can be applied at the river in confirmation of adult caddisfly identifica-

122 / IN THE KINNICKINNIC

tion. Members of both orders have microscopic surface features on their wings. Caddisflies have fine hairs, a trait responsible for the order name Trichoptera (try-KOP-ter-ah) (*tricho* - hair). Butterflies and moths have scales, leading to the name Lepidoptera (lep-ih-DOP-ter-ah) (*lepido* - scale). Hairs and scales are especially apparent with a hand lens.

A second characteristic, silk production, plays a role in the lives of both of these insects. Most people are familiar with the idea that butterfly and moth caterpillars spin silk for various purposes. The most obvious example is production of an enclosure in which to pupate. The caterpillar releases fine silk threads from its lower lip (labium) and methodically uses them to construct a cocoon. In the same way, caddisfly larvae produce and apply silk to form larval cases, nets, and retreats, as well as cocoons for pupation. In building the cases and cocoons caddisfly larvae add plant, rock, or sand bits acquired from the stream environment as an integral part of their construction.

When I talk with people about caddisflies, there is a common assumption that all larvae build portable cases. But common net-spinner larvae remain caseless. They use their silk to assemble a fine-meshed catch-net and fixed retreat. The net is attached to a rock or piece of wood and oriented perpendicularly to the current. It works by filtering suspended food materials, including organic debris, various invertebrates, algae, and diatoms, from passing water. This diet is predictably mixed, and it follows that common net-spinner larvae are omnivores. Individuals build silken retreats next to their nets, camouflaging them with sand or organic bits and exit their hideaways when necessary to feed on trapped materials. The fragile creations are disrupted as rocks or other anchor materials are removed from the water and they are not normally seen. G. B. Wiggins, who made significant contributions to our understanding of caddisflies, wrote about the exquisite nature of the seine-like nets and how they occur by the thousands in streams and rivers.

Net-spinner larvae can be recognized by noting a few key physical characteristics. With specimens in a tray of water, stretched out and crawling freely, one can see elongate, cylindrical, curving bodies, often described as worm-like or caterpillar-like. Larvae are of medium size, five-eighths inch long, and gray, brown, or greenish in color. They have three pairs of jointed thoracic legs and a pair of prolegs (accessory abdominal legs) on the last abdominal segment. The larva uses its prolegs to keep its posterior end in contact with the substrate.

Each of the three thoracic segments is covered dorsally with a pigmented, often dark brown or black, protective plate, a characteristic, along with numerous branched, ventral, thoracic and abdominal gills (accompanying illustration), that separates this caddisfly family, in the larval stage, from others. No wings or wing pads are present. The antennae are too small to be seen without magnification and there are no tails. Larvae that fit this description could be any of several species of caseless caddisfly immatures belonging to the family Hydropsychidae (hi-dro-SYK-ih-dee). This term, derived from the Greek bases *hydro* and *psyche,* refers (among several interpretations) to water butterfly. Of the common names applied to members of this group, the one with greatest entomological use is common net-spinners.

Adult net-spinners are often described, not surprisingly, as moth-like. They are dull-colored, hold their wings roof-like over the body when at rest, have long antennae, and no tails. They have no coiled sucking proboscis as in moths. The common name *sedge* is often applied to these insects in their adult form. A more specific and descriptive modifier may be added to *sedge* to indicate a particular species, for example, the name spotted sedge to represent the net-spinner *Ceratopsyche slossonae.*

In our region there is an impressive and ubiquitous presence of hydropsychids. Herbert H. Ross, in his *Caddis Flies or Trichoptera of Illinois,* wrote, "… various species of Hydropsychidae form the most abundant faunal element in most of the rivers and streams" of the Midwest. Hafele and Roederer make the point that net-spinners are the most important caddisfly living in many streams. My collection records for the Kinnickinnic support these kinds of assessments. In the Kinni, not only can these larvae be collected from any reach of the stream from its origin to the delta (table 5), collections can be made during every month of the year as well. The genus *Ceratopsyche* tends to be the most prevalent and diverse, with considerably fewer specimens from the genera *Cheumatopsyche* and *Hydropsyche.*

Caddisflies are a classic example of aquatic insects that develop through complete metamorphosis. The life cycle progresses from egg to larva to pupa to adult, as in the butterfly and moth developmental sequence we learn growing up. Eggs, deposited in water by the gravid female, hatch into tiny aquatic larvae. This worm-like stage eats and grows through five larval instars, each separated from the previous by a molting process. The last larval instar pupates within the protection of its retreat. After a few weeks a pharate adult—that is, an adult still within a loose pupal cover—will swim to the surface and exit from it. This insect is strikingly distinct from other life stages of the same species with its streamlined shape, wing pads, long legs, and antennae. It's just a swim away from becoming aerial. As it reaches the top of the water, the still enshrouded adult struggles with multiple challenges: It must break through the surface tension, burst and exit the pupal skin, and along the way not become one of many ingested by feeding trout.

All aspects of caddisfly growth and development set the stage for one of the most impressive biological phenomena a streamwatcher can observe, the transition of a fully aquatic creature into a terrestrial one. The emergence, or hatch, of caddisflies fosters expectation among observers and ultimately develops into a sense of natural culmination and confirmation. This event, however, is not entirely predictable. It carries with it certain unknowns—notably when it will actually happen, how extensive emerging numbers might be, and the degree of concurrence.

So we watch the stream carefully, starting in May and continuing through summer, for emergences, looking for dull-colored mottled insects popping out of the stream and appearing to float up from the water surface. Still in need of further wing and exoskeleton maturation, they take refuge in protected places, such as cracks, crevices, and nearby vegetation. We may see them fly again when they are fully developed. This time, in subdued light, they will be searching for a mate. Following copulation, females return to the water to release strings of eggs onto submerged objects.

Some emergences are truly extraordinary, impressing even seasoned fly fishers. Having spent untold hours on the stream in pursuit of wily trout, and experiencing these events repeatedly over the years, my colleague and friend, Ken Olson, refers to the emergence flights as "pure magic."

Saddle case-maker larva, *Glossosoma*

ABANDONED CASES
AND LIBERATED LARVAE

I t took me a while to realize, in my earlier stream sampling days, that certain caddisfly larvae are not always encountered residing in their cases. I'm not referring to common net-spinners or free-living caddisflies which never form a portable house. I mean a type that is recognized technically as a case maker and case dweller, that abandons the structure it created during the course of normal river life. This idea started to sink in when I was doing preliminary sampling in the Kinnickinnic River.

The larvae I was seeing were smaller than most of the caddisflies I previously collected and showed a distinctive pinkish body color. Needless to say, these would be under the microscope as soon as I got them back to the lab. I also noticed that when the samples were sorted, there would be a number of unoccupied cases, with close to the same count as these new larvae. I soon learned about a curious behavioral trait of these insects—they seemed to be extremely quick to free themselves from their cases when disturbed. This sort of personal revelation, made while carrying out the work of regular sampling, became the kind of incentive that would make even the most routine river collecting more than a perfunctory gathering of specimens.

I came to know this new creature as *Glossosoma*, a saddle case-maker caddisfly, and member of the family Glossosomatidae. I collected it from almost every sample site along the length of the river (table 5). Across the Upper Midwest, the family encompasses three genera: *Agapetus*, *Glossosoma*, and *Protoptila* (table 5), with one, two, and three species, respectively, included. Two species of *Glossosoma* occur in Wisconsin, *G. intermedium* and *G. nigrior*. In their annotated list of the caddisflies of Michigan Leonard and Leonard wrote of *G. nigrior*: "This is probably the most abundant and widely distributed species of caddis fly [sic] in the gravel-bottomed trout streams of Michigan."

A quick subsurface sample, made by picking up and examining a submerged rock, can provide the observer with an intriguing find and preliminary confirmation of saddle case-maker larvae at the same time. Individuals construct cases which are dome shaped (prefacing drawing), rounded over the dorsal (back) side and flat on the ventral (belly) side. A ventral band of materials connecting the sides of the dome is reminiscent of the cinch of a saddle. Picturing the case as similar to the shape of a tortoise shell is also useful for remembering the form. Following a tradition of calling adult caddisflies *sedges*, adults of saddle case-makers are referred to as *little sedges*.

Many caddisfly larvae of Midwestern rivers form conspicuous portable enclosures. These worm-like immatures incorporate bits of available mineral or organic materials, or both, in the construction of their cases. In fact it has been hypothesized that the adult common name *caddisfly* and the larval common name *caddisworm* were taken from the idea of having these bits included in the case. The term *cadace* (with a variety of spellings) is a word that historically referred to a ribbon of a particular type of yarn. Cadice men were mobile vendors of the 1600s who traveled with samples of cloth materials attached to their clothing as a way of displaying them.

A closer look at the saddle-shaped case of *Glossosoma* reveals construction with sand grains and small gravel pieces. The larva attaches these particles to each other piece-by-piece with tiny amounts of spun silk. Two openings are left on the underside: one for exposure of the front end of the body, the head and legs, and the other for the latter abdominal segments and prolegs (accessory legs). The front and rear of the structure can readily change when the larva reverses its position inside. The cases tend to have larger rock or sand particles placed in the middle with smaller ones on the ends and underside. The spaces between rock pieces permit water to freely circulate around the body of the larva. With this architecture they achieve protection from predation while grazing on exposed surfaces, and at the same time utilize flowing water for its oxygen, which is absorbed through the body surface.

A larva freed of its case is elongate, segmented, and has a pink or pinkish-tan color. The abdomen appears smooth with no gills present. The first thoracic segment, directly behind the head, has a plate-like dorsal covering. At the rear of the body the ninth abdominal segment also has a dorsal plate.

Larvae are small, three-sixteenths to three-eighths inch long, when fully developed.

Glossosoma is an organism of cool, fast moving streams where rocky, gravelly bottom substrates are present. The genus is assigned the lowest possible tolerance value—zero—in the Hilsenhoff Biotic Index, suggesting it is present only where there is no organic pollution. Larvae are herbivorous scrapers. They work surfaces of rocks ingesting *periphyton*, the thin layer of algae, diatoms, and debris covering rocks and wood. As they feed during summer, they pass through multiple molts and grow in size. My experience has been in collecting larvae from late summer through the fall as they get large enough to be noticeable. Once pupation has begun in late autumn or winter, larvae are rarely seen. Then, in the spring and summer, adults escape the pupal case and pupal skin and take flight. They present themselves in a moth-like way, small and dark brown. After mating, gravid females return to the stream to deposit eggs.

These small caddisfly larvae are notably selective when choosing construction materials for their cases. Imagine the larva picking an individual sand or gravel fragment based on its size, fastening it into the specific part of the dome, and then anchoring it with emitted silk. Additionally, and unlike many other caddisfly types which enlarge their existing cases with each molt, *Glossosoma* start a new case each time one is needed. So they exit the old case and become temporarily free-living. While free, they are utilizing the current, possibly for dispersal purposes, before settling into a different location and starting on the next case.

Glossosoma readily abandon their cases if disrupted and when responding to demands of growth. The story gets even more intriguing with closer scrutiny of what is drifting, as in studies carried out by Tom Waters at Valley Creek in Washington County, Minnesota. Waters acquired hourly samples from the creek over two-day periods at various times of the year. He found that *Glossosoma intermedium* larvae drift in the current after sunset and before sunrise. This pattern was most pronounced in August when a maximum mean drift rate of three hundred and fifty individuals per hour per foot of stream width occurred after sunset. Because all *Glossosoma* collected were free of their cases, it appeared their drift participation was caused by voluntarily abandonment. Was the purpose to construct larger cases, migrate to new locations, or carry out some other as yet undetermined function? The definitive reason remains unknown. Well-documented accounts of invertebrate behavior such as this one can challenge our assumptions, and increase our curiosity about the dynamic nature of stream communities.

～ノ丨ヽ～

Beside my microscope today a small lab dish holds abandoned *Glossosoma* cases and a roughly equal number of free, uncased *Glossosoma* larvae. All were sorted from river bottom gravel acquired during a November sample on a far upper reach of the Kinnickinnic River. Although all of these cases are approximately the same size and shape, each is an individualized composition. Sand and small gravel particles from near-white and dark charcoal to tan, yellow, and pink are adeptly arranged one piece thick to form rounded carapaces. The rocky fragments appear insecurely bonded, as if they might readily disarticulate. In fact they are efficiently held together with silk, the apparent looseness of their fabrication allowing for passage of water. They are exquisite. I never grow tired of admiring their perfection. They remind me of a late fall day when the sun was shining brightly, a brisk breeze was blowing, and the nascent river was running gin clear and ice cold.

Humpless case-maker larvae, *Brachycentrus occidentalis*

HUMPLESS DRIFTERS

I find that the proverbial phrase, *cycle of life*, comes to mind easily when I'm at the river making spring collections. Sights, smells, and sounds appearing at that time feel particularly significant, even though the cycle of plant and animal lives is progressing in some way (and in some other place for migrating species) throughout the year. Trees with fresh green leaves, great blue herons wading in a backwater, and caddisflies in flight above the stream are all welcome signs. These triggers and many others can evoke ideas about the season and what *cycle of life* means for living things in the larger sense.

In biology labs and classrooms, however, one more often hears the technical phrase, *life cycle*. The term *life cycle* accounts for all of the stages of life from the moment of fertilization of an organism until it, in turn, reproduces. When I go to the river to determine what insects are living there, I am looking beneath the surface, an exercise which almost entirely involves immature insects. If I happen by chance onto an insect emergence, which is a terrestrial adult (or near adult) event, I acknowledge that it does not directly add to my intended data set. It does, however, contribute another dimension to the larger picture. In insects, eggs, larvae, subimagos, pupae, and adult life stages are all elements of a *life cycle*, considered in sequence within the context of a single species.

One late spring afternoon *Brachycentrus* (bray-kee-SEN-trus) caddisflies were making their transition from water to air. With an abundance of adults in frenzied flight I realized the special opportunity I had to find aquatic precursors of the same species in my samples. My presence for this special occasion could only be described as good fortune. Adults were taking flight and, at the same time, I found the distinctive subsurface aquatic forms of the same caddisfly in my sorting tray.

When I conduct entomology clinics for anglers and other interested stream visitors, I encourage the practice of picking up a few submerged rocks to see what might be attached to or crawling on them. Using this approach in cold, fast flowing, unpolluted Midwestern trout streams, it is not uncommon to find the extremely numerous early caddisfly, *Brachycentrus*, in its larval form. I mention the issue of numbers because Brachycentridae, represented in the Kinnickinnic primarily by *Brachycentrus occidentalis*, appears to be the second most common family of caddisfly in the river. Only common net-spinners of the family Hydropsychidae are more abundant.

One of the more useful common names for *Brachycentrus* larvae, which makes reference to anatomical characteristics, is humpless case-maker. This name comes from the fact that larvae of this species lack both dorsal and lateral spacers (humps) on the first abdominal segment. The absence of these protruding bumps can be seen when a larva is removed from its case, and is especially noticeable when compared to non-brachycentrid examples. The humps play a role in water flow over respiratory surfaces of the body within the cases of most caddisflies. Close observation reveals the dark head and dorsal thoracic plates of the larva, unusually long middle and hind legs, and a green, orange, or tan body.

An additional feature of this caddisfly larva is a uniquely constructed case. With the shape of a gently tapered cylinder it is more or less round in cross section. The primary construction material is silk, which appears reddish brown to gray, interspersed with bits of flat plant fragments and sand grains. Routine observations made during sequential collections of this caddisfly indicate a square profile for the case in the earlier larval stages. Unlike other common Midwestern *Brachycentrus* such as *B. americanus*, which maintains this format through the last instar, the case of *B. occidentalis* becomes rounder with advancing stages. Oliver Flint in his summary of *Brachycentrus* notes that for cases in which silk becomes the primary material, as is true for the Kinnickinnic specimens, the ultimate case will be circular in cross section.

Brachycentrus larvae ingest diatoms, algae, plant detritus, and insects they obtain through filtering and grazing. With the case attached to the substrate, they extend the middle and hind legs into the current to filter out food particles. In the grazing process the case is unattached, and they scrape algae from the surfaces of substrate cobbles and gravel using mouthparts modified for the process.

The underwater world is complex, dynamic, and at times chaotic. River volume and flow rates change with rainfall and snowmelt. Currents and channels respond, sediments erode from one place and accumulate in another, vegetation and other natural debris disperse and collect. *Brachycentrus* larvae are not immune to these forces and they are not always securely attached to the substrate. Random detachment of occupied cases from their original places on rocks or pieces of wood puts them into the conveyance of drifting food organisms.

The susceptibility of drifting larvae is obvious, but attachment to materials does not assure safety. Trout are capable of actively dislodging caddisfly larvae from bottom substrates. Using scuba equipment, Gary LaFontaine observed trout feeding by poking their snouts into rocks, knocking larvae free, and readily ingesting the loosened insects. Fish were also observed to actively pull larvae from their attached positions. Those knocked loose but not eaten become part of the everyday drift. This predatory behavior is possible and effective because these larvae are often attached to the upper, exposed sides of rocks.

Brachycentrus larvae add to their vulnerability by participating in two instinctive behaviors. They engage in behavioral drift, an intentional severing of attachment for the presumed purpose of downstream distribution. While this detachment is voluntary, the end result can be just as ominous as if it were involuntary. Another behavior, which I first saw photographically recorded by entomologist Dean Hansen, is tethering or rappelling, where cased larvae allow themselves to be carried a short distance downstream, attached and controlled with a length of silk. Surely, neither of these activities goes unnoticed by observant, prey-seeking fish.

As spring progresses larvae molt repeatedly, growing through five instars (stages). After reaching full size, approximately one-half inch long, they attach their cases to substrate rocks and modify them into cocoons. Inside, pupation is carried out, worm-like larvae transforming into mature, winged insects. In a few weeks new adults exit the cocoons and swim to the surface. As is typical for caddisflies, these adults are pharate, indicating they remain enclosed within the pupal covering. The distinctive, streamlined pharate adults are often caught by the current as they free themselves and generate gases for buoyancy. Eventually they swim and float their way upward, remaining vulnerable to predation until they penetrate the film, push through a split in the pupal covering, and escape into the air. These flights generally start in the second or third week in April and extend through May. Newly emerged adults make their way to shaded streamside vegetation and other objects during the day. At dusk they take to the air, swarming over the water, and mate on the ground or vegetation. Females return to the river and deposit eggs by dropping them at the surface or placing them subsurface. This interpretation suggests that this *Brachycentrus* requires only one year to reach adulthood, and its life cycle is *univoltine*.

A relative of *B. occidentalis*, *B. americanus*, was reported by Hilsenhoff to have a *semivoltine* life cycle in colder streams of the northern two-thirds of Wisconsin. This means that the species requires two years to complete development. If the same pattern is true for its relative, *B. occidentalis*, there should be well-developed larvae in the river in late spring as a result of overwintering in that stage, and further growth still to come. In my larval sampling experience through a calendar year, however, few larvae were collected in April and May. Very small larvae reappear in June and then slightly larger ones are collected in July. They continue growing through the fall. Kinnickinnic collections suggest a univoltine life cycle with eggs deposited after emergence in late spring (by the end of May), eggs hatching, larvae growing through the summer, and mature larvae overwintering. Then in late spring they complete pupation and emerge.

To comprehend the total number of individual insects living in a river like the Kinnickinnic is almost beyond imagination. Some species, such as humpless case-maker caddisflies, are abundant throughout the Kinni (table 5). Viewing a hatch of this caddisfly on a short reach of river or seeing a cluster of their tube-cased larvae on a single rock are small windows into the vastness of this population. These observations can start us thinking back through their lives, enlightening us on how their success is made certain. We know survival of arthropod species is largely about reproductive potential, and humpless case-makers demonstrate this capacity well. With the deposition of untold sums of eggs, even decimation of the population by fish during the hazardous emergence period is limited. Appreciating the presence of unseen masses, literal products of the power of reproduction, assures us not only about the abundance of the river here and now but, when the time arrives next spring, that another successful emergence will occur—the *cycle of life* in persistent motion.

Alderfly larva, *Sialis*

THE ALDER AND THE ALDERFLY

People who explore streams, lakes, and swamps have most assuredly wrestled with a confounding, nearly impenetrable shrub on the banks and shorelines of various bodies of water. It can be a challenge to get through thickets of this species, an exercise that involves moving through a wet habitat while parting tangled woody stems as you go. Their springy resiliency can be frustrating because, when forced aside, they respond by pushing back vigorously to their original shape. This experience is the scourge of the alder.

Our typical alder of the Upper Midwest is *Alnus incana* subspecies *rugosa*, commonly known as speckled or swamp alder, a relative of common birch trees. In addition to its growth pattern and characteristic habitat, the species can be recognized by its leaves. They are thick and egg-shaped with double-toothed edges and a wrinkled upper surface with deeply impressed veins. The common name of the plant is derived from the speckling of its reddish-brown bark with *lenticels* (horizontal orangish-white warty pore formations). In winter the shrub stands out because of small, cone-like female catkins that persist long after dispersal of fruit the previous spring.

In late spring and early summer, insects, known more for their clinging and running dexterity than for their ability to fly, can be found on the leaves and branches of speckled alder. These adults were originally given the name alderflies in England because they were strongly associated with the streamside shrubs after their emergence. This common name is still used for members of the family Sialidae, order Megaloptera (*megalo-* large, *-ptera* wing), represented in Wisconsin and Minnesota by several species of the genus *Sialis*.

A good time to look for adult alderflies is when approaching a stream bank or shoreline on a warm afternoon from mid-May to mid-June. A promising place to find them is on leaves or branches of shrubs closest to water; the plant type doesn't really matter, but alders and willows are good examples.

Alderflies may be spotted in flight, although they are more likely to be seen actively moving on vegetation. Look for black or dark brown insects, one-half to five-eighths inch long, with wings positioned tent-like over their backs. They resemble dark caddisflies because of this characteristic, but alderfly wings are different, having rather bold, pronounced veins and a reflective sheen to their surface. Adults have no tails, a characteristic that allows them to be quickly distinguished from mayflies and stoneflies.

When sampling submerged debris with a net in slow water areas, alderfly larvae stand out because of their unusual lateral abdominal features and tail (prefacing photo). They have an elongate body divided into a squarish head with short narrow antennae, a distinctive three-part thorax, each segment bearing a pair of legs, and a tapering abdomen. Light-colored mottling is visible against a darker orange-brown background color of the head and thorax. The first through seventh abdominal segments each bear a pair of lateral, four- to five-segmented filaments. A single median caudal filament, or tail, extends from the end of the abdomen. No wing pads or gills are present like those of mayfly or stonefly larvae. These are truly unique insects. Once seen they are unlikely to be forgotten.

Alderflies have two relatives that occur in Wisconsin and Minnesota, fishflies and dobsonflies. Both are members of the megalopteran family Corydalidae. To date, neither has been collected from the Kinnickinnic. However, the larvae of dobsonflies, called hellgrammites, do occur in the Apple River, two watersheds north of the Kinni. Hellgrammites are known for their impressive large size (two to three inches long) and active predatory feeding habits.

➤⁄⁀⫶⬳

Alderfly larvae live in various lake habitats and the slower parts of streams. They occupy mud deposits primarily, especially those with leaf litter, sticks, and other accumulated debris. Larvae burrow through the mix feeding mainly on midge larvae. Alderfly larvae have well-developed chewing mouthparts and are particularly voracious predators. As they feed and grow, they pass through ten larval instars, a process requiring one to two years. At the end of the last stage, the larva leaves the water to find a site above the waterline, close to the edge of the stream, where they establish a pupation cell in the soil. There, a half to one inch below the surface, and over the course of up to two weeks, the pupa transforms into an adult. The adult emerges during the night and is ready to fly early the next day.

Adults fly only during daytime. They are usually found close to water, which supports the idea that they are not strong fliers. They live from a few days up to two weeks, and are not known to feed during that time. Mating occurs on leaves and twigs, after which females fly to oviposition sites. The strategy for egg placement is a truly incredible adaptation. Eggs are deposited by the hundreds in even, compact rows on leaves and small branches that overhang still or slow moving water. This remarkable instinctive positioning allows the newly hatched first-instar larvae to drop directly into appropriate larval habitat as it enters its new world.

◂╱╲▸

Sialid larvae can be found in silty sediments of the Kinni year around, but not in all locations. Larvae are uncommon in the lower Kinni, even in seemingly suitable habitat. My four downstream-most study sites yielded only one specimen in a pilot study; none were collected from those sites in a year-long study. By contrast, in the upper Kinni, larvae occupy every site (table 6). Ninety-seven percent of several hundred specimens were found at the eight upstream-most locations, starting two miles above River Falls and continuing to near the headwaters.

Observation of larvae year around suggests availability of this population as a food source for fish. Borger noted that larvae serve as an important food for trout during winter when general emergence activity is low and most immatures are small. He also suggested that alderflies are probably most susceptible to predation in the early spring when maturing larvae become active, reasoning that increased activity promotes drift, and drift leads to vulnerability. Adult alderflies are exposed to predation by fish when their flying and oviposition activities bring them to the stream.

◂╱╲▸

Nowhere are alderflies more important to humans than in the rich fly fishing tradition of Great Britain. Appreciation for this insect is expressed in numerous historic writings, including those of the Reverend Charles Kingsley. The cleric's *Chalk-Stream Studies* was first published in Fraser's Magazine in 1858 and again as part of his *Prose Idylls, New and Old* in 1873. Kingsley's approach to entomology was minimalist to be sure, as he espoused the need for six or seven flies as sufficient for any fisherman. After listing and describing these, one of which was the Black Alder artificial fly, he suggested, "These are enough to show sport from March to October; and also like enough to certain natural flies to satisfy the somewhat dull memory of a trout." One of his most colorful and poignant passages regarding alderflies is this one from *Chalk-Stream Studies*:

> Beloved alder-fly! would that I could give thee a soul (if indeed thou hast not one already, thou, and all things which live), and make thee happy in all aeons to come! But as it is, such immortality as I can I bestow on thee here, in small return for all the pleasant days thou hast bestowed on me.

━╱╲━

Put me a thicket of alder and I will happily plod my way through, net and sorting tray in hand, to encounter the variety of living things residing in a body of water. Likewise, I gladly seek out the siltiest and, some might say, least desirable part of the stream to experience the organisms that require fine sediment accumulation for survival. Why? Because the system is more than cobble and boulders breaking fast clear water into sparkling silver rapids. Thicket and mud have their rewards in fascinating creatures like alderfly larvae, multicolored beings with atypical anatomical adaptations. Plus, there is the uncommon quality of an insect in which larvae are aquatic while pupae and adults are terrestrial. Add to these features a distinctive upriver distribution and a year-around larval presence, and one has a noteworthy Kinnickinnic River insect, well worth our attention and understanding.

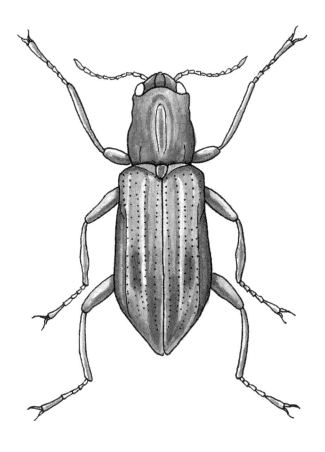

Riffle beetle adult, *Stenelmis*

BEETLES IN THE STREAM, AQUATIC INHABITANTS AND ERRANT TERRESTRIALS

I came across a comment involving the biological relationship between beetles and trout written by Dave Hughes, a respected contributor to the literature of fly fishing. He said that small beetles can be what fish are eating when we see them actively feeding, but, even when we try very hard, cannot see what insects they are feeding on. This suggestion struck me as significant for a couple of reasons. First, there is so much focus on mayflies and caddisflies in the popular lore of stream food webs that many organisms are left out of consideration and ultimately overlooked. Secondly, the reality is that beetles of notable variety are omnipresent in trout water. It would be an unusual occurrence to take a net sample from any Kinni substrate and not have beetle larvae or adults present.

The assortment of beetles we find in streams is a reflection of the worldwide diversity of the group. There are 350,000 species of beetles living on our planet. This represents about a quarter of all described living things. When J. B. S. Haldane, British biologist and mathematician, was asked what this preponderance said to him about creation, he suggested that the Creator must have had "an inordinate fondness for beetles." This impressive multiplicity carries through aquatic groups. There are 1,100 aquatic beetle species in North America. Over 350 of these occur in Wisconsin waters.

Sooner or later numbers like these prompt questions, such as: Why are there so many kinds of beetles? and, How did one type of organism attain such immense evolutionary success? The answers lie within critical interactions of genes and habitats. In a molecular genetics analysis calibrated with fossil evidence, Hunt and others demonstrated that species richness of beetles can be attributed to an extraordinary diversification event, a *superradiation*. This proliferative event occurred during the Jurassic Period, 145 to 208 million years ago and was followed by high survival of the derived lineages. Beetles were extremely successful at occupying new environments and, once these types became established, they persisted.

Evolutionary innovation is part of that larger success picture. Biologists recognize the wing configuration of beetles as one of the more extraordinary adaptations in the insect world, one that allows both protection and flight. The order name for beetles, Coleoptera, based on roots *cole* (sheath) and *pter* (wing), suggests the protective role of the *elytra* (EL-uh-truh), the first pair of wings. In most examples these are thick, hardened structures that cover a large portion of the dorsal side of the beetle body. They are hinged so that they lift forward and out of the way during flight. This exposes a membranous second pair of wings which unfolds and provides aerial propulsion. At rest, the elytra return to a covering position, meeting in a straight line down the middle of the back. This universal feature provides a convenient and reliable means of recognizing most beetle adults, no matter what kind they are.

Beetles develop by means of complete metamorphosis, indicating a life cycle based on eggs, larvae, pupae, and adults. This means that in addition to the variety of adult forms that would be found in water, there are also larval types one might want to consider. Larval beetles take on a variety of forms quite unlike those of the adults. They are often soft-bodied and light or medium colored compared to the dark or colorful adults. They lack elytra, show no wing or wing pad development at all, and have a distinctive head, thoracic legs, and a segmented abdomen. Curiously, in the case of aquatic beetle species, most do not transform to pupae in water, but instead form a pupal enclosure in the riverbank or elsewhere on shore.

Because beetles that happen to be in or on water may be more than aquatic residents, it's helpful to make the distinction between obligate aquatic species and terrestrial species that become "aquatic" by circumstances beyond their control. The first are water residents, commonly encountered by and routinely preyed upon by fish. The latter have fallen, or were blown by wind, into a realm in which they are totally unsuited to survive. They get eaten, too.

Some stream beetles are adapted to living in current and others are better suited for calmer water. To find the greatest number of families, one must sample from riffles to pools, mid-channel to margins, and surface to bottom. Attention to specific habitats like gravel substrates, vegetation, woody and other organic debris, and undercut banks, yields an assortment of beetle inhabitants.

When I did multihabitat sampling in the Kinni, I obtained several hundred specimens of two families of fast-water beetles. Most were members of the family Elmidae, commonly and simply known as riffle beetles, in several genera. The majority of the specimens, both larvae and adults, keyed to *Optioservus fastiditus*. These are small insects, under three-eighths inch long. The adults are black, elongate, and have long legs. The larvae are slender, with obvious segmentation. They occupy gravel substrates and stream vegetation where they function as herbivores. Larvae increase in size as they grow through six larval instars. They then leave the water to pupate in terrestrial locations. Adults have a post-emergence flight and return to stream gravel and vegetation to live. Three additional genera of elmids occur in the Kinnickinnic as well: *Ancyronyx*, *Stenelmis* (shown in the prefacing illustration), and *Dubiraphia*.

Another family of riffle beetles frequently collected was Dryopidae, commonly known as long-toed riffle beetles. All of these were identified as *Helichus striatus*. Dryopids live in environments similar to elmids and are also herbivores. They differ in that larvae are not aquatic. Both of these families were found throughout the length of the river (table 6) during all months of the calendar year, with *Helichus* absent at some of the upper river sites.

When sampling moves to lower energy, slower water habitats, a different array of beetles is collected. Any of these may be a component of the stream food web because of their behavior and abundance. Examples include predaceous diving beetles (Dytiscidae), whirligig beetles (Gyrinidae), water scavenger beetles (Hydrophilidae), and crawling water beetles (Haliplidae). Adult members of these families range in size from extremely small, under one-eighth inch long, to large, over an inch. The adults are primarily swimmers and their larvae are mainly crawlers. Some adults and many larvae are predatory. The voracious nature of larval dytiscids is recognized in the colorful common name, water tigers. As in the proverbial tale of the hunter becoming the hunted, these larval lifestyles expose the larvae as potential prey.

Because terrestrial beetles are found in every habitat in our landscape, it's easy to imagine that many species inhabit environments close to a stream. Any of the multitude of immature or adult beetles living on or near the shore of a lake or bank of a river can end up in the water; it's simply a matter of time, chance, and circumstance. If the number of species is any indication of the probability of terrestrial forms taking the plunge, then rove beetles (Staphylinidae), snout beetles and weevils (Curculionidae), ground beetles (Carabidae), and leaf beetles (Chrysomelidae) are the most likely candidates. Rove beetles and ground beetles are often associated with the ground and objects in contact with the soil; snout beetles and leaf beetles are mainly on foliage. Any of these ubiquitous non-aquatic examples might be floating on the stream surface, being carried along in mid-level drift, or tumbling helplessly over bottom substrates. Members of terrestrial families such as these are not in any way adapted for life in water. If they cannot quickly escape, their life will end there, one way or another.

A rewarding part of river invertebrate collecting, beyond the inspiration of working directly with local diversity, is recognizing the variety of aquatic locations in which organisms are likely to be found. After inferring habitat possibilities from surface cues, one can assess underwater features by looking into and through the water. The Kinni invites this kind of gazing. Its clarity allows peering into intricate waterscapes and taking in scenes of substrate rich in color and texture. There, for the observer to comprehend, are settings of beauty and wildness, filled with light and shadow. Under these cobbles and boulders, concealed in cracks and crevices, and in myriad cryptic spaces, insects and crustaceans flourish.

Beetles abound in these places. I look forward to finding them. Larval and adult beetle populations, along with other river inhabitants, change with transitions in the stream. Most significantly, when moving from fast water to slow, cobble to silt, woody debris to accumulated leaves, *the species change*. These faunal distinctions signify differences in habitats in the most meaningful way possible—reflecting qualities required of the beetle species living there.

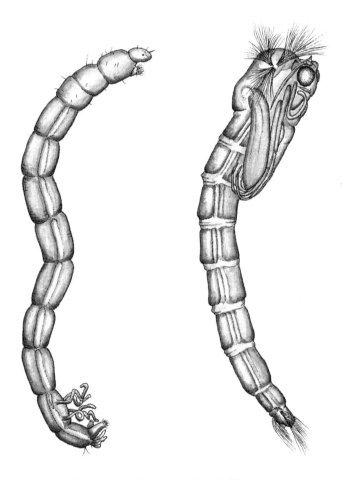

Midge larva (left) and pupa (right), *Chironomus*

SMALL IN SIZE, LARGE IN NATURE

One never knows what turns western Wisconsin weather will take when late February comes around. If you add afternoon air temperatures in the thirties to a clear blue sky, it can be a surprisingly nice day for a walk along the river. You might get the feeling that winter is actually winding down and giving way to spring. Snow cover normally lasts through this time of year, providing an optimal background for spotting emerging insects, whether they are seen actively flying from the river surface or landing on streamside objects.

Early in the course of my river insect studies, I was out on one of these unexpectedly warm winter days when a large number of small dark flies were rising up from the river below. Some were flying and others had settled onto the snow-covered rocks and long-dormant vegetation scattered over the bank. A passerby took notice of my attention to the activity and, noting the cloud of insects as well, inquired about what they might be. I shared my assumption that they were non-biting midges. It was gratifying to know that a casual observer was interested enough to ask about them.

One learns to do a certain level of field identification based on what is expected in concert with what one observes. With a closer look, the adults I saw that afternoon had a number of features that said *midge* to me: mosquito-sized (small), a long narrow body shape, long thin legs, one pair of slender wings, and absence of piercing mouthparts (apparent as a long proboscis if present).

It is understandable that the first thing said about midges relates to their small size. But we need to know that this idea pales in comparison to the extraordinary ecological significance of these creatures in natural systems. Midges meet a number of criteria that life scientists use to determine biological importance. One, they possess incredible diversity. They can make up 50% of the species present in an aquatic setting. In a standard technical reference on midges W. P. Coffman and L. C. Ferrington Jr. report there may be 20,000 species worldwide in this family and that there are most likely more than 2,000 species in North America. Wisconsin midge diversity is expressed in Hilsenhoff's aquatic insects summary where he provides a larval key for 103 aquatic chironomid genera of the state. Two, they occupy nearly every kind of aquatic habitat, including all varieties of stream and lake bottom substrates and deposits, suspended materials, algae, vascular plants, and fungal growths. We can expect them to be very common residents of most streams. Three, extremely large numbers of individuals can be present. High densities are the rule and not the exception. Coffman and Ferrington note that concentrations of 50,000 midge larvae per square meter are not uncommon.

The importance of midges in aquatic ecosystems is further exemplified by the wide variety of organic materials they ingest as larvae, and what ingests them. Larval feeding is based on highly adapted and variable mouthpart structures. Food procurement mechanisms range from filter feeding to scraping, gathering, shredding, and predation, the specificity of which results in the consumption of detritus, algae, plants, fungi, and other animals. Following through various food webs, midges at all life stages become the prey of most aquatic and some terrestrial predators, including other insects, fish, birds, and bats.

Midges are true flies, members of the order Diptera, and as such are distinguished from other adult insects by having one pair of wings (*di-* two, *-ptera* wing). Other examples of true flies are mosquitoes, black flies, and crane flies, all-in-all a collection of organisms well known to anyone who spends time outside in the summer. Some flies of interest to stream and lake watchers are not *true flies* because, among other things, they have four wings. These include dragonflies, mayflies, stoneflies, caddisflies, and many more. Note the clue provided in the entomological spelling and spacing convention. For true flies the *fly* portion of the name is emphasized by separating it from the descriptive term which precedes it, as in *house fly* and *horse fly*.

The term *midge* derives from the Middle English word *migge*. Used alone, and in accordance with the dictionary definition, it commonly refers to a member of the dipteran family Chironomidae (ky-row-NOM-ih-dee). Used more broadly, as with a descriptive adjective, midge can pertain also to other families of small flies. Some of these familiar to river hikers, canoeists, and fly fishers are the biting midges, also called punkies or no-see-ums, of the family Ceratopogonidae. Less seen are the non-biting dixid midges, family Dixidae, their characteristic U-shaped larvae found feeding at the surface of quiet backwaters. Both of these latter two midge types develop in slower, marginal waters of the Kinnickinnic.

Proficiency in chironomid identification requires considerable dedication and expertise. A limited number of people have the ability to identify midges beyond the family level. I had the unique opportunity to be guided by Len Ferrington of the Chironomid Research Group at the University of Minnesota through the initial levels of identification of larvae, pupae, and pupal skins (technically known as *exuviae*) that I collected during sampling studies of the Kinnickinnic River in 1999 and its South Fork tributary in 2000. Ultimately, Len expertly put the most specific names possible on the 2,688 and 703 specimens, respectively, from those collections. The 1999 main stem collections fell into five subfamilies of Chironomidae and represented 42 distinct types. From that base, and many additional hours experiencing these creatures in the river, I developed a great respect for them.

Midge presence in the Kinnickinnic was further documented in the first two seasons of biotic index sampling with which I was involved for the city of River Falls, Wisconsin, in 2004 and 2005. Following the Hilsenhoff Biotic Index (HBI) protocol, Kent Johnson and I obtained aquatic net samples from riffles at three specified locations upstream from the city. Three replications were done at each of these sites for two years, making a total of 18 samples. In addition to the calculated HBI numbers, numerical dominance values were determined from collection data. Midge larvae ranked in the top five families in numerical dominance in 16 of the 18 riffle samples. Numerically dominant chironomid genera in these collections were *Diamesa, Pagastia, Cricotopus, Eukiefferiella, Orthocladius,* and *Polypedilum (Uresipedilum)*.

꜀ꞈꞏ

Midges develop by complete metamorphosis. Prior to emergence of the flying adult, the life cycle follows an aquatic sequence of eggs, larvae, and pupae. Eggs are far too small to be seen in the field and identification of larvae is best made on more mature forms. So when sampling, I look for larger larvae, pupae, and pupal exuviae in the sorting tray, all of which can be found in the river year around.

Midge larvae are distinctive. They are elongate with segmented bodies, and lack jointed legs (prefacing illustration). They have two pairs of prolegs (short fleshy, unsegmented leg-like structures), a pair on the first thoracic segment and a pair on the last abdominal segment. Larvae also have a conspicuous head capsule and are missing obvious features that many other immature insects have, such as wing pads. Midge larvae pass through four instars or stages, separated by molts, becoming larger with each new exoskeleton. Many of these larvae construct silken tubes that can be observed when rocks are removed from the riverbed. When examining freshly obtained midge larvae, one sees an assortment of body colors: off-whites, yellows, oranges, greens, and browns. The larvae known as bloodworms that live in low oxygen settings possess hemoglobin and are bright red in color.

The midge pupa is a comma-shaped organism with a segmented abdomen and wing pads (prefacing illustration). Pupae, like larvae, develop in bottom debris. During the pupal stage, the fourth larval instar transitions to the adult. When adult features have developed, and influencing conditions of temperature and light have been met, the pupa begins its ascent to the surface. This stage is more correctly called a *pharate adult* (from *pharos*, a garment), because it is a mature adult over which the pupal skin temporarily remains and from which it must exit.

Time spent in the proximity of the Kinni during any month of the year, crossing a bridge, or hiking streamside, puts us into position to observe flying midge adults. If we think back in time from the point of this observation, we can appreciate the prior movement of pharate adults from the bottom of the stream to the top. This typically happens in large numbers. As with other insects that emerge at the surface, there is a period of time between splitting of the pupal skin and flight readiness of the adult. The new adult must extract itself from its cover and expand its wings, all while floating with the current. This drifting time and pupal swim which leads up to it are extremely vulnerable periods for a midge. Opportunistic trout readily consume them as they make this transition to terrestrial life. Coincidentally, it is this predatory behavior of fish that makes them susceptible to imitations presented by fly fishers.

Soon after emergence, eons-old behavioral routines bring males and females together. Often they fly *en masse* as numerous dark bodies excitedly swarm above the stream. Eventually, after mating and insemination, fertilized females return to the water to deposit eggs. This behavior creates yet another chance for fish to take advantage of an abundant food source.

The midge is a perfect organism on which to practice a simple idea. It's human nature to apply names to plants and animals we observe and then move on, without thinking beyond their initial recognition. This encounter presents an opportunity that should not be missed. With insects as ecologically important as midges it's rewarding to take the next step and expand on personal understanding of their connections in and with the river. As we perceive relationships and recognize context, we remember.

Barry Lopez wrote about the experience of taking children into the woods and how, over time, he learned to say less and less to them. In place of his inclination to mechanically name things, he and the children would look for something like a piece of bone or shell and together extrapolate from it to the connections the animal would have with its world. This produced, in turn, associations beyond the simple act of finding and naming to create a memory that was more likely to last. Becoming aware of midges and thinking of them in a larger river environment can generate the same kind of meaning for river watchers.

Random interaction among a flurry of small creatures, an onlooker, and myself on a late winter day shaped imagery for me that has lasted after the passing of many years. For someone interested in stream insects, and the curious split lives of those that transform from aquatic to terrestrial, the scene could hardly be more meaningful. To witness an event that culminates months, if not a year, of feeding, growth, development, and predator avoidance, adds to its appreciation. Qualities that make midges noteworthy—their vast numbers, abundant diversity, and ecological significance—substantiate the concept that small physical size should not be part of the evaluation of importance in nature.

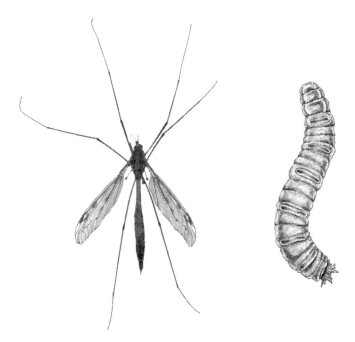

Crane fly adult and larva, *Tipula*

CRANE FLIES, LEATHERJACKETS,
AND MOSQUITO HAWKS

Sometimes while standing in the stream I try to put myself in the position and mind of a trout, thinking I may gain insight into how such a fish might be caught. I accept that more things are going on in that brain than I could ever imagine. For the most part I'm supposing that all piscine sensory and neural mechanisms are in high gear assessing two critically important issues: the movement and proximity of potential prey *and* the movement and proximity of potential predators. Basic to the biology of behavior is the cost versus benefit equation. The act of eating is necessarily balanced against the risk of being eaten.

The menu for the stream cafe can be overwhelming with its mayfly, caddisfly, and midge offerings. On the other end of the spectrum are prey items which come individually, and much less often, but which have appreciable nutritional value. An excellent example of this latter category of food organisms in the Kinnickinnic is the large crane fly larva. A trout's opportunity to ingest prey of this type might occur when a rainfall event of great enough magnitude to increase stream discharge, stirs up bottom substrates, and releases organisms normally secure there. In my fantasy setting I visualize a hungry fish lying in wait, spotting this enticing larva, and moving with as little effort as necessary to select it from the food choices in the conveying current.

The crane fly I'm imagining in this picture is the fully grown larva of the large crane fly, *Tipula* (prefacing illustration), common to the Kinni (table 6). This large insect, two inches and longer, is nearly cylindrical and legless. Its head end is rounded—usually the head itself is not visible, as it can be retracted into the thorax—and the tail end is blunt with six fleshy lobe-like processes. Segmentation is visible as indented rings along the length of the body. Various body colors of gray-green, dull orange-tan, off-whites, grays, and browns mean larvae can be well-hidden in river debris.

Several additional crane fly larvae of a considerably smaller variety live in the Kinnickinnic. These have the same basic body design as *Tipula* but with different external features. Structures used to separate them from their larger relative, beyond size, include a variety of characteristics, many associated with the posterior end of the body. Abdominal lobes and nearby spiracles (visible respiratory openings) vary in number, size, and shape. Creeping welts, which are traction devices located ventrally on the body (evident as elongate ovals in the *Tipula* larva illustration), can be present or absent, and prolegs also vary. This group presents an interesting assortment of worm-like larvae in a range of sizes and with a variety of adaptations for life in water.

➤〳〵➤

Crane flies, like midges, are members of the order Diptera (*di*- two and -*ptera* wing), the true flies. Adult true flies have the first pair of wings well developed for flight. The second pair of wings is modified into short, knobbed structures called *halteres* (hall-TIRZ), that vibrate extremely rapidly and work as sensors of change in flight direction. One pair of wings is the exception, not the rule, among insect orders. A few other adults have only one pair of wings, including some mayflies. In comparison with most Diptera, particularly examples such as house flies and horse flies, which are strong fliers, the flight of crane flies is a gentle flutter, creating the look of suspension in air.

Crane flies are members of the family Tipulidae (tih-PEW-lih-dee), a family name derived from the Latin *tipula* which means water spider. The term is, of course, inaccurate classification-wise, but does provide a useful initial image of adults. Tipulids adapted to aquatic habitats live in diverse environments from the margins of ponds and lakes to fast moving streams. This is a large family, second in number of species in the order Diptera only to the midges (Chironomidae). Greater than fifty species of crane flies live in the Midwest. Larvae of many species are aquatic or semiaquatic.

➤〳〵➤

As in all true flies, the tipulid life cycle is based on complete metamorphosis. The egg hatches into a small worm-like larva which is followed by a series of larvae (sometimes called *leatherjackets*), a pupa, and an adult. To become fully grown, larvae must pass through four instars, each separated from the previous by molting, or shedding of the larval skin. Larval instars are similar to each other in appearance, but become larger after each molt and continued feeding. Tipulid larvae fulfill various ecological roles in the river, including as shredders (*Tipula*) and predators (*Dicranota, Hexatoma, Limnophila, Pedicia*), with *Pilaria* a possible predator. An exception is *Antocha* which is a collector-gatherer.

Even for crane fly larvae that develop in water, it is typical for pupae to inhabit moist soil or shoreline debris, out of reach of fish. Adults emerge from the pupal skin and, after some time spent opening wings and completing development of the cuticle, they mate. The females then return to the water to deposit eggs on plants and other objects below the surface.

‒✎‶‑

Crane fly adults often make a startling visual impression because they resemble very large mosquitoes. Most people have seen them hovering up and down at a porch light on a warm summer night or resting on a window screen in the morning. There is nothing wrong with noticing the resemblance of these two true flies. Both have long, thin wings, an elongate body, and very long legs, but be aware that the majority of our common mosquito species are rarely over a half inch in length and most are smaller. Ironically, some of the large crane fly adults are known as mosquito hawks, implying predatory feeding, but these adults are not known to feed at all, and the name is better reserved for certain dragonflies.

A close look at the adults of many crane fly species reveals beautiful coloration, including characteristic patterns and intricate markings, on their slender bodies and spindly legs. Basic exoskeleton colors vary from browns, grays, and tans to oranges and yellows. The wings, too, can be quite striking: Some are transparent, some appear smoky, while others have distinctive dark or light areas, or both.

‒✎‶‑

I recall several occasions, when doing summer net sampling in the Kinnickinnic, next to a steep bank shadowed by overhanging vegetation, observing large numbers of small freshly emerged crane fly adults. At first, only a few were visible against the near vertical dark soil. As I looked more closely, I could see they were all moving upward, clinging to the bank and to each other, propelling themselves away from the water like dozens of tiny rock climbers ascending a wall at the same time.

These anecdotal observations correlate with finding substantial numbers of larvae of various smaller genera in bottom substrates of the Kinnickinnic (table 6). Some of these were *Antocha*, an interesting genus because their entire immature life, including pupal stage, is aquatic. I also collected relatively large numbers of *Dicranota* larvae from bottom gravels and debris and smaller numbers of *Hexatoma. Antocha, Dicranota,* and *Hexatoma* are all common residents of Wisconsin streams with *Tipula*. Collected in lower numbers from the Kinni were *Limnophila, Pedicia, Pilaria,* and *Hesperoconopa*, genera reported to be less common in the state.

Several of these genera have low tolerance of organic pollution as shown by their HBI values. Selected examples include *Hesperoconopa* (TV=1), *Hexatoma* (TV=2), *Antocha, Dicranota,* and *Limnophila* (TV=3). Tolerance values, TVs, are discussed in my essay, *Listening to Aquatic Insects*.

A substantial number of families of aquatic Diptera, in addition to midges (Chironomidae) and crane flies (Tipulidae), play a role in river food webs. True fly diversity in the Kinnickinnic, as demonstrated by net-acquired specimens, includes members of these families, as well: no-see-ums, also called biting midges or punkies (Ceratopogonidae), dixid midges (Dixidae), phantom crane flies (Ptychopteridae), black flies (Simuliidae), soldier flies (Stratiomyidae), snipe flies (Athericidae) (table 6), muscoid flies (Muscidae), and horse and deer flies (Tabanidae). The order Diptera is second only to the order Coleoptera in number of North American insect species. Diverse and prevalent populations of immature true flies are typical of Midwestern rivers like the Kinni.

༺༻

Crane flies can fall into the abyss of obscure aquatic insect groups, not because they are uncommon, but because they easily blend in with their surroundings or are confused with other insects.

A good place to start learning crane fly recognition is with adults, simply because this is the most visible stage. Look for them while exploring among vegetation and debris of the river bank or while wading close to shore. These long-legged mosquito-like organisms may be flying near the water or resting on streamside vegetation and other objects, especially in protected areas. The keys to distinguishing them from other flies are: 1) extremely thin and long legs (think *crane*, the bird) as well as a long body and long wings, and 2) medium to large size. Be alert to the idea that the legs may be distracting for in-flight identification, as they hang behind the body after takeoff and may be mistaken for the tails of unrelated adults.

Whether it's a spidery looking fly or a writhing larva that I happen across during sampling, I count on crane flies to inspire curiosity. I owe this interest to their diversity, not only in form, but in the many adaptations they have acquired to survive in water, on land, and in the air. Crane flies fill important roles in their respective habitats. The function of larvae as organic detritus feeders is especially noteworthy. Invertebrate and vertebrate predators utilize larvae as food sources, and adults are subject to predation by many animals, including other insects, amphibians, and birds. My visual impression of large soft-bodied larvae of crane flies as succulent tidbits for trout keeps this connection in the river food web active for me, and my imaginary trout in-waiting.

Scud adult, *Gammarus*

AN ABUNDANCE OF SCUDS

A call came each spring from Ms. Wilcox inviting me to visit St. Bridget Parish School and share my interest in insects with her fourth grade class. We started these sessions with pupil contributions on what makes an insect an insect and how they are important in the world. Students were impressively prepared on the subject by recent lessons. Then it was time for individual questions. Little arms and hands were raised high. Ms. Wilcox cautioned students against telling personal bug stories, knowing well they were coming. Following questions, we looked at a series of glass-topped display cases, the kind museum curators call their *ooh-aah* boxes. The ones I brought to show were filled with colorful butterflies and large beetles. Anticipating that active creatures would invite curiosity, I also took living specimens from insect cultures housed at my department. For example, mealworm life cycle stages (larvae, pupae, and adults) the children could pick up and closely observe (and most did!) served as a hands-on lesson in beetle metamorphosis.

I also wanted to show students some of the insects and crustaceans living in their local stream, the Kinnickinnic, and make a few points about river conservation. So on my way to the school, I stopped at the river to collect a variety of living examples and transported them to the classroom in an aquarium. In spite of a wide range of invertebrates visible in the water, the scuds were a special success. They attracted attention because the males were carrying females on their backs, a pre-mating ritual that can last several days. In fact most of the individuals in the tank had paired up and were swimming *in tandem*. The kids were wide-eyed and inquisitive. I explained that this is not actually mating; it's a courtship behavior. But it was, of course, a great conversation starter for a fourth-grade classroom.

⌐⁄⁄⎩∖⌐

Insects and crustaceans are the most visible invertebrates in a stream. Scuds are one of three kinds of macroinvertebrate crustaceans that inhabit the Kinnickinnic River. The other two types are aquatic sowbugs, sometimes called cressbugs, *Caecidotea racovitzai* (table 6), and crayfish, *Orconectes* spp.

So how are crustaceans similar to, and different from, insects? Like insects, crustaceans are arthropods. Members of the phylum Arthropoda have an exoskeleton, body segmentation (with segments grouped into regions or tagmata), and paired, jointed appendages. Insects have an exoskeleton made hard with proteins, three body regions (head, thorax, abdomen), one pair of antennae, and three pairs of non-branched appendages originating on the thorax (with none on the abdomen). Crustaceans differ from insects in that they have an exoskeleton hardened with calcium, three body regions often viewed as a cephalothorax and abdomen, two pairs of antennae, and most segments, including those of the abdomen, bearing a pair of appendages. Crustaceans often retain a primitive biramous, or two-branched, condition on some appendages.

With arthropods as the dominant organisms on Earth, it is curious that insects achieved their greatest success on land and in freshwater, and crustaceans had their primary success in the oceans. Exceptions to this generality include the very few insects that live in intertidal ocean environments and crustaceans like the scuds and crayfish, among others, that are well established in freshwater.

Scuds, which are also known as sideswimmers, freshwater shrimp, and amphipods, are extremely numerous in Midwestern streams and lakes and flourish in a variety of aquatic settings. It's not unusual to collect them in waters as different as a pristine trout stream and a shallow eutrophic pond. In contrast to the way we think about many aquatic invertebrates that emerge and become aerial adults following subsurface development, scuds never leave the water. Their entire life cycle from egg to adult is carried out below the surface. It's typical for scud generations to overlap so, whatever time of year a sample is taken, it will include a full range of growth stages and sizes.

The common scud of the Kinnickinnic River and its tributaries is *Gammarus pseudolimnaeus* (family Gammaridae, order Amphipoda). The species was named by Bousfield in the 1950s when he revised the freshwater amphipods inhabiting previously glaciated regions of North America. *G. pseudolimnaeus* is widely distributed throughout the Great Lakes region. It is likely that our location in west-central Wisconsin is near the northernmost edge of its distribution.

Close to eight hundred scud specimens acquired in a pilot survey of the Kinnickinnic and over two thousand specimens collected in a comprehensive survey were *G. pseudolimnaeus*. All seventeen river collection sites sampled from Kinnickinnic River State Park to north of Interstate 94 yielded specimens of this species (table 6). Additionally, in family-level biotic index sampling done on the South Fork of the Kinnickinnic River between March and May of a single year, Gammaridae made up ninety percent of macroinvertebrates collected. Accounts of scud numbers from other rivers often include words such as *incredibly numerous* and *surprisingly abundant*. These comments are appropriately applied to the Kinnickinnic and its tributaries as well.

As amphipod crustaceans, scuds appear quite different from the many and diverse insects with which most stream observers are familiar. The laterally flattened shrimp-like body is arched when they are not swimming. Two pairs of antennae extend forward from the head, followed by a number of ventrally positioned, serially arranged, paired appendages. These include multiple mouthparts, two pairs of grasping and pulling legs, five pairs of crawling and walking legs, three pairs of swimming legs, and three pairs of uropods. The latter are abdominal appendages used for pushing when the scud is crawling.

It's not unusual to find scuds in a variety of colors, some quite vivid. While they are commonly ivory, gray, or tan, they can also be yellow, orange, purple, blue, or olive. With this I add a word of caution. When crustaceans have been preserved in alcohol, they almost always look orange, pink, or red, like shrimp or lobster that have just been boiled for humans to eat. Then, with time in storage, they turn off-white or white. To see their true colors, it's a good practice to view fresh specimens.

Scuds may not be seen until the shallow debris or vegetation in which they are feeding or resting is disturbed. When that happens, they can be observed swimming with a unique darting movement. They straighten the body and use their three pairs of swimming legs to efficiently and quickly move from one place of hiding to another. The very name scud, akin to the Norwegian *skudda* (to push), and in English meaning to move or run swiftly, suggests this quick movement. The alternate name, sideswimmer, derives from a tendency to swim with a side, as opposed to the back, facing up.

When living specimens are brought into the lab, scuds readily position themselves under any cover present, and are only observed darting through open water when prompted. (Those in Ms. Wilcox's classroom were prompted often.) They are active at night in the stream and their presence as part of the nocturnal behavioral drift phenomenon was well documented by Waters. Pennak, author of the classic textbook and reference *Fresh-water Invertebrates of the United States*, characterized amphipods as requiring a narrow, cold temperature range, instinctively needing to be in contact with a substrate, and typically hiding in and among vegetation, debris, and stones in daytime to avoid light.

Scuds feed avidly on all types of plant and animal materials and are known to browse on surface debris covering plants and substrates of streams. They are well described as omnivorous scavengers. They are only rarely predaceous. Scuds are eaten by insects, amphibians, and fish, the latter being their primary predators. McCafferty noted they are an important food source for fish. Borger similarly commented in reference to their large numbers that it is no surprise they are eaten by trout.

I was working at a river site downstream from River Falls on a summer afternoon, the kind of day one might hope to recall whenever a good thought is needed. It had all the elements of a perfect day—penetrating sun, a few puffy cumulus clouds, and a light breeze. Specimens were coming in good numbers from a variety of substrates. The familiar chuckling of water moving over shallow riffles was the only noise I expected to hear. But, as I was looking through a subsample, I caught the sound of conversation. I couldn't have known this day would include another chance encounter with Dave Norling. He and a fellow angler were working their way upstream in several feet of water, cane rods in hand, with their canine companion, a golden retriever named Chief.

Dave asked what I was finding, so I invited him over to see the invertebrates in my sorting tray. He immediately focused on the scuds darting through the shallow water. Before long we were looking closely at the scud flies he had tied, comparing them with the living specimens. I noticed that Dave was particularly interested in the color variations of these crustaceans. We talked briefly about fishing and he kindly gave me an assortment of scud flies he created. One of the take-home notes for me was that, of all the possible scud colors, one was remarkably similar to Chief's fur. Apparently, as I gleaned from the discussion, other family pets were also sources for Dave's "family scud" fly pattern.

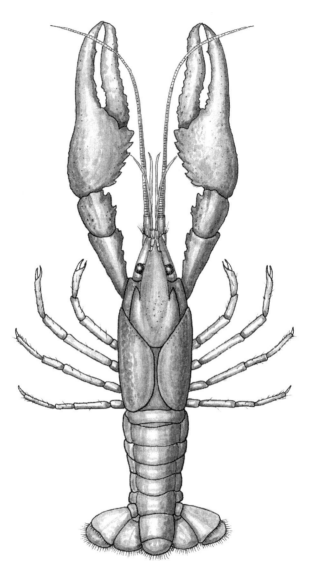

Crayfish adult, *Orconectes*

LESSONS OF THE RUSTY CRAYFISH

I recall my excitement as a young boy, interested in all things wild, the fun of fishing for crawdads, as we called them, not far from my home in Missouri. A friend and I would ride our bikes to the city park and stalk our prey at one of the small lakes there. The water was a light brown color, like coffee with creamer, murky to the point of making it impossible to see our quarry. In this typical Missouri lake we would have to use something other than a visual approach in our pursuit.

Our bait was a piece of raw chicken liver tied onto the end of a string. Positioned stomachs-down on the dock and hanging over the edge, we lowered the slippery mass until we felt it stop on the lake bottom. As we repressed every possible ounce of youthful impatience, the passage of what seemed like endless time would bring subtle vibrations up through the line to our hopeful fingers. This was a signal that one or more crayfish were grasping the liver with their daunting claws. We pulled the string up to the surface as slowly and steadily as anticipation would allow, so the catch were not alerted to their ensuing capture.

Sometimes the quarry would get used as fishing bait, but I was inclined to bring mine home for observation in an aquarium. In my mind this was a creature as exotic as any I could see at the city zoo. I was fascinated by the intricacies of crustacean anatomy, especially the numerous and diverse appendages. The shape and movement of each kind of extremity intrigued me and, with study, became some of my earliest examples of biological function and adaptation.

Little did I know that fifty years later I would be collecting crayfish, albeit very different species, in different ways, and for different purposes. Over many years my biology students and I collected crayfish from the Kinnickinnic River and its tributaries while working on class projects. I added crayfish specimens to our departmental reference collection whenever possible from my own stream invertebrate surveys, as well.

Most of the crayfish I found in the Kinnickinnic River and its South Fork tributary were native *Orconectes virilis*. Hobbs and Jass, coauthors of *Crayfishes of Wisconsin*, refer to papers of several workers, going back to 1883, who reported this species as the most common crayfish in the state. They reported also that this is the only crayfish that has been found in every Wisconsin county. The majority of my Kinni crayfish collections were from the lower dam area below Glen Park in River Falls to a sampling site within Kinnickinnic River State Park.

So the story is predictable to this point. It's no surprise when routine survey work supports expected outcomes. Then, while attending a meeting of the North American Benthological Society held in La Crosse, Wisconsin, I had the opportunity to have Ray Bouchard of the Philadelphia Academy of Sciences look at crayfish specimens I collected from the Kinnickinnic. The last species I expected him to find among the group was the rusty crayfish, *Orconectes rusticus*. He was examining specimens under the microscope when he stopped on one of particular interest. He separated the mouthparts so they could be clearly seen and invited me to take a look. I peered through the eyepieces as he explained that the blade-like incisor region of the mandible was confirmation of the *rusty*.

It would seem that identifying a crayfish called "rusty" would be a simple process. Common names, however, are inherently problematic and body colors and markings in arthropods can widely vary. Many descriptions of rusty crayfish contain these words: red or rust-brown spots on each side of the carapace (the shield-like cover of the head and thorax). However, an important qualification necessarily cautions the observer that the spots vary considerably in size, shape, and location, and *may not be present*. Technical keying and ultimate determination of the crayfish requires a magnified look at appendage and carapace characteristics with examination of a primary mouthpart, the mandible, for confirmation.

The rusty crayfish is native to the Ohio River Basin and states of Ohio, Kentucky, Tennessee, Indiana, and Illinois. The range of *O. rusticus* in Wisconsin is *disjunct*, in other words, not connected to the region of native distribution. Hobbs and Jass indicate the modern range of *O. rusticus* across a large part of Wisconsin. Reading further on distribution they state, "The occurrence of this species in the state is 'artificial' and closely approximates the location of lake districts and/or areas of dense human populations." All prevailing hypotheses regarding movement of this species from native to non-native regions implicate human conveyance in general and use of crayfish as fishing bait in particular. No historical or literature-based data points indicate the presence of rusty crayfish in the Kinnickinnic River.

᱋ᜩᜪ᱋

Biologists have appreciated for some time that the rusty crayfish has had unfavorable effects on Wisconsin lakes. Citing a number of earlier workers, Houghton and colleagues summarized the detrimental effects of this crayfish, indicating that they: 1) impact energy flow and decrease habitat by destruction of aquatic plants, 2) displace native crayfish with their aggressive behavior, large size, and fast growth, 3) feed on benthic invertebrates, such as snails, insects, and other crustaceans, and 4) consume eggs and fry of many fish species.

In the study by Houghton and colleagues, which is especially pertinent to the subject of crayfish in the Kinnickinnic River, the Prairie River in north-central Wisconsin was used to test the effect of the presence of *O. rusticus* on the density and diversity of aquatic invertebrates in a coldwater stream. The sections of the river chosen for analysis had three levels of rusty crayfish abundance: upper river - not colonized, middle river - intermediate colonization, and lower river - high abundance. The upper section is classified as a high-grade trout fishery. The lower section is considered a medium-grade trout fishery as the river widens downstream, has less groundwater influence, and is subjected to increased solar radiation. Following analysis of crayfish and macroinvertebrate populations, as well as multiple environmental factors, they concluded that "...the decrease in benthic invertebrate density was brought about by the increasing abundance of rusty crayfish."

An additional conclusion from the Prairie River study, was "...that colder water temperatures are keeping rusty crayfish from the upper reaches of the Prairie River." These authors point to previous studies by Mundahl and Benton who "...found that post-molting mortality in rusty crayfish dramatically increased when the temperature was held below 68°F, and rusty crayfish did not grow at temperatures below 57.2°F."

Summer temperature studies on the Kinnickinnic River in the mid-1990s conducted by Kent Johnson demonstrated warmer water conditions just below River Falls and its impoundments, compared to locations directly upstream from the city. Results of these analyses suggest the reason for limited distribution of the rusty crayfish in the river. To date, specimens of the crayfish have been found in the Kinnickinnic only from downstream of the lower dam to its convergence with the Rocky Branch tributary. It appears that this section may be the most hospitable part of the river for *O. rusticus* from a temperature perspective. On a watershed scale, for most of the calendar year and a significant part of summer, the habitat should be thermally unfavorable for this species.

The presence of rusty crayfish in the Kinnickinnic is the result of an unwelcome and potentially damaging species introduction. Ecological disruption of lakes resulting from presence of the species has been well documented, and now there are data showing detrimental effects in a north-central Wisconsin river.

There is much remaining to be learned about the rusty crayfish in the Kinnickinnic. Some strategies for finding out more might include: determining the full areal extent of the species in the main stem and tributaries, establishing a biomonitoring program in areas known to support reproduction and survival, and setting up continuing quantitative assessment to provide data on populations trends.

Efforts that further the coldwater regime of the river create an environment that is less supportive of the rusty crayfish. Keeping the river summer-cool is our best hope. Specific actions that we know are effective—establishing buffers, reducing imperviousness, retaining and treating storm water—all advance this goal.

PART III

No man steps in the same river twice, for it's not
the same river and he's not the same man.

Heraclitus (Greek, 535-475 B.C.)

Kinnickinnic River near its confluence with Rocky Branch

THE YIN AND YANG
OF LIVING IN CURRENT

W hat would it be like as an invertebrate, underwater in a rapid, sub-jected to the whims of a fast-moving and turbulent current, bounc-ing from one boulder to another, unable to determine your course, only to be ejected unceremoniously into a pool of calmer water at the end? What could make this nightmare scenario even more chilling would be your delivery into the proximity of a waiting trout, a large one that has earned its productive feeding lie at the upper end of the metaphorical prey conveyor belt.

My mental image of this situation is sharpened by a few such swims I experienced during whitewater canoeing and kayaking courses. The simple truth is that my human form has none of the adaptations necessary to survive this self-inflicted mistreatment and must rely on protective extras such as a PFD (personal flotation device) and helmet. It also doesn't hurt that one or more instructors have stationed themselves in appropriate downstream rescue positions to toss out a helpful throw line. This practice safeguards involuntary swimmers, such as myself, from further potential danger, something along the lines of a safety net.

For river insects and crustaceans it's hazardous to be swimming or drifting through open water—situations that are part of aquatic life. Many insects nav-igate from the river bottom to the surface just prior to emergence. Others get dislodged unintentionally in the course of everyday activities, or purposefully release themselves to be transported downstream as drift. Some must swim to the water-air interface because that is where they obtain oxygen. To be seen in open water is to be vulnerable. This is life or death. There is no safety net.

Unlike the aerial and terrestrial habitats in which many insects live, where air is the medium through which many go about their daily lives, water pro-vides special challenges, not the least of which is its density. Water is over seven hundred times as dense as air. We appreciate this quality when we walk through it. Knee-deep in the river a fly fisher endeavors to make progress in any direction. Moving upstream, against the current, adds water *movement* to the equation. When excessive effort becomes necessary to take individual steps, we might be inclined to adopt a strategy to avoid the worst of it.

Likewise, for the majority of river insects, adaptation to living in moving water is directed not so much toward struggling with strong current as it is about behavior patterns to avoid it. Most stream insects live among or under an array of substrate materials. When we take the time to look beneath the surface, avoiding reflecting light and deep shadows, the river reveals an abundance of microhabitats for aquatic invertebrates to occupy. Gravel, cobble, and boulders provide considerable non-current, or low-current, spaces. Likewise, plant life and debris, such as leaves and downed wood, supply numerous additional habitat possibilities.

～기〈～

Obviously, not all current related issues are resolved by avoidance. Many aquatic insects and crustaceans need to be directly in current for purposes of catching prey, filter feeding, obtaining oxygen, or a combination of these. The best way to see examples of adaptations related to water movement is to go straight to the river and pluck a rock from the streambed. Let most of the water drip away and look it over for clinging or attached critters. Some of the most common insects we find in the Kinni provide the best examples of features related to successful current life. Familiarity with these will carry over to recognition of similar characteristics in other organisms.

FLATHEAD MAYFLY LARVAE (HEPTAGENIIDAE)

To maintain a position in close proximity to the current, for the purpose of taking advantage of oxygen and food resources, it's adaptive to have a compressed body, one that is dorsoventrally (back-to-belly) flattened. This allows occupation of cracks and crevices among gravel, cobble, and other debris, avoiding stronger flow while still remaining in fast water. The flathead mayfly larva, *Stenonema vicarium*, is an example of this adaptation in a common Kinnickinnic insect. *Stenonema* and its relatives can disappear before one's eyes in the thin layer of water on an exposed rock. This body configuration not only allows for concealment, it also takes advantage of the area close to the surface of an underwater object, called the *boundary layer*, where current is reduced by frictional resistance. At the same time that the flathead larva is hidden in substrate and scraping algae from the surface of a rock, it can be making the most of water flow to obtain oxygen.

SMALL MINNOW MAYFLY LARVAE (BAETIDAE)

On a plucked rock we are likely to see small minnow mayfly larvae, such as *Baetis tricaudatus*, that possess a classic streamlined form, as the common name indicates, not unlike a typical fish. Baetids are known as strong swimmers and this shape is a factor in efficiency of movement. It also contributes to stability when the insect is poised on a rock. The hydrodynamic profile allows water to flow around it in a way that does not strip the insect from its position. Small minnow mayfly larvae also have an advantage that lesser size confers—lowered resistance to flow—a characteristic of many insects that live in moving water.

SPINY CRAWLER MAYFLY LARVAE (EPHEMERELLIDAE)

Anatomical features on the feet of certain larval insects allow them to grasp the smallest of irregularities on the surface of substrate materials. Minute hook-shaped claws—single for larval mayflies, paired for larval stoneflies, for examples—are located on the ends of the feet. (Keys may refer to these segmented feet as *tarsi*, singular *tarsus*, and may call the claws *tarsal claws*.) The tiny hooks are more-or-less curved, extremely small (!), and sharply pointed. When crawler mayfly larvae such as *Ephemerella* are resting or moving about rocky materials on the streambed, as when feeding, these microscopic hooks mean the difference between maintaining safe contact and drifting.

HUMPLESS CASE-MAKER CADDISFLY LARVAE (BRACHYCENTRIDAE)

Rocks picked from the Kinni often have small, cylindrical tubes attached, sometimes clustered together in large numbers. These cases, constructed by larval caddisflies, and which are often characteristic for a group or type, are made from materials like plant parts or sand grains that are bonded together with silk. The slightly tapering cases of the humpless case-maker, *Brachycentrus occidentalis*, are easy to find in the Kinni, both occupied and unoccupied. They represent an adaptation to current based on bonding to the substrate. Larvae attach their cases, with silk strands they produce, to rocks in strategic positions, for feeding and oxygen access. Empty, attached cases persist, and are found on rocks long after they have been abandoned.

〜丶〜

Previous descriptions may give the impression that insects in the stream are all nicely tucked away in safe places, protected from predation as they feed and respire. That is not to say that insects cannot be found in open water, there by chance or by instinct. A net or piece of screening placed in the stream perpendicular to the current samples downstream transport of temporarily suspended insects known as *drift*. A drift sample can be taken either at or below the surface, or both. The process takes very little effort, provides immediate feedback, and is one of the most practical and valuable learning techniques for understanding what is going on in the stream at a given time.

Below the surface all manner of larvae, pupae, and adults can be found drifting. The catch will include normally anchored or hidden insects inadvertently dislodged and swept up in or using the current for transport. It may also contain larvae and certain pupae making their way from bottom substrates to the surface, headed for emergence as adults, or for mayflies, emergence as subimagos. The drift composition depends on many factors, including the time of year, the hour of day, flow levels, and weather conditions.

Tom Waters of the University of Minnesota recognized three categories of drift almost 50 years ago: *constant drift*, the continuous and low level occurrence of most species at all times; *catastrophic drift*, that caused by physical disturbance of bottom fauna through flooding and bottom scouring, and perhaps the most intriguing, *behavioral drift*, that occurring in a repeated pattern at a certain time of night or day as an instinctive behavior of certain species.

Several prevalent Kinnickinnic insects and crustaceans engage in behavioral drift. The very common small minnow mayfly, *Baetis tricaudatus*, and the familiar scud, *Gammarus pseudolimnaeus*, are known to display night-active drift, along with certain stonefly and black fly larvae. Some caddisflies are day-active drifters and some are night-active. While significant study has been done on this behavior, there is still much to be understood. Certainly, drifting under cover of darkness has potential as an adaptation for avoiding predation. Though most drift patterns do not cover large distances, the activity is also an efficient dispersal mechanism.

—⁄⁊⁊⁊—

Standing knee deep in the stream I think about how moving water formed the valley through which the river now courses. With water pushing on my shins, I consider what this energy means for things living in the river. Every substrate perceivable here is subjected to some effect of current. To a greater or lesser extent these settings are populated by characteristic invertebrates, including insects and crustaceans.

I recall an essay by Barry Lopez in which he described photographing the flowing water of creeks and rivers near his home. Examining images captured in extreme light conditions, Lopez became interested in the patterns of flow that ordinarily remain unseen. He wrote about the complexity of uninterrupted laminar flow changing to turbulence around a single rock, something a sophisticated computer could not fully describe. This made me think about aquatic organisms living on and among these rocks and how they have solved the problems associated with maintaining contact, orientation, and movement with intricate mechanisms of adaptation.

Gullan and Cranston later reminded me of the relationship between river organisms and the convoluted flow issue when they put forward the idea that small-scale features of running water in natural settings are much more involved than were previously thought, that the interaction of current speed and body shape is not simple. I marvel when I think that aquatic organisms are dealing with flow chaos as an underlying feature of underwater life while so many other critical requirements for survival are being met.

—⁄⁊⁊⁊—

A studied look into the stream may reveal little in the way of insects and crustaceans living there, but they *are* present, on or under most of the things we *do* see: rocks, woody debris, aquatic plants. Some are clinging to the surfaces of these objects, taking advantage of adaptations such as body shape and claws.

Many are positioned outside of the fast current in sheltered spaces under boulders and cobble, in gravel, sand, and silt, and within accumulated organics like hardwood leaves. In this variety of places river invertebrates are actively feeding, growing, and, whenever possible, avoiding predation. Highly adapted anatomical features and physiological processes combined with sophisticated behavioral patterns assure that they flourish, in water from swiftly moving to barely moving.

How often can we appreciate our world on parallel scales, with moving water sculpting physical environments the size of watersheds and, at the same time, shaping the micro- and macroscopic biological adaptations on which our six-legged river inhabitants depend?

South Fork of the Kinnickinnic, Third Street bridge area,
UWRF campus, normal flow, 4 May 2000

South Fork of the Kinnickinnic, Third Street bridge area,
UWRF campus, flood event, 1 August 2001

INSECT SURVIVAL IN
EXTREME STREAMFLOW EVENTS

When persistent rain leads up to the day targeted for sampling aquatic invertebrates, I can only imagine what is happening with the river. All that lies between data acquisition and disappointment will be a quick look at the water. Two scenarios play out in my mind. One is the river moderately elevated, slightly turbid, usual features visible, the influx of water accommodated. *Probably O.K.* The other is a noisy torrent, opaque with suspended silt, bobbing with flotsam, threatening to go over—or already over—its banks. *Not so good.*

The sound of water grows as I approach the river. Through the trees the tops of choppy brown waves are showing. Closer, the river looks chaotic. Familiar riffles and prominent boulders have disappeared under the extra volume. This isn't what I hoped to find. For reasons of sampling efficacy and personal safety the sample will have to wait until another day.

An experience of this kind leads to questions. What's happening to the living things you expected to find? Surely insects and other river organisms are being pushed downstream in the maelstrom of silt and sand, drifting wood, and other organic debris. You're wondering to what degree the underwater community is being disrupted by these forces? Will it return to the order that existed before and, if so, how and when?

A single Midwestern storm can quickly change stream conditions. A series of downpours can overwhelm multiple watersheds. This is what happened in the Minnesota and Wisconsin portions of the Driftless Area during the third week of August 2007. The Driftless Area is a region of steep hillsides, deep valleys, and cold, clear trout streams. The vulnerable landscape was ravaged by unrelenting rainfall, ranging from eight to twenty inches over a period of a few days. Just over fifteen inches of rain fell on one of those days. This twenty four-hour data point was reported as the heaviest daily rainfall ever recorded in Minnesota by an official National Weather Service observing station. Rivers flooded, homes and businesses were damaged and lost, people died. Fortunately, most rainfall events are not record breaking, but one like this opens our eyes to nature's possibilities and forces us to think about what future atmospheric changes may bring.

It's useful to have a general sense of river flow when preparing to work or recreate in the water. This can be derived from previous days of observing, or attention to recent or ongoing precipitation amounts, or all of these, combined with past experiences. A significant rain event can increase flow dramatically and flow can remain high for several days, or longer. With time one gains an appreciation of these pulses, and schedules work or recreation around them.

River observers can stay aware of Kinnickinnic flow remotely by accessing real-time data from the U.S. Geological Survey gaging station in the lower Kinni valley. The recording gage, located upstream from County Trunk Hwy F, is identified as USGS 05342000. It transmits discharge, precipitation, and gage height numbers to the United States Geological Survey web site where it is stored for use by resource managers, water scientists, and the public. The discharge data in standard cubic feet per second (cfs) is very useful in understanding river fluctuations and for decision-making related to going to the lower Kinni. A web search based on "USGS 05342000" brings up the site. Additional details are available there, including the web page: "Water Science Glossary of Terms," which can be accessed from the main page through the link *Explanation of Terms*. There the reader can find definitions and explanations of river-related words, including discharge, base flow, groundwater, particle size, runoff, sediment, turbidity, thermal pollution, and many others.

━╱╲━

When I first became interested in the biological effects of increased stream volume, like that following heavy or extended rainfall, I needed to add the rich terminology of hydrology to the lexicon of river ecology. I came to know the flow volume of the river per unit of time as its *discharge*. Modifications in discharge, especially significant increases, noticeably influence the physical part of the stream environment. Hydrology and river biology became for me intimately intertwined.

Of critical importance to the aquatic invertebrate community is *scour*, also known as *channel scour*, where cutting of the streambed occurs and suspended materials are transported by water. The sound of the word *scour* suggests its potential. From the Latin *excurare*, which translates literally as to clean off, to scour means clearing, digging, or removing by, or as if by, a powerful current of water. The ability of water to pick up and move sediment particles is discharge dependent. Obviously, larger materials such as boulders and cobble are less likely to erode than sand and silt, but when enough force is exerted, they too are moved. One simply needs to visit the stream enough times, especially during spring, to observe impressive redistribution of silt and sand substrates, as well as large scale movement of gravels, cobbles, and woody debris.

When sediments are dislodged from the streambed, so too are some resident organisms. As discharge increases, more aquatic invertebrates become part of the drift. An observer standing near the rushing water during a flooding event might be mesmerized by the appearance of the frenzied surface and forget that substantial energy is being translated to substrates, habitats, and living things below. If forces are great enough to denude the streambed and sweep away community members, repopulation becomes necessary to restore the natural order.

On July 18, 1993, catastrophic flooding occurred in the Baxter's Hollow region of Otter Creek south-southwest of Baraboo, Wisconsin. The creek rose six feet, possibly more, after nearly eight inches of rain fell in the area. In what might be called a stroke of good fortune, the insect species of the stream had been previously documented—almost annually since 1963—by William Hilsenhoff and his students. In 1984 and 1985 they carried out an intensive biotic index project at Otter Creek to develop a correction factor for the existing HBI protocol. Otter Creek insects were also compiled in 1990 and updated in 1992. The pre-flood fauna was well documented. So in 1994 circumstances were ideal for obtaining post-flood insect data that could be compared with pre-1993 records.

Results of this study showed that "substantial changes" occurred in the insect fauna in the high gradient portion of the creek. All silt and debris, and almost all sand and gravel in these sections were carried away. Pools and riffles were eliminated. What remained was an almost continuous run (fast deep water) over cobble and larger rocks. Insect changes included: increased numbers of some species, reduced numbers of other species, and probable elimination of several species. Hilsenhoff predicted that silt, sand, and debris would return to these areas with time and that insects would follow: "Insects eliminated by the flood can return if suitable habitat exists, because adults of almost all species fly long distances." But he also suggested that, because of the extreme alteration in some habitats, it was unlikely that some of the populations would reoccupy their pre-flood locations.

━╱╲━

Stream biologists recognize four mechanisms by which aquatic invertebrates recolonize areas where population decline has occurred. These are drift, vertical movement, aerial contributions, and upstream movement. A number of ingenious in-stream experiments have been designed and carried out in attempts to determine the key features and relative importance of each of these possibilities. However, no clear pattern seems to fit all situations. Having so many variables influencing stream and population dynamics, coupled with a wide range of impact situations, means that each event will have a different combination of recovery mechanisms.

Drift conveys individuals that can play a role in recolonization. As previously noted, when displacement is caused by a scouring discharge, it is referred to as *catastrophic drift*, exactly what I am imagining as I view the tumbling water of the stream. The significance of drift can be seen from two perspectives, one as the cause of displacement and the other as a recolonization mechanism. As long as an upstream reach or reaches of the river serve as a viable source of organisms, drift can act as a replacement mechanism downstream from that location.

Another basic mechanism relies on the proclivity of organisms to occupy locations in protected spaces, within substrates. The post-event recovery mode in this case is referred to as *upward migration* or *vertical movement*. Wallace and Anderson suggest that stream insects respond to increased flow and rebound accordingly after the event: "Presumably, some portion of the benthic community seeks refuge deeper in the substrates during floods; insects are difficult to find at such times, but normal population levels are found soon after the flows subside."

Two additional possibilities for recovery are *aerial sources* and *upstream migration*. Aerial sources involves adults flying into the denuded area and depositing eggs to initiate a new generation, as noted in the Otter Creek recovery prediction. Upstream migration relies on either adult or immature insects crawling or swimming through water and settling in affected places.

Whether they remain sheltered in-place or return to their habitat of origin by drifting, moving upstream, or arriving aerially, insects and other arthropods, in general, have the *reproductive potential* to fill a void once they get there. This is based on two intrinsic qualities. One is the large number of eggs customarily deposited per female, and the other is the relatively short length of time required to complete a generation, the specifics of both being affected by the kind of insect in question. The ability to repopulate and speed of resident recovery also depend on the geographic extent of the affected streambed and the proximity of viable sources of recolonizing individuals.

When flash flooding hits trout streams, we don't have to be there to visualize increasing discharges, scoured substrates, and catastrophic drift. Likewise, it's easy to imagine how removal and displacement of individual aquatic invertebrates vary with the severity of the event. Removal of species from areas that were previously inhabited, rearranged substrates, and reestablished habitats can create opportunity. Insects and crustaceans *will* repopulate, given a healthy stream environment, sometimes faster than we might expect.

The common net-spinner caddisfly larva, *Ceratopsyche*, feeds
by filtering fine materials from the current using
a catch-net constructed with spun silk

PREDATORS, GRAZERS, SHREDDERS, AND COLLECTORS

I have the greatest respect for fish. I fully acknowledge that my chances in a matchup with a trout are not so good. In a desperate attempt to provide myself with psychological support, I have calculated that my brain is 1,400 times larger than that of my prey. It doesn't seem to help. So if I suggest that trout feeding mechanisms are less diverse than that of their many potential prey items, namely insects and crustaceans, it is not to denigrate the many subtleties of behavior utilized or the successes that fish have as they acquire invertebrates as food. No question, a sophisticated predatory approach to energy and nutrient acquisition allows these finned creatures to grow and reproduce with great efficiency. But predation is just one of an arsenal of methods that aquatic invertebrates employ to acquire resources.

In Biology 101, students learn that all energy of importance to the majority of living things starts with the sun. Plant life in a variety of forms, including algae in aquatic settings, provides the conversion of light energy to chemical energy. The capture of light energy is rooted in the biochemical reactions of photosynthesis, with output in the form of readily useable and storable molecules. (A 1970's bumper sticker asked the question: "Have you thanked a green plant today?") The products of this conversion are the energy-laden sugars, starches, and other carbon-based compounds that we as humans derive, along with our herbivorous animal relatives, by eating plant materials.

From there energy passes through the *food chain*. Actually, because food chains intertwine, the passage occurs more realistically through a complex *food web*. Normal progression involves a series of classic feeding types which includes *herbivory* (ingesting living plant materials), *carnivory* (ingesting live prey), and *detritivory* (feeding on dead animal or plant material). When we look at biological communities as diverse as prairies, forests, oceans, and rivers, energy flow follows a standard sequence: 1) initial energy capture by green inhabitants, 2) passage to herbivores, 3) through a series of carnivores, and then 4) exploitation of remains by detritivores. This progression illustrates community structure as a series of feeding, or *trophic*, relationships. Each step is referred to as a *trophic level*. Communities typically have no more than four or five trophic levels because energy is inefficiently transferred through the system, and every participant uses some energy along the way.

Organisms that feed on more than one trophic level (as in eating both vegetable and animal substances) are called *omnivores*; the process is *omnivory*. As in humans and black bears, food is not simply animal or vegetable in nature, it's a mixture dependent in part on what is available when hunger prevails. When I picture a hungry black bear, I can just as easily see it eating a bunch of ants as a stem full of blueberries. If you look into the mouth of a bear, raccoon, or human, it is not hard to figure out the adaptations of the mouth and teeth, structured for the various foods the species eats. When a similar analysis is done of arthropod mouthparts, anatomical details reveal the nature of foods eaten, as well.

With the study of aquatic invertebrate feeding came the realization that virtually all aquatic insects are ultimately omnivores. Rarely do aquatic insects fall cleanly into one of the three conventional food web categories: carnivory, herbivory, or detritivory. This is due to the fact that their feeding is not precise. They are adapted anatomically and physiologically, like the raccoon, to ingest and digest multiple food types.

Because of the lack of specificity in assigning individual insects or groups of insects to the role of omnivory, and because the majority of aquatic insects fall into this increasingly non-descript category, K. W. Cummins, ultimately working with R. W. Merritt, developed a more practical and ecological categorization plan, dividing stream aquatic invertebrates into *functional feeding groups*. In this approach food sources are distinguished by: 1) particle size (detrital categories), 2) presence of chlorophyll (periphyton, primarily algae, especially diatoms, attached to surfaces of rock, wood, and plants), and 3) the high protein content of typical animal prey.

Using this method aquatic ecologists distinguish four primary categories of stream insect foods. The first is the most intuitive. This is *prey* in the form of various small living invertebrates subject to ingestion by predators. The second is *periphyton*, found on many aquatic surfaces. The third is *coarse particulate organic matter* (CPOM) consisting of plant parts (miscellaneous leaves, twigs, branches, logs, etc.) and green plants (both floating and rooted), larger than one millimeter (one twenty-fifth of an inch) in size. The last is possibly the most challenging of the four to imagine because it accounts for ingestion of items less than one millimeter in size. This is the *fine particulate organic matter* (FPOM) that includes fragmented CPOM, unattached living or dead organic materials, and microorganisms.

Directly associated with each food category is a *functional feeding group*. *Predators* ingest or suck the body fluids of prey. *Scrapers*, also called *grazers*, eat periphyton. *Shredders* feed on CPOM. *Collectors* consume FPOM. As a healthy, coldwater stream, the Kinnickinnic River has numerous invertebrate representatives of each group.

When I go to the stream, my tasks center on the *what*, *where*, and *when* of insect life. I do not collect data on the *how*, that is, how insects obtain the energy and nutrients necessary to live, grow, and reproduce. The feeding habits of many common aquatic species can be gleaned from published literature sources. Also, as previously noted, much can be inferred from mouthpart morphology and constructed devices such as collecting nets.

Would it be difficult to find insect or crustacean examples of these feeding groups in the Kinnickinnic? Absolutely not. Let's hike down there and see what we can discover. I'll take the net. You grab the sorting tray. We will start with the basic approach of picking up streambed rocks. After that we can use the D-net to look for living things in mixed or deeper bottom substrates or in piled-up materials like silt or leaf packs.

Wading into a riffle one of us reaches into the water and extracts a saucer-size rock. With a close look we find a flathead mayfly larva, *Stenonema*, easily identified by not only its flat head, but also its flattened body and three widely spread tails. We infer that the larva is *scraping* the thin layer of algae, detritus (non-living particulate organic matter), and small animal life, such as first instar midge larvae, from the hard stone surface with its mandibles. We can also call this *grazing*, implying an analogy with our more selectively herbivorous domestic field animals. Other examples we could find are feeding in the same way, including *Glossosoma*, the saddle case-maker caddisflies, with their tortoise shell-like cases, and small elongate riffle beetle larvae *Optioservus fastiditus* and *Helichus striatus* of the families Elmidae and Dryopidae.

Just a few feet away, box elder and willow leaves have accumulated among the submerged branches of a broken tree limb, held in place by the current. Within the mass giant stonefly larvae and crane fly larvae are *shredding* the leaves, reducing the coarse organic materials to fine particles. *Pycnopsyche* caddisfly larvae, recognizable by the sticks attached longitudinally to (and extending well beyond) their cases, feed similarly. Their life cycle begins with the hatching of eggs programmed to correspond with the leaf fall in autumn. If we are there in late winter, we may find larvae of the winter stonefly *Taeniopteryx* shredding similar materials. All that's left after these detrital processors are done are skeletonized remains, leaf shapes consisting only of supportive veins. Importantly, fragments of energy- and nutrient-laden organic materials are drifting with the current, setting up opportunities for collectors, both filtering and gathering.

Downriver a net-spinning caddisfly larva (such as the larval *Ceratopsyche* pictured in the prefacing photo) is *collecting* drifting particles by *filtering* the current with its silken net. It awaits nearby in its retreat and exits to harvest the fine plant and detrital materials. Black fly larvae, of which there are many in the Kinni, are often seen clustered together on rock surfaces. Attached by the end of their abdomen, hooked to a pad of silk they have spun and head hanging downstream, they filter fine particles from the moving water with fan-like mouth brushes.

Among cobble and gravel materials of the streambed, a spiny crawler mayfly larva, *Ephemerella*, is hunting through spaces and over surfaces, *collecting* fine sediment and detrital fragments. The particles aren't attached to objects, so this collecting is a *gathering* process. Some small minnow mayflies, *Baetis*, and little stout crawlers, *Tricorythodes*, are gatherers, as well as the scuds and non-biting midge larvae we would get with almost any substrate sample.

Movement of the spiny crawler attracts the attention of a fragile-looking yellow patterned stonefly larva actively searching the substrate for prey. Using its efficient mandibles in a classic act of *predation*, it attacks, kills, and ingests the mayfly larva. Energy is transferred via yet another link in the food web. The handsome larval perlid stonefly *Paragnetina*, the eye-catching alderfly larva *Sialis*, and the impressive waterscorpion, *Ranatra*, are other common predators we might happen upon. Our perspective on these unseen carnivores may not immediately transfer from the concept, say, of Canada lynx and showshoe hares, but aren't there more similarities than differences among all predator-prey relationships?

For anyone interested in family identification and then following up on feeding categories of specimens, a useful resource is Bouchard's 2004 *Guide to Aquatic Invertebrates of the Upper Midwest*. Organisms are arranged by order and family in Appendix A, with feeding groups indicated in the column labeled FG. Feeding groups are described in detail in Appendix C.

⌐⟋⎮⟍⌐

Thinking about these diverse relationships brings to mind Darwin's *entangled bank metaphor*:

> It is interesting to contemplate an entangled bank, clothed with many plants of many kinds, with birds singing on the bushes, with various insects flitting about, and with worms crawling through the damp earth, and to reflect that these elaborately constructed forms, so different from each other, and *dependent upon each other in so complex a manner*, have all been produced by laws acting around us.

Energy flow, as in *who eats whom or what*, binds the river community together. Food webs rely on many individual strands, each representing energy transfer from one species to another. It's natural for humans, when engaged in discussion about trophic levels and food webs, to use the terms *up* as we do with energy passage and *higher* when comparing ultimate carnivores to herbivores. But, in spite of their *lower* position in the typical food web diagram and lesser size, river macroinvertebrates deserve attention because they establish essential energy connections between producers and endpoint carnivores. At the same time, many of them are responsible for the process of breaking down river debris while releasing and acquiring its available energy. In seemingly simple acts of obtaining food, insects and crustaceans fulfill critical roles. These contribute, in turn, to long-term stability of the river ecosystem.

Lower Kinnickinnic River

A "HELL HOLE OF DEVIL'S BROTH"

I was making plans for a field trip designed to acquaint a group of UW-River Falls campus visitors with the Kinnickinnic River. The guests were college biology teachers, so I chose to visit sites along the river where I felt discussion could be generated, especially regarding aquatic life. In field trip tradition, we would stop and climb out of the van at various sites, often overlooks and bridge crossings, to view the river and talk about the nature of the watershed. Somewhat longer stops were planned at a cold, lucent feeder spring, a graceful waterfall, an expansive delta, an aging hydroelectric dam, and the site of a fish kill event of the previous year.

Part of my preparation as trip leader included selecting issues of human and natural history to introduce along the way. As I did this, I encountered a range of descriptions of human-river interaction. When I began, I was aware of recent river health issues, but I was generally uninformed about the way the Kinni was treated in the past, particularly before the 1950s. This exercise reminded me of how important it is to understand what the river has endured since settlement, and how fortunate we are that many protections are now in place. I appreciate, too, that the return of the river to good health is the result of extensive commitment and effort by numerous agencies, organizations, and institutions, and support of the public.

━✦━

Unsettling details of Kinnickinnic River history are portrayed by J. J. Prucha and N. A. Foss in their book *Kinnickinnic Years*. These authors describe a large effluent pipe which discharged most of the city's raw sewage into the middle pond several hundred feet below the Maple Street bridge. The water was populated with carp and few additional species, only fish that could survive the putrid anaerobic conditions. They point out that trout fishing in the river was mostly confined to the upper sections of the river, before the sewage treatment plant was built at the lower pond in 1936. Another source of pollution during that era was a creamery that discharged directly into the river between the Maple Street and Cedar Street bridges. Whitish rinse water and creamery waste discolored the river into the upper parts of the lower pond. Some trout survived in the lower Kinni where reaches were fast and well aerated.

River conditions of the earlier time were also expressed in an article from the July 31, 1930, *River Falls Journal* (including original capitalization; edited for length):

> There are some …springs along the stretch, one by the old brewery site, but no TROUT were seen there, the BROTH was probably too strong there, and the only TROUT seen in that vicinity were floaters. Then there was in the early days …the spring in the flat below Lake George, a beautiful clear spring with a large volume of flow. A starch factory operated from this spring for years. This spring has been covered up with the DEV-IL'S BROTH for so many years that most of us have forgotten about it and no doubt the TROUT couldn't find it if they tried.

> [W]e used to have fine fishing from source to mouth, from twenty-five to thirty miles of as fine a STREAM as GOD ever made …, until our domestic and industrial sewerage began to be dumped into it in ever increasing quantities. Since then our fishing area has been cut in half. See the pictures which were taken on MONDAY, July 28, and some day watch from the Maple Street bridge and see the struggles of some poor trout as he struggles in vain to keep going in this HELL HOLE of DEVIL'S BROTH, and then go to your alderman or the mayor and ask them to do something to restore OUR OWN KINN-ICKINNIC to its original state of purity. IT CAN BE DONE. OPEN YOUR MOUTH AND SAY SOMETHING.

Surely these comments represent a low point from which we have emerged, never to see again. These days we have our own issues that may be considerably less obvious than past point sources of pollution, but current pollution sources do have their own brand of detrimental consequences.

Today the primary threat to the river is nonpoint source pollution from agricultural and urban land uses in the watershed. Snowmelt and rainfall on these surfaces wash a multitude of pollutants into the river. In agricultural areas, these pollutants include sediment, fertilizers (phosphorous and nitrogen), herbicides, pesticides, and the organic waste produced by livestock. In urban areas, pollutants from impermeable surfaces include sediment, fertilizers (phosphorous and nitrogen), metals, and hydrocarbons (gas, oil, and antifreeze). These issues are characterized in the video *A Storm on the Horizon*, produced by Kent Johnson and Andy Lamberson of the Kiap-TU-Wish Chapter of Trout Unlimited.

Fortunately, the days when cattle could graze on the river bank and obtain water from the stream, practices that led to considerable bank erosion and manure deposition, were greatly reduced when the Wisconsin DNR carried out fencing projects in the 1950s. Fencing promoted stream bank stability and created buffer zones between agricultural land and the river. Both of these measures contributed to reduced organic pollution and sediment runoff.

PARKER CREEK FISH KILL

I was scouting potential macroinvertebrate sampling sites in May of 1998 when I heard that Parker Creek sustained a significant fish kill. This was a troubling thought. Parker was rated Class I, indicating a stream in which trout populations are sustained by natural reproduction. It was also known as a rearing area for Kinni trout. Prior insect-based biomonitoring placed Parker stream water quality in the Very Good category, and standardized habitat analysis for the confluence section qualified it as Good.

I recall one of the first times I waded into Parker Creek, near its convergence with the Kinnickinnic, and realized I was witnessing the flow of a critical source of water for the river main stem. I quickly learned, too, that Parker can stand on its own as an idyllic stream. That day I stood in riffles so clear I could look down, next to my waders, and see streambed materials as through a pane of perfectly clear window glass. Rounded gravels and cobbles of every shape and hue shone through. I reached below the surface to check a rock for insects and was surprised by the cold temperature of the water that passed over my hand on that warm summer day.

Aquatic life is readily contemplated here. On and under these rocks, in spaces between them, and throughout the water above, all forms of coldwater organisms were living: microbes, algae, plants, invertebrates, and fish. It was a vibrant underwater community, a biological Eden, with diverse habitats and high-quality water. All that I had heard and read about Parker Creek was true. It was cold and clean, fed by seeps and springs, and sustained a population of wild native brook trout.

Initially, thinking about the kill, brook trout came to mind, but they weren't the only casualty. Nongame fish, crayfish, and aquatic insects were also destroyed. An estimated 3,500 to 4,000 brook and brown trout died in Parker Creek (97% of the population in the 4.5 mile tributary) and another 4,000 brown trout were killed where Parker empties into the main stem of the Kinnickinnic (40% of the population in a 1.5 mile section). Aquatic animals do not do well when subjected to oxygen depletion and ammonia toxicity, both results of manure runoff. These living things died from the combined effects of suffocation and poisoning.

Analysis of the event showed these contributing factors: 1) 10,000 gallons of liquid manure spread initially on one acre of a thirty-six acre field adjacent to an intermittent tributary of Parker Creek, followed on the same day by 2) a 1.75 inch rainfall, 3) the application of 360,000 gallons of liquid manure over the next three days with little incorporation, and 4) a rainfall of 0.5 inch. Manure was spread within 25 feet of the intermittent stream channel.

Ken Schreiber, Wisconsin DNR Water Quality Biologist, summarized what went wrong in a 1999 report. Schreiber noted these points: lack of manure incorporation into the soil, manure spread on already wet soils before a rain event, large amounts of manure spread in relation to receiving capacity of the soil, discharging on the field via a large hose making for non-uniform manure distribution, and an inadequate vegetated buffer between the field and the intermittent stream channel.

The farm operator in this case pled no contest, admitting neither guilt nor liability, and was fined $200 for "Depositing or Permitting to be Deposited Noxious Substances: Deleterious Substances, in violation of Wisconsin Statutes 29.9965(1) (b)11." All four parties, including the defendant, his attorney,

St. Croix County District Attorney, and DNR Warden agreed on a series of stipulations "to prevent any future or similar incidents through voluntary compliance with a nutrient management plan."

Directives in the plan were: 1) no manure applications within 50 feet of environmentally sensitive areas, 2) immediate incorporation (within 48 hours) of manure application within 200 feet of environmentally sensitive area outside of the 50 foot zone, 3) an annual review of the plan by county officials, 4) the plan must be followed for 10 years, and 5) conservation/grassland buffers of minimum 100 foot width to be established on both sides of the designated waterway, also maintained for 10 years.

Common sense decisions on critical issues would have gone a long way to lessen the seriousness of this adverse event: attention to soil moisture and weather conditions, incorporation of manure into the soil, allowing the field to dry prior to adding more manure, and observing a reasonably wide, vegetated buffer zone. Any or all of these choices would have benefited the fish and insects that perished in Parker and the Kinni that May, because of unfortunate decision making.

THERMAL POLLUTION

The sun was just coming up one morning as I was driving by the abandoned Red Owl grocery store. Steam rose in backlit wisps from the surface of the asphalt parking lot wet from the previous night's rain. I think back to this scene and revisit its imagery often. It reminds me of what summer downpours mean for the nearby river through a sequence of events that is all too predictable.

The July day was coming to an end with a warm and muggy evening. To the west sunlight was increasingly dimmed by enormous anvil-shaped cumulonimbus. After dark, thunder rumbled over the city and the clouds opened up. The rain provided welcome water for lawns, gardens, and trees. It also fell onto concrete and other solid surfaces that were hot from the afternoon sun. Cold raindrops were becoming warm water trickles that would all too quickly become heated runoff. The scale of this event was multiplied over the entire urban landscape. It was taking place on every street, sidewalk, driveway, and rooftop. All impervious surfaces in the developed environment of the city were preventing the natural infiltration of water into the soil.

The storm water drain in the gutter just below the Red Owl parking lot carried the heated water away. It entered a storm sewer pipe that ran under the street and, in a surprisingly short distance, reached its outfall at the river. The aquatic habitat in this reach of the stream was by most accounts good for trout and insects. The storm water resulting from a 1.34 inch rain increased the river water temperature from 56°F to 66°F. This stream water was undergoing *thermal pollution* and aquatic creatures, like the fish and insects, were experiencing a phenomenon known as *thermal shock*.

In his literature review and study of urbanization and storm water management, John Galli reported on the effects of thermal pollution on aquatic insects, particularly on sensitive groups. Generalizing from several sources, he suggests that water temperatures above 63°F are often considered above optimum for stoneflies, mayflies, and caddisflies and those above 70°F severely stress most coldwater organisms.

He also refers to research indicating that: 1) aquatic insects in general show little capacity to acclimate or compensate for temperature changes, 2) variation of 2.8°F to 3.6°F from the normal temperature regime can reduce adult insect size and ability to produce viable offspring, 3) sensitive species could be eliminated by temperature increases of between 3.6°F and 5.4°F, and 4) high shock temperatures, those which approach upper lethal limits, may affect growth and long-term survival. He predicted severe effects on coldwater insects for moderately and highly urbanized sites and several storm water management sites, with severe restriction or elimination of stoneflies. Similarly for these study sites, he expected that many mayfly and caddisfly species would be eliminated, restricted, or stressed, as well.

The effect of storm water runoff on Kinnickinnic and South Fork temperatures is well understood today because of critical studies which document water temperature changes. Research, both long-term and ongoing, centered in and around the city of River Falls, was begun by the Kiap-TU-Wish Chapter of Trout Unlimited in 1992 under the direction of Kent Johnson.

Johnson established five primary temperature recording stations, each strategically placed to monitor a unique setting: one upstream from the city near Quarry Road (a control site without storm water impacts), one near Division Street in downtown River Falls (a site directly impacted by storm water runoff), and two downstream from the city and its hydropower impoundments, in upper and lower Glen Park. A fifth station was placed on the UW-River Falls campus to record water temperatures in the South Fork tributary where storm water impacts are also evident. Each site utilizes data-logging thermometers set to continuously record stream temperatures every ten minutes from April to October. Data sets from thermographs located downstream from storm water outfalls typically showed rapid increases in river water temperature (temperature spikes) following summer rainfall events. Many years of temperature monitoring at Division Street have shown that temperature spikes of some magnitude and duration occur after most rainfall events during the summer season (June-August) (rain events less than 0.1 inch may be an exception).

The Kinnickinnic studies documented storm water-caused temperature spikes of up to 10°F and river temperatures rising to 78°F and above. These are significant numbers when compared to previously studied biological impacts of thermal regime disruption. Galli, who investigated elevated temperature effects on fish as well as invertebrates, concluded: "All trout species are extremely sensitive to thermal pollution/stress. Sustained elevated water temperatures over 70°F are generally considered to be stressful, while those at or above 77°F are usually lethal."

Bell, after reviewing the literature, summarized: "Studies tend to agree that the stream distribution of healthy adult brown trout is largely bounded by the 66°F thermal physiological limit, with a maximum not to exceed 72°F for an extended period. In the thermal window of 66-72°F, brown trout may be physiologically stressed and living at the edge of their survival tolerance."

Among data presented for brook trout by the Wisconsin DNR at the 2014 Driftless Symposium held in LaCrosse, Wisconsin, were the upper optimal temperature of 61°F and the upper thermal limit (MDAT, maximum daily average temperature) of 75°F. Numerous resources referenced in the summary by Raleigh, *Habitat suitability index models: Brook trout*, reported research based maximum temperatures at or near 77°F for this species.

There is no shortage of research indicating the vulnerability of brown and brook trout to thermal pollution. Likewise, we understand that temperature extremes comparable to those for trout species severely stress most coldwater organisms, including stoneflies, mayflies, and caddisflies. Add to such realities Kinnickinnic-specific data showing water temperatures approaching these levels during storm water runoff events. Connecting the dots creates a predictable pattern: rainfall -> impervious surfaces -> storm sewer pipes -> river water -> river inhabitants, that occurs repeatedly through the summer months. We don't have to be present at the river to picture the events falling in line late on a July evening when the thunder cracks and rain begins to fall. We know that an inevitable sequence is being set in motion, that thermal spikes and warmer river water are more than a possibility, and that river creatures from trout to stoneflies are experiencing potentially detrimental thermal effects.

Kinnickinnic evidence further demonstrates that city owned and managed dams increase downstream water temperatures. Not only do the impoundments create unfavorable thermal conditions for coldwater fish in these locations, they can provide a suitable thermal environment for detrimental introduced species.

EROSION AND SEDIMENTATION

I've hiked to the river a number of times with sampling gear in hand only to be turned back because the water was clouded with sediment. Although this didn't happen often, when it did, it was related to fast and high water resulting from a rainfall event. Suspended sediment, causing the water to appear turbid (or opaque and muddy), is the transport stage of materials resulting from erosion at a point of origin. Then, predictably, in lower energy segments of the river, the eroded materials are deposited on the streambed.

Finding places where sediment originates is not difficult. Just walk along the river and find a soil bank cut by water, or a place where cattle have trampled a bank by grazing or watering, or a cultivated field in close proximity to the stream, or a location where construction of various types, including roads, is occurring. Yes, stream bank erosion is a natural process, but it can also be unnatural. High levels of imperviousness in urban areas and sloped terrain or drain tiling in agricultural areas deliver abnormal amounts of water in addition to sediment to stream channels, which are forced to adjust via channel erosion, causing unstable stream banks.

When the water is clear, you can determine an important depositional characteristic by looking at bottom substrates to see if there are spaces among the gravel and cobble. *Embeddedness* is a measure of filling of spaces among those substrate materials, gaps which are particularly important as habitat for immature mayfly, stonefly, and caddisfly development. The small sediment particles contributing to embeddedness are sand, silt, and clay. The greater the embeddedness, the greater the impact on macroinvertebrates. And the problem extends beyond macros, as salmonid fish are also affected by sediment. Fish avoid suspended sediment and do not reproduce well when embeddedness is high, because fine sediment is covering the gravel substrate preferable for spawning.

THE FUTURE

In neither historical nor recent accounts did anyone intentionally set out to bring harm to the river or its inhabitants. Injury in noted examples occurred out of ignorance or lack of consideration of damage that would occur if best possible practices were not observed. It is more than obvious today that we cannot expect the river to remain healthy if we dump raw sewage or dairy waste products into it. But what present-day subtleties do we need to understand to continue to protect and improve the status of the river?

Many well-qualified individuals, in both professional and volunteer roles, understand the challenges we face today and will experience in the future. They have logical solutions and approaches. Kent Johnson and Andy Lamberson provide straightforward suggestions in *A Storm on the Horizon*: 1) practice watershed-wide planning, 2) reduce imperviousness, 3) minimize soil erosion, 4) establish vegetated river buffers, 5) retain and treat storm water runoff, and 6) protect sensitive areas. Ignorance and carelessness are not on our resolution list.

━┓╻┗━

The field trip through the watershed I planned for the visiting biology teachers was, by all accounts, a success. How could it not be, spending the better part of a day in sight of the Kinnickinnic with curious and attentive colleagues? At the various stops insightful questions were raised and stories were shared. We saw the good and the not so good. Many of the participants were from places where their local river was in serious need of attention. The day provided a great opportunity to demonstrate how a community values its river, a conversation made easy by having a river such as the Kinni to value.

ADDENDUM TO A "HELL HOLE OF DEVIL'S BROTH"

At the risk of using a well-worn cliche', there is a thermally significant ele-phant in the room. We all know that our atmosphere has been changing since the industrial revolution in the late 1700s. Today, atmospheric carbon dioxide (CO_2) measurements exceed all known historical records of this greenhouse gas. CO_2 levels continue to rise, with no alleviation in sight. Supporting infor-mation from respected sources such as Scripps Institution of Oceanography, NASA, and NOAA is easy to find, and the National Geographic *Climate Issue* is a must-read. These sources and many more provide ample evidence of escalat-ing CO_2 levels; increasing global temperatures; melting glaciers, polar ice, and permafrost; and rising sea levels. Unfortunately, when changes are described as "global," it makes them seem far away in space and time. However, the Wis-consin Initiative on Climate Change Impacts (WICCI) brings this issue close to home. WICCI's signature report: *Wisconsin's Changing Climate: Impacts and Adaptation*, describes the impacts of climate change on the quality and quantity of the state's water resources and suggests adaptation strategies where possible. If we recognize that climate change is the inevitable large picture we face, especially pertaining to temperature, the question arises: Is there hope for our coldwater streams?

People who love rivers are willing to stand up for their protection. They believe, correctly, that they can have an effect on the issues of a particular watershed. Individuals and groups can—and do—influence policies, including those related to development and dams in urban environments, and issues of buffer zones and feedlots in rural settings. But how will we address what looms in the future?

We can't predict with precision the impact that large-scale climate change will have on our rivers. We can be sure, however, that it will not be good. We should further realize that the greatest harm will come to organisms in coldwater settings—like the Kinnickinnic, where warming temperatures are already evident. A recent assessment of Kiap-TU-Wish's 1992-2009 Kinn-ickinnic River temperature monitoring data by the Wisconsin Department of Natural Resources noted that a warming trend in water temperature has been occurring at the Quarry Road and Upper and Lower Glen Park monitoring sites, consistent with the observed warming trend in Wisconsin air temperature during the same time period. The Kiap-TU-Wish data suggest that stream temperature warming has not necessarily occurred in short-term peaks, but rather as temperature increases measured over broader lengths of time during the summer. Due to the warming influence of the two Kinnickinnic River hydropower impoundments in River Falls, the observed warming trend is proportionately greater at the Upper Glen Park monitoring site and begins at a much higher baseline temperature, indicating that the river downstream from River Falls will be much more sensitive to any future impacts of climate change. In spite of the current warming trend, Kinnickinnic River temperatures remain suitable for trout, based on thermal tolerance limits noted by Wehrly and his coauthors. The question is, how long will these favorable cold-water conditions persist as temperatures continue to increase?

It's clear that aquatic insects in general do not acclimate well to temperature change. The work of Galli and others highlights the deleterious effects of increased water temperatures on growth and reproduction of many of these creatures. The consequences of elevated temperatures would likely fall first on species such as stoneflies, restricting the places in which they could live or eliminating them entirely. Ultimately mayflies, caddisflies, and other important community members would be affected in similar ways. It's agonizing to imagine the Kinnickinnic without the cold-adapted species that make it exceptional, its stoneflies and other susceptible invertebrates gone because of the failure of the human species to act responsibly.

Kent Johnson taking an HBI sample
for the North Kinnickinnic River Monitoring Project

LISTENING TO AQUATIC INSECTS

Wouldn't it be great if you could ask the inhabitants of a river how things are going? What if you could hear them talk about the living conditions in the river over the weeks, months, or years they have been there? Well, with insects, the simple presence or absence of a family, genus, or species in the water says a lot. Also, the relative numbers of each can contribute to a numerical assessment where an abundance of those intolerant of unhealthy conditions translates into a robust positive response. Do aquatic invertebrates talk to us? Sure they do. With analysis of sampled insects, a story of the river is told that we can clearly understand.

Projects focused on river health require initial assessment which is then followed by regular and continuous monitoring. Will changes occur? Will the health of the river be maintained? What parameters should be measured to assess its status? How should limited resources be allocated to obtain relevant physical, chemical, and biological measurements? These and other questions face officials, institutions, and conservation-oriented groups working to maintain or improve river quality.

One choice in regard to understanding the biological health of a river is a procedure developed and refined at the University of Wisconsin-Madison Department of Entomology. This is the macroinvertebrate-based bioassessment protocol known as the Hilsenhoff Biotic Index, or HBI, named for its developer aquatic entomologist William Hilsenhoff. Details of this tool were first published in 1977. Hilsenhoff modified and refined his protocol, describing updates in a series of papers from 1982 to 1998. In 1988 he added a Family-level Biotic Index (FBI) procedure designed to be used as a rapid field-assessment tool. Both HBI and FBI protocols rely primarily on insects and crustaceans, and to a lesser extent on other invertebrates. The Wisconsin Department of Natural Resources in conjunction with the University of Wisconsin-Stevens

Point originally adopted and has continued to use the HBI as its primary macroinvertebrate bioassessment protocol.

Several factors make aquatic insects good water evaluation organisms. First and foremost is the idea that insect species live in water for extended periods, responding to the variety of conditions that have transpired during their lives. This continuity factor is lacking in sampling techniques that represent a single point in time. Second, numbers of individuals in insect populations are often high, making protocol-required counts efficient to obtain. Finally, the diversity of insects and their varied responses to environmental circumstances make it possible to place groups or species into a hierarchy of tolerance categories.

Biotic index techniques such as the HBI and FBI rely on a foundation of data from previously collected organisms and details that correlate species, genera (pl. of genus), and families with levels of water quality. Prior records allow a *tolerance value* (TV) to be assigned to each of the specific kinds of organisms normally collected. The tolerance values in the HBI and FBI are determined relative to the degree of organic pollution in the water. Aquatic invertebrates are negatively impacted by organic and nutrient enrichment as well as by reduction of dissolved oxygen accompanying organics. Ultimately, this combination affects the ability of arthropod species to survive.

In both the HBI and FBI a higher TV value (*e.g.*, 10) represents a higher degree of tolerance to pollution and a lower number (*e.g.*, 0) indicates a lesser degree of tolerance. When an index is calculated, based on one hundred and twenty-five organisms, the result is a value that can be translated into a qualitative determination. When intolerant insects live successfully in a given environment, it follows that it is less organically enriched, has a lower calculated biotic index, and falls into a higher category of water health.

～⁄⫯～

The City of River Falls set a strong example of river stewardship when it adopted its 2002 Storm Water Management Ordinance. This regulation was designed to protect the Kinnickinnic River from the negative impacts of storm water runoff associated with new development and redevelopment projects. Then, in 2004, it pursued a plan to evaluate the effectiveness of this action with an infiltration-based storm water management project in the then-new Sterling Ponds subdivision on the northwest side of town. Multiple monitoring techniques would contribute to this evaluation effort under the name North Kinnickinnic River Monitoring Project (NKRMP). Short Elliot Henderson (SEH), the project consultant, provided support for monitoring and reporting.

Project organization began with a meeting of the startup committee. The group consisted of Reid Wronski and Kristy (Ketcher) Treichel, City of River Falls; Ken Schreiber, Wisconsin DNR; Kent Johnson, Kiap-TU-Wish Chapter of Trout Unlimited; and myself, UWRF. Base flow surveys and temperature monitoring were obvious tools to include. These would be organized and carried out by the City of River Falls, with SEH support. The committee felt, as well, that biomonitoring would be a valuable complement to base flow and temperature monitoring, so Kent and I volunteered to initiate and maintain an annual macroinvertebrate monitoring series based on the Hilsenhoff Biotic Index (HBI).

Three Kinnickinnic sampling sites were included in the HBI segment of the project (Note that NKRMP site locations, names, and numbers are different from those used in the author's 1999 and 2001 faunal surveys): Site 1 (North Main) was the site of potential impact, located below the confluence of Sumner Creek (and water flowing from Sterling Ponds) with the Kinni. Site 2 (Swinging Gate) and Site 3 (Hebert-Hagen) served as control or reference locations, upstream from the Sumner Creek inflow. Kent and I carried out HBI river sampling in 2004 and 2005. Samples for 2004 were sorted and processed in the lab at UWRF by myself; lab sorting and processing of the 2005 samples were completed by biology graduate student Zane McCallister. Identification, index calculation, and report generation were done by the Aquatic Biomonitoring Laboratory (ABL), University of Wisconsin-Stevens Point. Starting with the 2006 samples and continuing under city support through 2012, annual HBI collections were carried out by Kent Johnson; John Wheeler, UWRF; and Joe Gathman, UWRF.

As a project sub-consultant for Short Elliot Henderson (SEH), Kent coordinated all monitoring work and prepared annual project reports. Data analysis and reporting demonstrate the value of both long-term monitoring and employment of a multifaceted monitoring approach. The *City of River Falls, North Kinnickinnic River Monitoring Project, 2014 Report* describes the macroinvertebrate monitoring results and their relationship to temperature monitoring data:

The comparability of mean annual macroinvertebrate HBI values at Sites 1-3 during the 2004-2012 period indicates that no storm water impacts were apparent at Site 1, downstream from Sumner Creek and the Sterling Ponds subdivision. In fact, the mean 2004-2012 macroinvertebrate HBI values at Sites 1-3 indicate that the best water quality was evident at Site 1. The mean 2004-2012 macroinvertebrate HBI value at Site 1 (3.46) was indicative of excellent water quality, while the mean 2004-2012 macroinvertebrate HBI values at Site 2 (4.01), and Site 3 (3.69) were indicative of very good water quality. The 2004-2012 macroinvertebrate monitoring results nicely corroborate the 2004-2012 Kinnickinnic River and Sterling Ponds temperature monitoring results, which indicated that the summer temperature regimes in the Kinnickinnic River at Sites 1-3 were generally excellent for coldwater macroinvertebrate communities, and the Sterling Ponds storm water management practices were effectively treating storm water, as intended by the River Falls Storm Water Management Ordinance.

A summary of project results from 2004 through 2012, and additional aspects of the project, are available at the City of River Falls web pages under the heading Kinni River Monitoring.

NKRMP officially ended with termination of project funding, the city considering it had enough information to demonstrate the effectiveness of its storm water ordinance at Sterling Ponds. However, commitment to macroinvertebrate monitoring on the north Kinni remains active. John Wheeler sought and received UWRF support for HBI continuation through an additional biennium. Johnson and Wheeler completed the 2016 collections in May of that year. Pending funding they plan to maintain biennial HBI data collections at Sites 1-3. This is a particularly useful data set for the community into the future, documenting water quality before the river flows into the urban environment and shortly after it enters the city below Sumner Creek.

─╱╲─

River enthusiasts appreciate the special qualities of the Kinnickinnic, but few are likely aware that the river is inhabited by a significant array of organic pollution-intolerant macroinvertebrates. Among the examples that follow are some of the most prevalent Kinnickinnic insects. Note that many are members of groups that tend to disappear when water is degraded for various reasons. These are the stoneflies, mayflies, and caddisflies, orders Plecoptera, Ephemeroptera, and Trichoptera.

Examples of Kinnickinnic stoneflies having low tolerance values are in the genus *Taeniopteryx* (winter stoneflies) TV=2 and *Isoperla slossonae* (one of the little yellow patterned stoneflies) TV=2. Four mayflies have similar values, *Baetis tricaudatus* (a small minnow mayfly) TV=2, *Stenonema vicarium* (a flathead mayfly) TV=2, and *Ephemerella excrucians* TV=1 and *E. needhami* TV=2 (spiny crawler mayflies). Among the caddisflies, low tolerance examples are *Brachycentrus occidentalis* (a humpless case-maker) TV=1, *Ceratopsyche alhedra* TV=3, and *C. alternans* TV=3 (net-spinner caddisflies).

These values are stated for the purpose of example and viewed alone have only anecdotal meaning. Consider their influence on the HBI value when a significant number of them are tallied among the minimum 125 specimens in its calculation. The highest Kinnickinnic index values for which Johnson and I were responsible in 2004 and 2005 were 4.203 and 4.451, values which translate to the very good water quality category. Those same years the lowest values were 2.766 and 2.792, determinations that represented the excellent water quality range.

─╱╷╲─

In-stream sample collection methods are the same for the HBI and FBI. Each is acquired from a riffle or shallow run where the current is greater than one foot per second. An aquatic net is placed against the stream bottom and a foot, or both feet, are used to disrupt substrates immediately upstream. Current carries the freed materials into the net. Care is taken to assure that a minimum debris sample of eight ounces (one cup) is achieved, an amount sized to contain the required number of macroinvertebrates. For validating purposes the HBI requires three samples, known as replicates, that are taken from the same area of the stream. Also, for HBI processing, the material is returned to the lab where a randomized extraction of one hundred and twenty-five specimens is carried out. A qualified taxonomist identifies each specimen to genus or species. The FBI is designed to have one hundred specimens picked in the field and requires identification to family, a process that can be done with significantly less training. The HBI, as the more technical, laborious, and costly level, is the appropriate procedure for government and resource management departments and research settings. The FBI conversely is less technical, fast, and can be used effectively for initial or cursory analyses.

The FBI can be a useful tool in educational settings. It demonstrates the application and value of biomonitoring while encouraging students to learn identification with an immediate purpose. While teaching college entomology, I structured several of my fall lab periods as a series of aquatic insect related field exercises utilizing family level identification. The class formalized a working hypothesis based on site comparison, typically evaluating locations upstream and downstream of town. Small teams did FBI sampling, macroinvertebrate identification, tolerance value assignment, and biotic index calculations to provide data for hypothesis acceptance or rejection. I felt this was beneficial not only for biology majors in the class but also for horticulture and agronomy students who would potentially be influencing watersheds with future land management practices.

The FBI has also been successfully used as an educational tool at the secondary level. I was fortunate to have the experience of teaching a graduate summer session class for high school teachers, devoted entirely to FBI use by their students.

—⁓⁓—

People who frequent a river for the purpose of birding, catching a fish, paddling a canoe, or simply finding the peace and tranquility that a stream brings by watching it run are more likely to carry on this activity if the water is of high quality. Personal river impressions may be based on appearances such as clarity of water or more specific experiences or observations as in number and sizes of fish caught. These are valid and fulfilling subjective personal judgments. For the scientific record, however, correctly acquired, numerically based, repeatable data are the starting point on which valid technical decisions are made. With a proven, standard approach these numbers can be the foundation for evaluating management practices, including the application of appropriate protections that may be indicated.

Junction Falls on the Kinnickinnic River, 1865
(Photo courtesy of UWRF Archives
and Area Research Center)

POSTSCRIPT

Looking into moving water, into even the clearest of spring-fed streams, with sunlight reflecting, shadows obscuring, and riffles jumping, is less than revealing of invertebrate creatures. Catching the flash of a brown trout skittering away is a real possibility, but seeing diminutive and often concealed river life is not something that happens with a casual look.

The water surface is more than a visual barrier. It's a conceptual one as well. We don't instinctively connect with the alien milieu of the underwater world. It exists beyond our eyes and out of our minds. The insects and crustaceans that live there are in many respects invisible.

An exception to this imperceptibility occurs when certain aquatic insect adults, or pre-adult stages, emerge from the water for reproductive purposes. Impressive emergences of mayflies and caddisflies are memorable experiences for river watchers. But these fleeting events, based on short-lived individuals, can leave an observer with the impression of a diminished sense of their larger importance. This stage-specific brevity, combined with an assumption that local species are already well known and that interesting and unfamiliar things are found only somewhere else, discourages the possibility of revelations close at hand.

I came to know the Kinnickinnic through its living things. The insect and crustacean life captivated my curiosity. There were many unknowns surrounding these organisms, and innumerable questions about them that needed answers. Then, with timing not of my making, I became the benefactor of an unusual opportunity: a chance to advance the documentation of species in a river community for which many assumptions existed but for which there was limited technical evidence. Curiosity, questions, and opportunity came together to create the sparks that ignited my journey.

Experiences on the Kinnickinnic changed my perspective of the river in ways I had not anticipated. They not only expanded my ideas on flowing water, habitats, and inhabitants, they enlightened me on concepts of time and landscape. As I stood in the shadows of the weathered dolostone walls of the lower Kinni, I thought of the valley and course of the river as spaces once occupied by ocean bottom, and tried to fathom the unimaginably large volume of rock that eroded away since its origin. Instead of descending into the valley on a simple path, I came to think of my approach to the river as a walk through geologic, as well as real, time.

While sampling in winter, I pictured the surrounding topography entombed under three-quarters of a mile of Pleistocene ice. With images of glaciers melting and biotic communities returning, I envisioned Paleoindians thriving on the landscape, hunting on the prairie and oak savannas and fishing the stream well into the 1800s. I could imagine surveyor James M. Marsh and his crew in the fall of 1847 as they finished platting the valley and surrounding areas in anticipation of Euro-American settlement. Within sight and sound of the river it was easy to appreciate the wild and unspoiled nature of the region at that time.

During this journey I experienced the river from its spring and wetland origins to the expansive delta at its confluence with the St. Croix River. I dealt with river structure, attempting to understand how riffles and pools and other elements of configuration affected invertebrate habitation. With exploration of much of the continuous running water of the river system, and detailed sampling of the main stem and South Fork tributary, I saw the range of habitats that such a stream can possess. I watched the river change with the seasons, saw it flow openly under groundwater influence through the coldest months of the year, and observed it in its most unrestrained states during periods of melting snow and heavy rain.

The times I remember most vividly, however, were those when encountering the magnificent invertebrate life of the river, detailed in these essays. From some of the most common organisms: the scud (*Gammarus*), the spiny crawler mayfly (*Ephemerella excrucians*), two small minnow mayflies (*Baetis tricaudatus* and *B. brunneicolor*), the common net-spinner caddisfly (*Ceratopsyche slossonae*), and the humpless case-maker caddisfly (*Brachycentrus occidentalis*) to those less common, like the burrowing mayfly (*Hexagenia*) and brushlegged mayfly (*Isonychia*), I felt their presence and importance in the Kinnickinnic. It may be that they represent a less than expected array of species, the expression of a parallel reality—high productivity and low diversity—resulting from unique stream conditions or unknown idiosyncrasies of biogeographic history. Perhaps the distinctive nature of the fauna will generate further questions, encourage interest, and promote discussion.

In the end it is my sincere hope that readers find this community of aquatic invertebrates compelling, that the stories herein promote a new or renewed perspective on the river we affectionately call *The Kinni*, and that this exceptional natural resource inspires conservation-minded people, fly fishers, and all manner of river watchers into the future.

> Aquatic insects are like good friends.
> They're always there when you need them.

Part IV

In the depths of the unknown one finds something new.

—Charles Baudelaire

GLOSSARY

abdomen	The third and hindmost region of the insect body. In aquatic insects the abdomen is where the posterior extensions, cerci and median caudal filament, originate and is the location of gills in some groups.
Acari	The arachnid order including aquatic mites.
Amphipoda	The crustacean order including scuds, organisms also known as sideswimmers, amphipods, and freshwater shrimp.
anterior	Of or nearer the front end of the body; further forward in position.
arthropod	A member of the phylum Arthropoda, characterized by a segmented body, jointed appendages, and an exoskeleton based on chitin; includes insects, crustaceans, and arachnids.
associate	The process of correlating the immature stages of an insect's life with the adult. Often accomplished by rearing adults from collected larvae.
benthic	Literally means bottom, as of a stream, but is commonly used by aquatic biologists to refer to aquatic locations between the surface and the bottom.
biodiversity	The range of organisms present in a given ecological community or system; includes the interactions of species, their dependency on one another, and the role of each in the community.
biomonitoring	The use of biological responses to assess existing status or changes in water quality; often involves the use of indicator species or indicator communities, especially macroinvertebrates.
biotic	Of or relating to life. The opposite is abiotic.
biotic index	A numerical representation of environmental quality in which living organisms are sampled, identified, counted, and a single value (metric) is calculated. See HBI and FBI.
bivoltine	Having two generations per year.
boundary layer	The thin layer over the surface of an object submerged in moving water where current is reduced by frictional resistance.

burrower	A mayfly behavioral category based on creation of burrows dug into soft substrates. *Hexagenia* is a burrower.
carnivore	An animal that eats other animals.
cast skin	The exoskeleton released by a molting arthropod. Also called a shed skin or an exuviae.
catch-net	A net formed with silk to filter particles from moving water.
caudal	Referring to the posterior or tail end of an organism.
cercus	One of a pair of appendages at the posterior end of an insect body. (plural = cerci)
character, characteristic	A feature or trait used to differentiate one organism from another.
Class I trout stream	A high-quality stream where trout populations are sustained by natural reproduction.
climber	Aquatic insects associated with roots along stream banks and aquatic plant stems. Larvae of dragonflies and damselflies are examples.
clinger	A mayfly behavioral category based on flat-bodied larvae that hold to substrate with claws, typically in fast water, as in the heptageniids *Stenonema* and *Stenacron*.
cocoon	A silk case in which a pupa develops.
Coleoptera	The insect order including beetles.
collector	A macroinvertebrate that consumes fine particulate organic matter (FPOM). Collectors can be further divided into filtering collectors and gathering collectors.
common name	The name given to an organism outside of formal scientific nomenclature. These names are often regional and highly variable.
community	The interacting species of microorganisms, plants, and animals inhabiting a given area.
complete metamorphosis	An insect developmental sequence in which the stages are egg, larva, pupa, and adult.
crawler	A mayfly behavioral category based on mayfly larvae that swim inefficiently and move primarily by walking, as in *Ephemerella* (spiny crawlers) and *Tricorythodes* (little stout crawlers).
crepuscular	Active in twilight, either at dawn or dusk, or both.
Cretaceous Period	The geological period from 144 to 66 million years ago.

crustacean	Primarily aquatic arthropods with multiple body regions and multiple pairs of legs; includes scuds and crayfishes.
cryoprotectant	A biochemical such as glycerol, or a sugar or protein that functions as an antifreeze compound.
cuticle	The equivalent of the exoskeleton in arthropods, indicating a non-cellular covering secreted by an underlying epidermis.
Decapoda	The crustacean order including crayfish.
degree day	A measure of heat accumulation required for development in an ectothermic organism, calculated from a determined threshold temperature.
detritivore	An organism that eats detritus of plant or animal origin.
detritus	Non-living particulate organic matter.
diapause	A period of dormancy or arrested development during which growth and metamorphosis stop.
diatom	A single-celled alga known for its patterned silicon-based cell wall.
dichotomous key	A written tool used to identify living things. A dichotomous key is arranged as a series of character-based couplets in which a decision must be made based on observation of the unknown organism. Each choice leads to additional couplets until identification is completed. Also called a taxonomic key or simply a key.
Diptera	The insect order including true flies.
diversity	See biodiversity.
D-net	A net designed to collect aquatic organisms. The net hoop is shaped like the letter D. The flat side is placed on the bottom of the stream and substrates are disturbed, usually with a foot just upstream, allowing the current to propel insects and other living things into the net. Also called a kick net, dip net, or aquatic net.
dorsal	Referring to the back or upper side of an organism.
drift	The downstream transport of insects and other invertebrates in and by the current.
dun	The winged mayfly stage between the larva and adult. The technical equivalent is subimago.
ecosystem	The organisms of a particular habitat and their abiotic (nonliving) environment interacting to produce a stable system.

ectotherm	An organism in which body temperature is based on, and reflective of, the ambient temperature.
elytron	A thickened, horny, or leathery front wing, as in adult beetles. (plural = elytra)
embeddedness	The degree to which coarse gravel and cobble are surrounded or covered with sand, silt, or other fine substrates.
emergence	The process in aquatic insects where the adult, or subimago, exits the larval or pupal covering at the surface of the water. Commonly called a hatch.
entomology	The study of insects.
Ephemeroptera	The insect order including mayflies.
EPT index	A generic richness measure (metric) based on the percentage of a sample that consists of mayflies (Ephemeroptera), stoneflies (Plecoptera), and caddisflies (Trichoptera).
exoskeleton	The external, non-living covering in arthropods providing support and protection. In arthropods the exoskeleton can vary from thin and flexible to thick and rigid.
exuviae	The shed skin of a larva or pupa at metamorphosis. Also called a cast skin.
family	The classification level below the order and above the genus.
Family-level Biotic Index	A water-quality evaluation metric designed by W. L. Hilsenhoff and based on tolerance values assigned to the family level of aquatic insects and crustaceans.
fast seasonal life cycle	A one-year (univoltine) life cycle in which rapid larval growth follows an extended egg or larval diapause.
fauna	The animals of a region or particular environment. The adjective form is faunal.
FBI	Family-level Biotic Index.
feeding lie	A position in which an animal such as a fish places itself in order to catch prey.
film	The surface of water.
fly	1) A member of the order Diptera, characterized by having two wings. A term also used in the names of flying insects in many other orders, including: dragonfly, mayfly, stonefly, alderfly. 2) A fly fisher's imitation, consisting of a fishhook with feathers or other materials added to make it appear as an insect. Also known as an artificial.
fly fishing	The type of fishing in which an artificial fly is cast with a fly rod.

functional feeding groups (FFGs)	A classification of aquatic macroinvertebrates based on morpho-behavioral mechanisms used to acquire foods. The groups refer primarily to modes of feeding or to the food-acquisition system and not to the type of food per se.
genus	The first of the two Latin- or Greek-based names forming the scientific name, traditionally capitalized. Also underlined or printed in italics along with the species name to distinguish them from regular text. (plural = genera)
grazer	A macroinvertebrate that eats periphyton. Also called a scraper.
groundwater	Water emerging from seeps and springs, previously located in rock fractures and pores of underground materials.
habitat	The place where an organism lives.
haltere	The knob-like, modified second pair of wings in adult Diptera (true flies).
hatch	The emergence of a subimago (dun) or imago (adult) insect from its aquatic habitat. The technical equivalent is emergence.
HBI	Hilsenhoff Biotic Index.
herbivore	A plant-eating animal.
Heteroptera	The insect order including true bugs.
Hilsenhoff Biotic Index	A water-quality evaluation metric based on a technique designed by W. L. Hilsenhoff based on tolerance values assigned to the genus or species level, or both, of aquatic insects and crustaceans.
imago	An adult, sexually-mature insect.
imperviousness	The blockage of normal infiltration of precipitation into the ground, caused by, but not limited to, urban development such as parking lots, roads and driveways, and rooftops.
incomplete metamorphosis	An insect developmental sequence in which the stages are egg, larva, and adult. Lacks a pupal stage.
insect	Arthropods with three body regions, three pairs of legs, and (commonly) wings in adults.
instar	A stage of larval arthropod between successive molts.
invertebrate	Literally, an animal without a backbone. Includes many stream animals such as insects, crustaceans, planaria worms, nematodes, horsehair worms, leeches, clams, and snails.
Isopoda	The crustacean order including aquatic sowbugs.
Jurassic Period	The geological period from 208 to 144 million years ago.

key	See dichotomous key. Also used as a verb, as in *to key*, meaning to use a key for identification.
larva	A term widely used in zoology to indicate the immature stage of an animal; in arthropods larva is used both for insects with incomplete metamorphosis and those with complete metamorphosis. (plural = larvae)
lateral	Referring to the side of an organism.
leaf pack	An underwater collection of tree or shrub leaves, often piled on a snag or other submerged objects, comprising a unique habitat for aquatic invertebrates.
macroinvertebrate	An invertebrate large enough to be seen without magnification. Often used in plural form as a collective term for insects and crustaceans.
macrophyte	A macroscopic green plant living in water.
main stem	The main course of a river, excluding its tributaries.
median	In the middle.
median caudal filament	The single middle appendage arising from the posterior end of the insect body; the middle tail.
Megaloptera	The insect order including alderflies and related insects.
membranous	In insect wings, meaning thin and more or less transparent.
metamorphosis	A change in form during development.
metric	A measurement or value representing selected qualities of a community.
molt	The process in which arthropods replace the previous and outgrown cuticle or exoskeleton with a new, soft, and expandable one.
natural	Indicating the living example of an insect or crustacean, in contrast to an artificial.
niche	The role that an organism fulfills in its ecological community.
nonpoint source pollution	Pollution for which sources cannot be traced to a single point. Examples include eroding farmland, construction sites, urban streets, and barnyards. Pollution from these sources commonly reaches water bodies through runoff.
nymph	The immature stage of an arthropod, occurring between the egg stage and adult; used in insects with incomplete metamorphosis.
Odonata	The insect order including dragonflies and damselflies. The term odonate is a common name that refers to members of the order.

omnivore	An organism that eats both living plant and living animal material.
order	The classification level above the family that separates insects into major groups, for example: order Ephemeroptera, mayflies; order Plecoptera, stoneflies; and order Trichoptera, caddisflies.
Ordovician Period	The geological period from 490 to 450 million years ago.
organism	A living thing.
oviposit	To deposit or lay eggs.
penes	Plural for penis; part of the male insect genitalia. The penes are used in identification of adult insects because they typically differ between or among different species.
periphyton	Algae, bacteria, other microorganisms, and non-living organic matter attached to any submerged surface, commonly rocks, wood, and plants.
Permian Period	The geological period from 286 to 245 million years ago.
pharate adult	The swimming form of the adult caddisfly that exits the puparium still covered by a loose pupal skin.
photoperiod	The daily cycle of light and dark that affects the behavior and physiological functions of living things.
Plecoptera	The insect order including stoneflies.
Pleistocene	The geological period from 2.6 million years ago to approximately 11,700 years ago. Also referred to as the Ice Age.
point source pollution	Sources of pollution that have discrete discharges, as from a pipe or outfall.
pool	A deeper area of stream with slow water velocity and no surface turbulence.
posterior	Of or nearer the rear or hind end of the body; further back in position.
predator	An organism that ingests, or sucks the body fluids of, another organism, its prey, for food.
productivity	The amount of energy or material formed by an individual, population, or community in a specific time period.
proleg	An unsegmented leg-like structure, typically paired, on the thorax of some fly larvae and last abdominal segment of caddisfly larvae, sometimes bearing hooks for attachment.
pupa	The insect stage between larva and adult, can be active or inactive, uncovered or concealed in a cocoon. (plural = pupae)

puparium	A hardened case in which pupation occurs, formed from the last larval exoskeleton.
pupate	To transform from a larva to a pupa.
pupation	The process of transforming from a larva into a pupa.
reach	A continuous stretch or expanse of a river, especially a straight section.
riffle	A shallow area of stream with fast water and obvious surface turbulence.
riparian	Of or relating to the bank of a river.
run	An area of stream with moderate to fast current and a smooth surface, often deeper than a riffle.
scientific name	The genus name plus the species name of an organism, creating a binomial, the formal published name of an organism. It is italicized or underlined by tradition to distinguish it from surrounding text.
scraper	A macroinvertebrate that eats periphyton. Also called a grazer.
sedge	A common name for an adult caddisfly.
seep	A place where groundwater reaches the surface, or adds to the volume of the river subsurface, more slowly than from a spring.
semivoltine	Two years required per generation.
seston	Swimming or floating organisms and non-living matter in a body of water.
shredder	A macroinvertebrate that consumes coarse particulate organic matter (CPOM).
slow seasonal life cycle	A one-year (univoltine) life cycle in which eggs hatch quickly after they are deposited, larvae grow slowly through the year, and most adults emerge early in the year.
snag	A downed limb or tree in the stream.
sp.	The abbreviation for species (singular); used after the genus name where the genus is known but the species is undetermined.
spacing hump	Bump-like projection on the thorax of a caddisfly larva that creates a space through which water moves between the larval body and the case.
species	The second of the two Latin- or Greek-based names of scientific nomenclature. The species name is underlined or placed in italics, as is the genus, and is not capitalized. Species names are not expressed in the absence of the genus name or its abbreviation.

spinner	The adult mayfly stage. The technical equivalent is imago.
spp.	The abbreviation for species (plural); used after the genus name where the genus is known but more than one species is undetermined or multiple species are being referred to nonspecifically.
sprawler	An aquatic insect that crawls or rests on surfaces of substrates with legs spread. Larval examples exist in many insect groups.
subimago	The technical name for the winged mayfly life stage that precedes the adult. The stage of mayflies that emerges from the water. Also called a dun.
substrate	The materials on or in which organisms physically live.
swimmer	A mayfly behavioral category based on swimming proficiency. Often subdivided into small swimmers (baetids) and large swimmers (*Isonychia*).
synonymy	In taxonomic revision, indicating that two or more species names are actually one in the same species. Synonymize is the verb form.
tail	A posterior extension of the insect abdomen. The paired ones are together called cerci, the middle one is the median caudal filament.
taxon	A taxonomic group or the name applied to it. (plural = taxa)
taxonomy	Study of the principles of scientific classification. Sometimes used as an equivalent of the term classification.
teneral	The status of a recently molted insect in which the new exoskeleton is soft and without color.
terrestrial	A term referring to insects or other living things that originate from and live in non-aquatic sources. Includes creatures such as grasshoppers, leafhoppers, beetles, and ants.
thermal pollution	The degradation of water quality by any process that changes ambient water temperature.
thermal shock	A large and rapid change of temperature considered with respect to its effects upon living organisms.
thorax	The middle region of an insect body, the location of legs and, in adults, wings.
tolerance value (TV)	A numerical value assigned to an organism or group representing its ability to withstand adverse conditions such as organic pollution.
Trichoptera	The insect order including caddisflies.
trophic	Of or relating to nutrition.

turbidity	A quality of water in which carried sediment creates a muddy, unclear condition.
type specimen	The specimen designated as the type of a species by the original author (namer) at the time the species name and description were published (type is shorthand for holotype).
univoltine	Having one generation per year.
ventral	Referring to the belly or lower side of the organism.
watershed	An area encompassed by a divide and draining to a particular watercourse or body of water.
wing pad	The developing folded and compacted wing on the thorax of mayfly and stonefly larvae, covered by larval exoskeleton.

NOTES

ABBREVIATIONS USED IN THE NOTES

AE: W. Patrick McCafferty, *Aquatic Entomology: The Fishermen's and Ecologists' Illustrated Guide to Insects and Their Relatives*, (Boston: Jones and Bartlett Publishers, 1981).

AIB: William L. Hilsenhoff, "An improved biotic index of organic stream pollution," *Great Lakes Entomologist* 20 (1987).

AIW: William L. Hilsenhoff, "Aquatic insects of Wisconsin, keys to Wisconsin genera and notes on biology, habitat, distribution and species," *University of Wisconsin-Madison Natural History Museums Council Publication* 3, G3648 (1995).

GAI: R. William Bouchard Jr., *Guide to Aquatic Invertebrates of the Upper Midwest: Identification Manual for Students, Citizen Monitors, and Aquatic Resource Professionals,* (St. Paul: University of Minnesota, 2004).

NAG: Gary A. Borger, *Naturals: A Guide to Food Organisms of the Trout,* (Harrisburg: Stackpole Books, 1980).

PREFACE

ix   *amid rolling hills where big bluestem prairie once flourished*: Big bluestem (*Andropogon gerardii*) was the dominant plant of historic tallgrass prairie (mesic prairie), once common and now rare. Wisconsin Department of Natural Resources, "Mesic Prairie," http://dnr.wi.gov/topic/EndangeredResources/Communities. asp?mode=detail&Code=CTHER074WI.

ix   *"the damnedest prettiest falls you ever seen."*: Edward D. Neill and J. Fletcher Williams, *History of Washington County and the St. Croix Valley, including the Explorers and Pioneers of Minnesota, and Outlines of the History of Minnesota* (Minneapolis: North Star Publishing Company, 1881), 199. *Damnedest* was expressed as d_____st in Neill and Williams.

ix   *fifty river and creek miles are of the highest classification given to Wisconsin trout streams*: Karen Voss, ed., *Nonpoint Source Control Plan for the Kinnickinnic River Priority Watershed Project* (Wisconsin Department of Natural Resources Publication WT-522, 1999), 3. http://dnr.wi.gov/topic/nonpoint/documents/9kep/Kinnickinnic_River-St_Croix_Co.pdf.

x   *biotic indices done by the Wisconsin Department of Natural Resources*: WDNR biologist Ken Schreiber kindly provided me with report copies, Ken Schreiber, personal communications, 1996, 1998.

x   *insects and crustaceans that live specifically in riffles*: The Hilsenhoff Biotic Index
     protocol, used routinely by the WDNR, recommends obtaining samples
     from a specific habitat, "preferably …a riffle area" with a few alternatives
     suggested: other fast-water, rock- or gravel-bottom settings, or snags. William L.
     Hilsenhoff, "An improved biotic index of organic stream pollution," *Great Lakes
     Entomologist* 20 (1987): 34.

x   *Specimens were collected, identified, and ultimately archived*: Approximately 26,000
     specimens were archived for future reference.

x   *based primarily on data assembled from …2001 with additional results from a similar
     project*: Sampling details for the 2001 project are described in the essay
     "Opportunity, Serendipity, Strategy." During a previous study in 1999, 322
     D-net subsamples were taken, compared to the 1020 D-net subsamples in
     2001.

x   *I planned to structure them around the most common Kinnickinnic insect and crustacean
     species I was encountering through routine sampling*: Just over half (13 out of 20) of the
     Part II essays represent taxa that made my most prevalent list for 2001. Into
     the mix of stories I added: 1) uncommon types like *Hexagenia* and *Isonychia* and
     2) less common examples of note such as giant stoneflies, saddlecase maker
     caddisflies, and rusty crayfish, among others.

xi   *"…continued strangers to the productions of their own climate."*: Martin Martin, *A Voyage
     to St. Kilda, 1697* (London: Dan Browne, 1698).

xi   *shares the wisdom of his mentor and friend Roger Deakin*: Robert Macfarlane, *The Wild
     Places* (New York: Penguin Books, 2007), 225.

HEADWATERS

8   *Downstream, at the USGS gage*: United States Geological Survey, "USGS
     05342000 Kinnickinnic River Near River Falls, WI," http://waterdata.usgs.
     gov/wi/nwis/uv/?site_no=05342000

8   *qualitative habitat rating of Good*: Ken Schreiber, *Kinnickinnic River Priority Watershed
     Surface Water Resource Appraisal Report* (Wisconsin Department of Natural
     Resources, West Central Region, 1998), Appendix 5.

8   *procedure involving multiple quantitative stream attributes*: Wisconsin Department of
     Natural Resources, *Guidelines for Evaluating Habitat of Wadable Streams* (Bureau
     of Fisheries Management and Habitat Protection, Monitoring and Data
     Assessment Section, 2000).

8   *brook and brown trout populations …at nearly 600 and over 5,000 fish per mile*:
     Schreiber, *Kinnickinnic River Priority Watershed Surface Water Resource Appraisal Report*,
     Appendix 5.

8   *coldwater stream*: Tom Waters expressed the idea that the term "coldwater"
     is probably not the most accurate description that we can apply to trout
     streams such as the Kinnickinnic. Because of groundwater supply, the Kinni is
     relatively warm in winter. He suggested we use the term "summercool," adding
     that it is finding increased usage. Tom Waters, e-mail message to author, April
     12, 2001.

8   *historic moist soil environments, like the Kinnickinnic Wet Prairie State Natural Area*: Wisconsin Department of Natural Resources, "Wisconsin State Natural Areas Program Kinnickinnic Wet Prairie (No. 583)," http://dnr.wi.gov/topic/ Lands/naturalareas/index.asp?SNA=583.

8   *report this outflow at more than 700,000 gallons per day*: Kinnickinnic River Land Trust, "Ecology," http://kinniriver.org/kinnickinnic-river/ecology/.

9   *From what appears as a slough*: Marty Engel, forwarded e-mail message, August 25, 2002.

9   *survival of cold-adapted aquatic invertebrates*: Alan V. Nebeker and Armond E. Lemke, "Preliminary studies on the tolerance of aquatic insects to heated waters," *Journal of Kansas Entomological Society* 41 (1968): 417-418.

9   *in year-around temperature monitoring of a large spring*: Kent Johnson, telephone conversation with author, September 28, 2015.

10   *conceptually synonymous with fertility and biological productivity*: James T. McFadden and Edwin L. Cooper, "An ecological comparison of six populations of Brown Trout (*Salmo trutta*)," *Transactions of the American Fisheries Society* 91 (1962): 53-62.

ROCK AND WATER

14   *The rock layers underlying …composing its bluffs and walls*: Valuable suggestions were provided by Michael Middleton, e-mail message to author, December 15, 2016, and Kerry Keen, e-mail message to author, December 3, 2014, during the development of this Kinnickinnic valley bedrock section.

14   *entire Kinni valley*: This phrasing is used throughout the essay collection to denote the Kinnickinnic River valley from its headwaters to its confluence with the St. Croix River.

15   *These rock layers were eroded, notably during the Ice Age:* A. C. Runkel, "Minnesota at a Glance Ancient Tropical Seas - Paleozoic History of Southeastern Minnesota," Minnesota Geological Survey, rev. 6/2002, http://purl.umn.edu/59447.

16   *each hill there as a burial ground*: Robert Macfarlane, *The Wild Places*, 173.

16   *Pre-Wisconsinan*: The use of the term pre-Wisconsinan indicates the glacial events that preceded the most recent activity, known as Wisconsinan.

16   *Pre-Wisconsinan deposits have been well documented*: Robert W. Baker, "Pleistocene History of West-Central Wisconsin," 31st Annual Midwest Friends of the Pleistocene Field Conference, Friends of the Pleistocene Field Trip Guide Book 11 (1984); Robert W. Baker, "Evidence for Glacial Lake River Falls, Paul Cudd and Sons Incorporated Gravel Quarry," in *Paleogeography and Structure of the St. Croix River Valley*, edited by Ian S. Williams, 53rd Annual Tri-State Geological Conference (1989); Robert W. Baker, J. F. Diehl, T. W. Simpson, L. W. Zelazny, and S. Beske-Diehl, "Pre-Wisconsinan glacial stratigraphy, chronology, and paleomagnetics of west-central Wisconsin," *Geological Society of America Bulletin* 94 (1983): 1442-1449. I appreciate Bob Baker's willingness to review my glacial history paragraphs for accuracy, e-mail message to author, March 19, 2017.

16   *Ice, estimated to be nearly three-quarters of a mile thick*: Ice thickness of 1100 to 1200 meters for the River Falls location at Pre-Illinoian maximum was derived from a computer model developed by Howard Mooers. Bob Baker, e-mail message to author, March 17, 2017.

17   *When I became interested in the settlement-era vegetation of the Kinnickinnic area*: R. W. Finley, "Map of the Original Vegetation Cover of Wisconsin," (North Central Forest Experiment Station, St. Paul: USFS-USDA, 1976). Wisconsin Geological and Natural History Survey. Downloads and prints available through University of Wisconsin-Extension, https://wgnhs.uwex.edu/pubs/000386/.

17   *hand-written notes of Deputy Surveyor James M. Marsh*: James M. Marsh, "Field Notebook 151 (Exterior Boundary Surveys)," in *Wisconsin, Commissioners of Public Lands, Surveyor's Field Notes, 1832-1865*. Microfilm (1847) accessed via UWRF University Archives & Area Research Center.

18   *prairie and savanna ...remnants ...restorations*: Learn about the St. Croix Valley Chapter of The Prairie Enthusiasts at these web sites: http://www.theprairieenthusiasts.org/content.asp?contentid=221; https://www.facebook.com/TPESCV.

18   *agriculture occupies 78% of the area*: Voss, *Nonpoint Source Control Plan*, 3.

18   *That standard characterization was expressed*: Jim Humphrey and Bill Shogren, *Trout Streams of Wisconsin and Minnesota*, 2nd ed. (Woodstock: Backcountry Guides, 2001), 167-168.

18   *Wadable stream habitat evaluation data*: Marty Engel, personal communication, 1998.

RIVER INVERTEBRATES

23   *brachiopods*: Brachiopods are bottom-dwelling, shallow marine forms that resemble bivalved molluscs. About 325 species are living today; 12,000 species are known from fossils. Some attach to substrates and others burrow.

23   *The French naturalist Jean-Baptiste de Lamarck*: Jean-Baptiste de Lamarck, *Natural History of Invertebrates*, 7 vols. (1815–1822).

24   *her comprehensive six-volume treatise*: Libbie H. Hyman, *The Invertebrates*, 6 vols. (New York: McGraw-Hill, 1940-1967).

25   *"first determiner of what macroinvertebrates we collect..."*: Kent Johnson, e-mail message to author, September 17, 2015.

25   *as pointed out by Hilsenhoff*: Hilsenhoff, "An improved biotic index of organic stream pollution," 35.

OPPORTUNITY, SERENDIPITY, STRATEGY

29 *like DuBois's insects of the Brule River of northern Wisconsin*: Robert B. DuBois, "Aquatic insects of the Bois Brule River System, Wisconsin," *Wisconsin Department of Natural Resources Technical Bulletin* 185 (1993); William L. Hilsenhoff, Jerry L. Longridge, Richard P. Narf, Kenneth J. Tennessen, and Craig P. Walton, "Aquatic insects of the Pine-Popple River, Wisconsin," *Wisconsin Department of Natural Resources Technical Bulletin* 54 (1972).

29 *or a similar lab at the University of Minnesota*: Several people suggested that Tom Waters or one of his students at the University of Minnesota had carried out invertebrate work in the Kinni, but this was not the case. Tom Waters, e-mail message to author, January 4, 2002.

29 *distribution of mayflies of the Upper Midwest*: R. Patrick Randolph and W. Patrick McCafferty, "Diversity and distribution of the mayflies (Ephemeroptera) of Illinois, Indiana, Kentucky, Michigan, Ohio, and Wisconsin," *Bulletin of the Ohio Biological Survey* 13 (1998). The five species of larval mayflies recorded from the Kinnickinnic River were: *Acentrella ampla, Baetis brunneicolor, Baetis tricaudatus, Baetisca laurentina,* and *Ephemerella needhami.*

30 *a key resource brought to my attention a series of Hilsenhoff Biotic Index (HBI) samples*: Ken Schreiber, *Kinnickinnic River Priority Watershed Surface Water Resource Appraisal Report* (Wisconsin Department of Natural Resources, West Central Region, 1998), 16.

30 *Ken provided me with detailed summaries of the HBI results*: Ken Schreiber, personal communication, 1996, 1998.

31 *to speak with him informally after the session*: It is often said that the most important part of an academic meeting is the discussion that occurs apart from the formal presentations.

31 *Lenat was testing a technique to assess water quality using aquatic invertebrates*: David R. Lenat, "Water quality assessment of streams using a qualitative collection method for benthic invertebrates," *Journal of the North American Benthological Society* 7 (1988): 222-233.

33 *much biodiversity is yet to be found the old-fashioned way*: Edward O. Wilson, *The Diversity of Life* (Cambridge: Harvard University Press, 1992), 150.

33 *provided me with particularly useful data*: Marty Engel, personal communication, 1998.

33 *quantifiable stream information using standardized field protocols*: Wisconsin Department of Natural Resources, *Guidelines for Evaluating Habitat of Wadable Streams* (Bureau of Fisheries Management and Habitat Protection, Monitoring and Data Assessment Section, July, 2000).

LOOKING AND LEARNING

40 *starting with kingdom and progressively subdividing*: The standard mnemonic for remembering the sequence of hierarchal levels is: "King Phillip comes over for good soup." Undergraduate zoology students have invented many others, some of which are best not repeated.

40 *Today all known living things have a singular scientific name*: International Commission on Zoological Nomenclature (ICZN), "What's in a name? Scientific names for animals in popular writing," 2016, http://iczn.org/content/what%E2%80%99s-name-scientific-names-animals-popular-writing#.

42 *the following are those I've found most useful*:

Gary A. Borger, *Naturals: A Guide to Food Organisms of the Trout* (Harrisburg: Stackpole Books, 1980).

R. William Bouchard Jr., *Guide to Aquatic Invertebrates of the Upper Midwest: Identification Manual for Students, Citizen Monitors, and Aquatic Resource Professionals* (St. Paul: University of Minnesota, 2004). *Printed copies of this guide are available from Dr. Leonard C. Ferrington Jr., University of Minnesota, ferri016@umn.edu. They are $39.95 each plus $1.50/copy handling for single orders. More information is available at: http://www.entomology.umn.edu/faculty-staff/leonard-ferrington.*

Rick Hafele and Scott Roederer, *An Angler's Guide to Aquatic Insects and Their Imitations* (Boulder: Johnson Books, 1995).

W. Patrick McCafferty, *Aquatic Entomology: The Fishermen's and Ecologists' Illustrated Guide to Insects and Their Relatives* (Boston: Jones and Bartlett Publishers, 1981).

42 *contains keys to orders, families, and genera*: William L. Hilsenhoff, "Aquatic insects of Wisconsin, keys to Wisconsin genera and notes on biology, habitat, distribution and species," *University of Wisconsin-Madison Natural History Museums Council Publication* 3, G3648 (1995).

42 *The Appendix of McCafferty's Aquatic Entomology book*: W. Patrick McCafferty, *Aquatic Entomology: The Fishermen's and Ecologists' Illustrated Guide to Insects and Their Relatives* (Boston: Jones and Bartlett Publishers, 1981).

43 *An especially useful web site for larval identification to the family level*: Moriya M. Rufer and Leonard Ferrington Jr., "Volunteer Stream Monitoring Interactive Verification Program (VSM-IVP), Version 1," September, 2006, http://midge.cfans.umn.edu/vsmivp/.

43 *An aerial net, also called an insect net or butterfly net, is extremely useful*: A good source for insect nets of all types is BioQuip Products: www.bioquip.com.

PUTTING A NAME ON A MAYFLY

48 *My first step in identification*: AIW, 6.

48   *The go-to key for Ephemerella was in a journal article*: Richard K. Allen and George F. Edmunds Jr., "A revision of the Genus *Ephemerella* (Ephemeroptera: Ephemerellidae) VIII, The Subgenus *Ephemerella* in North America," *Miscellaneous Publications of the Entomological Society of America* 4 (1965): 249-253.

48   *I began corresponding*: Randolph and McCafferty, "Diversity and distribution of the mayflies (Ephemeroptera) …," *Bulletin of the Ohio Biological Survey* 13 (1998).

49   *Resolution of many Ephemerella issues*: Luke M. Jacobus and W. Patrick McCafferty, "Revisionary contributions to North American *Ephemerella* and *Serratella* (Ephemeroptera: Ephemerellidae)," *Journal of the New York Entomological Society* 111 (2003).

50   *associated two Au Sable River adult males with their immature forms*: Justin Leonard, "The nymph of *Ephemerella excrucians* Walsh," *Canadian Entomologist* 81 (1949).

A UBIQUITOUS PRESENCE

57   *Nine species had been documented for the state of Wisconsin*: AIW, 11.

57   *Tom was particularly familiar with Valley Creek*: Tom Waters, e-mail message to author, April 12, 2001.

58   *a larger daytime-emerging sulphur and a smaller evening-emerging sulphur*: Mike Alwin, e-mail message to author, April 4, 2006.

58   *abundant in unpolluted, fast streams during fall and early spring*: AIW, 4-5.

58   *longer in E. needhami (eight months) and shorter in E. excrucians (two months)*: The same monthly data for larvae were recorded in 1999 and 2001.

58   *Edmunds and Waltz point out that diapause*: G. F. Edmunds Jr. and R. D. Waltz, "Ephemeroptera," in *An Introduction to the Aquatic Insects of North America*, eds. Richard W. Merritt and Kenneth W. Cummins (Dubuque: Kendall/Hunt Publishing Company, 1996), 126.

58   *Looking to the river bottom for mayfly life cycle chronology data*: Study of size classes month by month would be a reasonable project to add to the to-do list.

58   *combined with revisions detailed in the 2003 Jacobus-McCafferty paper*: Luke M. Jacobus and W. Patrick McCafferty, "Revisionary contributions to North American *Ephemerella* and *Serratella* (Ephemeroptera: Ephemerellidae)," *Journal of the New York Entomological Society* 111 (2003).

WONDERFUL MYSTERY

61   *In a conversation I had with angler and writer Jim Humphrey*: Jim Humphrey, personal communication.

62   *eloquently described in a July 1989 article*: J. R. Humphrey, "The Kinnie," *Fly Fisherman Magazine*, July, 1989, 32-35, 59-61.

62 *George Edmunds and his coauthors published a relevant analysis*: George F. Edmunds Jr., Steven L. Jensen, and Lewis Berner, *The Mayflies of North and Central America* (Minneapolis: University of Minnesota Press, 1976), 5.

63 *ability of aquatic insects to tolerate organic and nutrient pollution*: AIB, 37.

63 *photo …depicting an "idyllic" riverine scene*: Currier Land Company brochure, ca. 1900, accessed from UWRF Archives and Area Research Center.

63 *These efforts included installing in-stream habitat structures*: Voss, *Nonpoint Source Control Plan*, 222.

63 *kinds of direct and indirect nutrient enrichment expressed in the Edmunds document*: Edmunds, Jensen, and Berner, *The Mayflies of North and Central America*, 5.

64 *water temperatures upstream of River Falls had dropped 10°F*: Voss, *Nonpoint Source Control Plan*, 222.

64 *Here is what we know*: I appreciate and acknowledge Kent Johnson's contribution to the substance and clarification of the points on this topic. Kent Johnson, e-mail message to author, December 5, 2016.

64 *based on 1996 WDNR habitat analysis*: Marty Engel, personal communication, 1998.

64 *Improved water clarity and less-organic sediment mean less filterable food*: Luke Jacobus, e-mail message to author, April 5, 2016.

64 *a significant decrease in Kinnickinnic water temperatures since the 1950s*: Voss, *Nonpoint Source Control Plan*, 222.

64 *temperature requirements (degree days) are insufficient for development of Hexagenia limbata*: Kent Johnson, e-mail message to author, December 5, 2016.

65 *The forelegs are used to gather in food …from surrounding mud*: Calvin R. Fremling, "Methods for mass-rearing *Hexagenia* mayflies (Ephemeroptera:Ephemeridae)," *Transactions of the American Fisheries Society* 96 (1967): 409.

65 *Studies show that the main food source is the sediments*: R. Dermott, "Ingestion rate of the burrowing mayfly *Hexagenia limbata* as determined with ¹⁴C," *Hydrobiologia* 83 (1981): 502.

65 *selectively obtain organic matter with a high caloric content*: Melvin C. Zimmerman and Thomas E. Wissing, "Effects of temperature on gut-loading and gut-clearing times of the burrowing mayfly, *Hexagenia limbata*," *Freshwater Biology* 8 (1978): 276.

66 *I can envision a sequence that would show with entomological support*: In the plan I'm imagining, there would be species summaries for the following historical periods: pre-Euroamerican settlement (1850), before the dawn of the conservation movement (1900), just as early conservation efforts focused on the Kinnickinnic (1950), the start of the twenty-first century (2000), and well into the coming era of climate change (2050). I can only encourage further analysis in the future.

LIFE AFTER THE SOLSTICE

70   *the high end of the optimal range for growth and survival*: Schreiber, *Kinnickinnic River Priority Watershed Surface Water Resource Appraisal Report*, 13.

71   *T. allectus …was the only one confirmed*: AIW, 11.

71   *Long slender hairs …gather habitat trash*: Justin W. Leonard and Fannie A. Leonard, *Mayflies of Michigan Trout Streams* (Bloomfield Hills: Cranbrook Institute of Science, 1962), 34.

71   *the time of the summer solstice*: I had saved a small scrap of paper on which I made notes while talking to Jim Humphrey about tricos. He told me they emerge consistently on June 21, that you could "set a clock by it." Jim Humphrey, personal communication, 2004.

71   *R. J. Hall and his colleagues studying Tricorythodes allectus …in Minnesota*: Ronald J. Hall, Lewis Berner, and Edwin F. Cook, "Observations on the biology of *Tricorythodes atratus* McDunnough (Ephemeroptera: Tricorythidae)," *Proceedings of the Entomological Society of Washington* 77 (1975): 45-48.

72   *This is generation one, members of which develop at different rates*: NAG, 54.

FLATHEADS IN PARADISE

75   *the flatheaded or flathead mayfly*: AE, 106; GAI, 58.

76   *Of the ten genera and twenty-three species of the family Heptageniidae*: AIW, 11. Many of the ten genera of heptageniids recorded by Hilsenhoff as occurring in Wisconsin are described as uncommon, rare, or very rare.

77   *sporadically seen on the Kinnickinnic between mid-May and mid-June*: Humphrey and Shogren, *Trout Streams of Wisconsin and Minnesota*, 169.

78   *Carboniferous Period, 360 to 299 million years ago*: University of California Museum of Paleontology, "The Carboniferous Period," 2011, http://www.ucmp.berkeley.edu/carboniferous/carboniferous.php.

78   *Extensive swamp forests existed across much of the landscape*: William Purves, David Sadava, Gordon Orions, and H. Craig Heller, *Life, The Science of Biology*, 7th ed. (Sunderland: Sinauer Associates, Inc., 2004), 451.

78   *lycopods (clubmosses) up to 40 meters tall*: Purves et al., *Life, The Science of Biology*, 579.

78   *land snails, insects, spiders, scorpions, and millipedes*: University of California Museum of Paleontology, "The Carboniferous Period," 2011, http://www.ucmp.berkeley.edu/carboniferous/carboniferous.php.

78   *primitive wing-joint mechanisms of mayflies and dragonflies*: These two orders of living insects with several extinct orders form the informal grouping Paleoptera (or Palaeoptera) (*paleo*- old, *-optera* - wing) indicating the wings cannot be folded against the body when at rest. The related adjectival term is *paleopterous*. Contrasting terms are Neoptera and *neopterous*.

78   *sclerite pattern arranged differently*: Donald J. Borror, Charles A. Triplehorn, and
      Norman F. Johnson, *An Introduction to the Study of Insects*, 6th ed. (Philadelphia:
      Saunders College Publishing, 1989), 33.

IN SEARCH OF LARGE SWIMMERS

83   *In their Pine-Popple River study*: William L. Hilsenhoff, Jerry L. Longridge,
      Richard P. Narf, Kenneth J. Tennessen, and Craig P. Walton, "Aquatic insects
      of the Pine-Popple River, Wisconsin," *Wisconsin Department of Natural Resources
      Technical Bulletin* 54 (1972): 12.

84   *he characterized Isonychia larvae as*: AIW, 5.

84   *In the study of the Pine-Popple River system*: Hilsenhoff et al., "Aquatic insects of the
      Pine-Popple River, Wisconsin," 12.

84   *in a study of the Brule River*: Robert B. DuBois, "Aquatic insects of the Bois Brule
      River System, Wisconsin," *Wisconsin Department of Natural Resources Technical
      Bulletin* 185 (1993): 16.

THINKING SMALL

89   *Over two dozen species of baetids are found*: AIW, 11.

90   *known widely for large population numbers*: Fred L. Arbona Jr., *Mayflies, the Angler, and
      the Trout* (Tulsa: Winchester Press, 1980), 47.

90   *write of numerically impressive hatches*: Leonard and Leonard, *Mayflies of Michigan
      Trout Streams*, 88.

90   *mention the omnipresence of Baetis in those reaches*: Humphrey and Shogren, *Trout
      Streams of Wisconsin and Minnesota*, 169.

FLYING DRAGONS AND DAMSELS

93   *with the caution that the activity regimes*: There is no question that dragonflies ingest
      mosquitoes, but the two flying insects are active at different times of day.
      Mosquitoes are crepuscular (being active at dawn and dusk) and dragonflies are
      mostly diurnal (active during daylight, especially midday). The consumption
      of mosquito larvae by dragonfly larvae (underwater) is likely significant. Greg
      Seitz, "Dragonfly Paradise," *Minnesota Conservation Volunteer*, July-August, 2016,
      12-13.

93   *"mosquito hawk" …used in conjunction with dragonfly adults*: AE, 127.

94   *In a review of Paleozoic arthropod fossils*: William A. Shear and Jarmila Kukalova-
      Peck, "The ecology of Paleozoic terrestrial arthropods: the fossil evidence,"
      Canadian Journal of Zoology 68 (1990): 1807-1834.

95   *Larvae of the only two Wisconsin genera of broad-winged damsels*: AIW, 17.

A CASE OF COOL TIMING

99   *exit the water …from late January to early April*: NAG, 72.

100   *small winter stoneflies, winter stoneflies*: GAI, 83, 86.

100   *brown stoneflies*: GAI, 84

100   *roll-winged stoneflies*: GAI, 84.

100   *because of their propensity to stay burrowed in substrate*: GAI, 84.

101   *entered a state of suspended growth and development known as diapause*: AIW, 18; K. W.
        Stewart and P. P. Harper, "Plecoptera," in *An Introduction to the Aquatic Insects of
        North America*, eds. Richard W. Merritt and Kenneth W. Cummins (Dubuque:
        Kendall/Hunt Publishing Company, 1996), 218 (Table 14A).

101   *the presence of antifreeze materials complements behavioral freeze-avoidance strategies*:
        Richard E. Lee, "Insect cold-hardiness: To freeze or not to freeze," *Bioscience* 39
        (1989): 308-313.

MACROINVERTEBRATE CANARIES

105   *a perfect match for the common stonefly*: The term *common stonefly* is used here to
        refer to a specific family of stoneflies, Perlidae. See AE, 160 and GAI, 85. An
        alternative name for this family is *golden stoneflies*. The terms "common stonefly"
        and "perlid" are used interchangeably in this essay in reference to the family.

106   *the EPT metric, a generic richness calculation*: Richard A. Lillie, Stanley W. Szczytko,
        and Michael A. Miller, *Macroinvertebrate Data Interpretation Guidance Manual*
        (Wisconsin Department of Natural Resources PUB-SS-965, 2003), 11.

LITTLE YELLOW PATTERNED STONEFLIES

109   *patterned stoneflies*: GAI, 85.

110   *eleven species of Isoperla from rivers across Wisconsin*: AIW, 23.

111   *suspended development known as diapause*: AIW, 19.

111   *may be related to evasion of fish predation*: J. Bruce Wallace and N. H. Anderson,
        "Habitat, life history, and behavioral adaptations of aquatic insects," in *An
        Introduction to the Aquatic Insects of North America*, eds. Richard W. Merritt and
        Kenneth W. Cummins (Dubuque: Kendall/Hunt Publishing Company, 1996),
        69.

A SHEEP IN WOLF'S CLOTHING

115   *for many months, feeding them on elm leaves*: Phillip H. Harden, *The stoneflies
        (Plecoptera) of Minnesota*, PhD diss., University of Minnesota, 1949, 40.

115   *acquisition by collectors*: Kenneth W. Stewart and Bill P. Stark, *Nymphs of North American Stonefly Genera (Plecoptera)* (Denton: University of North Texas Press, 1993), 428.

117   *both species are widely distributed in Wisconsin*: AIW, 19.

117   *found a definite geographic separation of the two species in Minnesota*: Phillip H. Harden and Clarence E. Mickel, "The stoneflies of Minnesota (Plecoptera)," *University of Minnesota Agricultural Experiment Station Technical Bulletin* 201 (1952): 10.

117   *Pteronarcys proteus was reported to have twelve instars*: R. P. Holdsworth Jr., "The life history and growth of *Pteronarcys proteus* Newman," *Annals of the Entomological Society of America* 34 (1941): 496.

117   *only male larvae could be determined morphologically*: Harden and Mickel, "The stoneflies of Minnesota (Plecoptera)," 9.

118   *a standard procedure ... for determining water conditions*: AIB, 37.

118   *von Humboldt expressed this idea in the early 1800s*: Andrea Wulf, *The Invention of Nature: Alexander von Humboldt's New World* (New York: Alfred A. Knopf, 2015), 87; John Muir conveyed a similar idea in his book, *My First Summer in the Sierra*, when he wrote: "When we try to pick out anything by itself, we find it hitched to everything else in the universe." originally published in 1911 in the *Atlantic Monthly* directly from his journal entry of July 27, 1869. John Muir, *My First Summer in the Sierra* (Project Gutenberg, May 26, 2010), 158.

NAKED CADDISFLIES

121   *two branches of the superorder Amphiesmenoptera*: Ralph W. Holzenthal, Roger J. Blahnik, Aysha Prather, and Karl Kjer, "Trichoptera. Caddisflies," Last modified July 20, 2010, http://tolweb.org/Trichoptera/8230/2010.07.20.

122   *how they occur by the thousands in streams and rivers*: Glenn B. Wiggins, *Larvae of the North American Caddisfly Genera (Trichoptera)*, 2nd ed. (Toronto: University of Toronto Press, 1996), 3.

123   *impressive and ubiquitous presence of hydropsychids*: Herbert H. Ross, "The Caddis Flies, or Trichoptera, of Illinois," *Bulletin of the Illinois Natural History Survey* 23 (1944): 76.

123   *the most important caddisfly living in many streams*: Hafele and Roederer, *An Angler's Guide to Aquatic Insects and Their Imitations*, 142.

ABANDONED CASES AND LIBERATED LARVAE

127   *one, two, and three species, respectively*: AIW, 33.

127   *In their annotated list of the caddisflies of Michigan Leonard and Leonard wrote*: Justin
      W. Leonard and Fannie A. Leonard, "An Annotated List of Michigan
      Trichoptera." *Occasional Papers of the Museum of Zoology, University of Michigan* 522
      (1949): 4.

128   *cloth materials attached to their clothing*: Holzenthal et al., "Trichoptera. Caddisflies,"
      http://tolweb.org/Trichoptera/8230/2010.07.20.

129   *The genus is assigned the lowest possible tolerance value*: AIB, 38.

129   *studies carried out by Tom Waters at Valley Creek*: Thomas F. Waters, "Diurnal
      periodicity in the drift of stream invertebrates," *Ecology* 43 (1962): 316-320.

HUMPLESS DRIFTERS

134   *the ultimate case will be circular in cross section*: Oliver S. Flint Jr., "The Genus
      Brachycentrus in North America, with a Proposed Phylogeny of the Genera of
      Brachycentridae (Trichoptera)," *Smithsonian Contributions to Zoology* 398 (1984): 4.

135   *observed trout feeding by poking their snouts into rocks*: LaFontaine, *Caddisflies*, 82.

136   *a semivoltine life cycle in colder streams ...of Wisconsin*: William L. Hilsenhoff, "The
      Brachycentridae (Trichoptera) of Wisconsin," *Great Lakes Entomologist* 18 (1985):
      151.

THE ALDER AND THE ALDERFLY

141   *noted that larvae serve as an important food for trout during winter*: NAG, 145.

141   *The cleric's Chalk-Stream Studies*: Charles Kingsley, "Chalk-Stream Studies." in
      Prose Idylls, New and Old, transcribed from the 1882 Macmillan and Co. edition
      by David Price, Project Gutenberg, November 5, 2014, http://www.gutenberg.
      org/files/7032/7032-h/7032-h.htm.

BEETLES IN THE STREAM, AQUATIC INHABITANTS AND ERRANT TERRESTRIALS

145   *cannot see what insects they are feeding on*: Dave Hughes, *American Fly Tying Manual*
      (Portland: Frank Amato Publications, 1986), 27.

145   *an extraordinary diversification event, a superradiation*: Toby Hunt et al., "A
      comprehensive phylogeny of beetles reveals the evolutionary origins of a
      superradiation," *Science* 318 (2007): 1913-1916.

147   *both larvae and adults, keyed*: William L. Hilsenhoff and Kurt L. Schmude,
      "Riffle beetles of Wisconsin (Coleoptera: Dryopidae, Elmidae, Lutrochidae,
      Psephenidae) with notes on distribution, habitat, and identification," *Great Lakes
      Entomologist* 25 (1992): 191-213.

148   *settings of beauty and wildness*: Macfarlane, *The Wild Places*, 173.

SMALL IN SIZE, LARGE IN NATURE

151   *there may be 20,000 species worldwide in this family*: William P. Coffman and
      Leonard C. Ferrington Jr., "Chironomidae," in *An Introduction to the Aquatic
      Insects of North America*, eds. Richard W. Merritt and Kenneth W. Cummins
      (Dubuque: Kendall/Hunt Publishing Company, 1996), 635.

152   *a larval key for 103 aquatic chironomid genera of the state*: AIW, 58-70.

152   *concentrations of 50,000 midge larvae per square meter*: Coffman and Ferrington,
      "Chironomidae," 636.

153   *Following the Hilsenhoff Biotic Index (HBI) protocol*: AIB, 31-39.

153   *Midge larvae ranked in the top five families in numerical dominance*: Numerical
      dominance indicates the contribution of a taxon to the total number of
      individuals in a sample. Description and interpretation of the metric is
      discussed in Lillie, Szczytko, and Miller, *Macroinvertebrate Data Interpretation
      Guidance Manual*, 19.

155   *the experience of taking children into the woods*: Barry Lopez, "Children in the
      Woods," in *Crossing Open Ground* (New York: Vintage Books, 1989), 147-151.

CRANE FLIES, LEATHERJACKETS, AND MOSQUITO HAWKS

158   *Greater than fifty species of crane flies live in the Midwest*: AIW, 71.

158   *Larvae of many species are aquatic or semiaquatic.*: Borror, Triplehorn, and Johnson,
      An Introduction to the Study of Insects, 535.

159   *shredders ...and predators*: George W. Byers, "Tipulidae," in *An Introduction to
      the Aquatic Insects of North America*, eds. Richard W. Merritt and Kenneth W.
      Cummins (Dubuque: Kendall/Hunt Publishing Company, 1996), 568-570
      (Table 23A).

159   *a collector-gatherer*: Byers, "Tipulidae," 568-570 (Table 23A).

160   *all common residents of Wisconsin streams*: AIW, 57.

160   *genera reported to be less common in the state*: AIW 57.

160   *Several of these genera have low tolerance*: AIB, 38-39.

160   *The order Diptera is second only to the order Coleoptera*: Borror, Triplehorn, and
      Johnson, *An Introduction to the Study of Insects*, 147.

AN ABUNDANCE OF SCUDS

164   *Crustaceans differ from insects*: Cleveland Hickman Jr., Larry S. Roberts, Allan
      Larson, and Helen I'Anson, *Integrated Principles of Zoology*, 12th ed. (New York:
      McGraw-Hill, 2004), 378.

161   *The species was named by Bousfield in the 1950s*: E. L. Bousfield, "Fresh-water amphipod crustaceans of glaciated North America," *Canadian Field-Naturalist* 72 (1958): 55-113.

165   *a number of ventrally positioned, serially arranged, paired appendages*: Robert W. Pennak, *Fresh-water Invertebrates of the United States* (New York: John Wiley & Sons, 1978), 451-452.

166   *presence as part of the nocturnal behavioral drift*: Thomas F. Waters, "The drift of stream insects," *Annual Review of Entomology* 17 (1972): 253-272; Thomas F. Waters and Jay C. Hokenstrom, "Annual production and drift of the stream amphipod *Gammarus pseudolimnaeus* in Valley Creek, Minnesota," *Limnology and Oceanography* 25 (1980): 700-710.

166   *the classic textbook and reference Fresh-water Invertebrates of the United States*: The most recent edition of this text, the 4th, published in 2001, is now authored by Douglas Grant Smith under the title *Pennak's Freshwater Invertebrates of the United States*. It includes amphipods and other crustaceans, but not insects, the author citing the emergence of a separate and comprehensive literature on aquatic insects.

166   *characterized amphipods as requiring a narrow, cold temperature range*: Pennak, *Fresh-water Invertebrates of the United States*, 455.

166   *they are an important food source for fish*: AE, 389.

166   *no surprise they are eaten by trout*: NAG, 167.

LESSONS OF THE RUSTY CRAYFISH

170   *reported this species as the most common crayfish in the state*: H. H. Hobbs III and Joan P. Jass, *The Crayfishes & Shrimp of Wisconsin (Cambaridae, Palaemonidae)* (Milwaukee: Milwaukee Public Museum, 1988), 85-86.

170   *the only crayfish that has been found in every Wisconsin county*: Ibid., 94.

170   *appendage and carapace characteristics with examination of a primary mouthpart, the mandible*: Ibid., 22.

170   *The range of O. rusticus in Wisconsin is disjunct*: Hobbs and Jass, *Crayfishes & Shrimp of Wisconsin*, 76.

171   *summarized the detrimental effects of this crayfish*: David C. Houghton, Jeffrey J. Dimick, and Richard V. Frie, "Probable displacement of riffle-dwelling invertebrates by the introduced rusty crayfish, *Orconectes rusticus* (Decapoda: Cambaridae), in a north-central Wisconsin stream," *Great Lakes Entomologist* 31 (1998): 13-24.

171   *previous studies by Mundahl and Benton*: Neal D. Mundahl and Michael J. Benton, "Aspects of the thermal ecology of the rusty crayfish *Orconectes rusticus* (Girard)," *Oecologia* 82 (1990): 210-216.

172   *Summer temperature studies on the Kinnickinnic River*: Kent Johnson, *Urban Storm
        Water Impacts on a Coldwater Resource*, Second World Congress of the Society of
        Environmental Toxicology and Chemistry (SETAC), Vancouver, BC, Canada,
        1995, http://www.rfcity.org/DocumentCenter/View/97.

172   *establishing buffers, reducing imperviousness…*: Kent Johnson and Andy
        Lamberson, "A Storm on the Horizon," Kiap-TU-Wish Chapter, Trout
        Unlimited video, uploaded February 22, 2011, https://www.youtube.com/
        watch?v=d2qVo5fRcT4.

THE YIN AND YANG OF LIVING IN CURRENT

180   *recognized three categories of drift*: Thomas F. Waters, "The drift of stream insects,"
        Annual Review of Entomology 17 (1972): 253-272.

181   *the complexity of uninterrupted laminar flow changing to turbulence*: Barry Lopez,
        "Learning to See," in *About This Life* (New York: Vintage Books, 1998), 228-
        229.

181   *the interaction of current speed and body shape is not simple.*: P. J. Gullan and P. S.
        Cranston, *The Insects: An Outline of Entomology*, 2nd ed. (Oxford: Blackwell
        Science, 2000), 222.

INSECT SURVIVAL IN EXTREME STREAMFLOW EVENTS

185   *Just over fifteen inches of rain fell on one of those days*: Minnesota Department of
        Natural Resources Climate Journal, "Heavy Rains Fall on Southeastern
        Minnesota: August 18-20, 2007," http://www.dnr.state.mn.us/climate/
        journal/ff070820.html.

186   *heaviest daily rainfall ever recorded*: Minnesota Department of Natural Resources
        Climate Journal, "24-hour Minnesota Rainfall Record Broken August 19,
        2007," http://www.dnr.state.mn.us/climate/journal/24hour_rain_record.
        html.

186   *U.S. Geological Survey gaging station*: The USGS gaging station is operated in
        cooperation with Trout Unlimited, Kinnickinnic River Land Trust, and the
        City of River Falls.

186   *A web search based on "USGS 05342000"*: "USGS 05342000 KINNICKINNIC
        RIVER NEAR RIVER FALLS, WI," http://waterdata.usgs.gov/nwis/uv
        /?site_no=05342000&agency_cd=USGS.

187   *On July 18, 1993, catastrophic flooding occurred in the Baxter's Hollow region of Otter
        Creek*: William L. Hilsenhoff, "Effects of a catastrophic flood on the insect fauna
        of Otter Creek, Sauk County, Wisconsin," *Transactions of the Wisconsin Academy
        of Sciences, Arts and Letters* 84 (1996): 103-110.

188   *Stream biologists recognize four mechanisms*: D. D. Williams and H. B. N. Hynes,
        "The recolonization mechanisms of stream benthos," *Oikos* 27 (1976): 266.

188   *it is referred to as catastrophic drift*: Waters, "The drift of stream insects," 254.

188   *suggest that stream insects respond to increased flow*: J. Bruce Wallace and N. H. Anderson, "Habitat, life history, and behavioral adaptations of aquatic insects," in *An Introduction to the Aquatic Insects of North America*, edited by Richard W. Merritt and Kenneth W. Cummins (Dubuque: Kendall/Hunt Publishing Company, 1996), 44.

PREDATORS, GRAZERS, SHREDDERS, AND COLLECTORS

192   *developed a more practical and ecological categorization plan*: Kenneth W. Cummins, "Trophic relations of aquatic insects," *Annual Review of Entomology* 18 (1973): 183-206.

193   *algae, detritus…, and small animal life, such as first instar midge larvae*: Cummins, 1973, 197.

194   *Pycnopsyche caddisfly larvae …feed similarly*: Cummins, 1973, 188, Figure 2.

194   *hatching of eggs programmed to correspond with the leaf fall in autumn*: Wiggins, 1996, 348.

195   *following up on feeding categories …a useful resource*: Bouchard, 2004, 225.

195   *Darwin's entangled bank metaphor*: Charles Darwin, *On the Origin of Species* (London: John Murray, 1859), 489. Italics within the quote were added by the author (CG).

A "HELL HOLE OF DEVIL'S BROTH"

197   *numerous agencies, organizations, and institutions, and support of the public*: These include, alphabetically: City of River Falls, Friends of the Kinni, Kinnickinnic River Land Trust, Pierce County Land Conservation Department, St. Croix County Land Conservation Department, Trout Unlimited (Kiap-TU-Wish Chapter), University of Wisconsin-River Falls, and Wisconsin Department of Natural Resources.

197   *Unsettling details of Kinnickinnic River history*: John J. Prucha and Norman A. Foss, *Kinnickinnic Years* (Syracuse: Arrow Printing, 1993), 36-39.

198   *River conditions of the earlier time were also expressed*: *River Falls Journal*, "Izaak Walton League to the Rescue," July 31, 1930. Permission to reprint excerpt granted by publisher Steve Dzubay, June 15, 2015.

199   *characterized in the video A Storm on the Horizon*: Kent Johnson and Andy Lamberson, "A Storm on the Horizon," Kiap-TU-Wish Chapter, Trout Unlimited video, uploaded February 22, 2011, https://www.youtube.com/watch?v=d2qVo5fRcT4.

200   *An estimated 3,500 to 4,000 brook and brown trout died*: Ken Schreiber, *The Parker Creek fish kill, a consequence of current manure management practices in Wisconsin* (Wisconsin Department of Natural Resources, West Central Region, 1999).

200   *Analysis of the event showed these contributing factors*: Ibid.

200   *summarized what went wrong in a 1999 report*: Ibid.

200   *"Depositing or Permitting to be Deposited Noxious Substances ..."*: State of Wisconsin, Circuit Court Document, St. Croix County, Case No. 98 FO 779, 14 January 1999.

201   *Directives in the plan were*: Ibid.

202   *a phenomenon known as thermal shock*: Johnson, "Urban Storm Water Impacts on a Coldwater Resource," http://www.rfcity.org/DocumentCenter/View/97.

202   *effects of thermal pollution on aquatic insects*: John Galli, *Thermal Impacts Associated with Urbanization and Storm Water Management Best Management Practices*, (Sediment and Stormwater Administration of the Maryland Department of the Environment, Baltimore, MD, 1990), 128-133.

202   *Research, both long-term and ongoing, centered in and around the city*: Johnson, "Urban Storm Water Impacts on a Coldwater Resource," http://www.rfcity.org/DocumentCenter/View/97.

202   *Johnson established five primary temperature recording stations*: Johnson, "Urban Storm Water Impacts on a Coldwater Resource," http://www.rfcity.org/DocumentCenter/View/9.

203   *investigated elevated temperature effects on fish as well as invertebrates*: Galli, "Thermal Impacts," 139-141.

203   *Bell, after reviewing the literature, summarized*: John M. Bell, *The Assessment of Thermal Impacts on Habitat Selection, Growth, Reproduction, and Mortality in Brown Trout (Salmo trutta L.): A Review of the Literature* (Applied Ecological Services Project 05-0206, Vermillion River EPA Grant #WS 97512701-0, 2006), 15-16.

203   *data presented for brook trout*: Paul Cunningham, Matt Diebel, Joanna Griffin, John Lyons, Matt Mitro, and John Pohlman, "Adaptation Strategies for Brook Trout Management in the Face of Climate Change," 7th Annual Driftless Area Symposium, LaCrosse, Wisconsin, 2014.

203   *Numerous resources referenced in the summary*: Robert F. Raleigh, *Habitat suitability index models: Brook trout* (U. S. Department of Interior, Fish and Wildlife Service, FWS/OBS-82/10.24, 1982), 6.

204   *city owned and managed dams increase downstream water temperatures*: Kent Johnson. *Evaluating the Thermal and Hydrological Impacts of Kinnickinnic River Hydropower Impoundments in River Falls, WI, Summary of Monitoring Results* (Kiap-TU-Wish Chapter, Trout Unlimited, 2014).

204   *High levels of imperviousness*: Kent Johnson, e-mail message to author, September 17, 2015.

205   *fine sediment is covering the gravel substrate preferable for spawning*: Thomas F. Waters, ed., *Sediment in Streams: Sources, Biological Effects, and Control*, Monograph 7 (Bethesda: American Fisheries Society, 1995).

205   *straightforward suggestions*: Johnson and Lamberson, "A Storm on the Horizon," https://www.youtube.com/watch?v=-d2qVo5fRcT4.

ADDENDUM TO A "HELL HOLE OF DEVIL'S BROTH"

206   *At the risk of using a well-worn cliche', there is a thermally significant elephant in the room*: Kent Johnson of the Kiap-TU-Wish Chapter of Trout Unlimited provided significant input on the writing of this addendum (as well as on the Thermal Pollution section of the previous essay) with his knowledge of thermal issues and the literature of climate change. I welcome not only his expertise, but his ability to make complex issues understandable for all readers. Kent Johnson, personal communication, May 7, 2017.

206   *atmospheric carbon dioxide (CO_2) measurements exceed all known historical records*: Scripps Institution of Oceanography, University of California San Diego, "The Keeling Curve," 2017, https://scripps.ucsd.edu/programs/keelingcurve/. The viewer can see an up-to-date summary graph ranging from one week to 800,000 years of CO_2 data, as well as the latest CO_2 reading from the Mauna Loa Observatory in Hawaii.

206   *Supporting information from respected sources*: National Aeronautics and Space Administration, "Climate change: How do we know?" 2017, https://climate.nasa.gov/evidence/; National Oceanic and Atmospheric Administration, "Climate Change & Global Warming," 2017, https://www.climate.gov/news-features/category/96/all.

206   *the National Geographic Climate Issue is a must-read*: National Geographic, *The Climate Issue*, November 2015.

206   *WICCI's signature report: Wisconsin's Changing Climate: Impacts and Adaptation, describes the impacts*: Wisconsin Initiative on Climate Change Impacts, "Wisconsin's Changing Climate: Impacts and Adaptations," Nelson Institute for Environmental Studies, University of Wisconsin-Madison and the Wisconsin Department of Natural Resources, Madison, Wisconsin, 2011, http://www.wicci.wisc.edu/publications.php.

206   *A recent assessment of Kiap-TU-Wish's 1992-2009 Kinnickinnic River temperature monitoring data*: Matthew Mitro, John Lyons, and Sapna Sharma, "Coldwater Fish and Fisheries Working Group Report," *Wisconsin Initiative on Climate Change Impacts*, 2011, http://www.wicci.wisc.edu/report/coldwater-fish-and-fisheries.pdf

206   *consistent with the observed warming trend in Wisconsin air temperature during the same time period*: Christopher J. Kucharik and Shawn P. Serbin, "Impacts of recent climate change on Wisconsin corn and soybean yield trends," *Environmental Research Letters* 3 (2008): 1-10. http://iopscience.iop.org/article/10.1088/1748-9326/3/3/034003/pdf.

207   *Kinnickinnic River temperatures remain suitable for trout*: Mitro, Lyons, and Sharma, "Coldwater Fish and Fisheries Working Group Report," 2011.

207   *based on thermal tolerance limits noted by Wehrly and his coauthors*: Kevin E. Wehrly, Lizhu Wang, and Matthew G. Mitro, "Field-based estimates of thermal tolerance limits for trout: incorporating exposure time and temperature fluctuation," *Transactions of the American Fisheries Society* 136 (2007): 365-374.

LISTENING TO AQUATIC INSECTS

209   *macroinvertebrate-based bioassessment protocol*: AIB, 38-39.

209   *Details of this tool were first published in 1977*: William L. Hilsenhoff, "Use of arthropods to evaluate water quality of streams," *Wisconsin Department of Natural Resources Technical Bulletin* 100 (1977).

209   *Family-level Biotic Index (FBI) procedure*: William L. Hilsenhoff, "Rapid field assessment of organic pollution with a family-level biotic index," *Journal of the North American Benthological Society* 7 (1988): 65-68.

210   *adopted its 2002 Storm Water Management Ordinance*: City of River Falls, "2002 Storm Water Management Ordinance," http://www.rfcity.org/index.aspx?NID=262.

211   *North Kinnickinnic River Monitoring Project*: City of River Falls, "Kinni River Monitoring," http://www.rfcity.org/index.aspx?NID=254.

211   *macroinvertebrate monitoring results and their relationship to temperature monitoring data*: City of River Falls, "North Kinnickinnic River Monitoring Project, 2014 Report," http://wi-riverfalls.civicplus.com/ArchiveCenter/ViewFile/Item/147.

PART IV

221   *"In the depths of the unknown …"*: Baudelaire's poem ending with this line was published in 1857. Charles Baudelaire, "VIII," in *"Les Fleurs du Mal" ("The Flowers of Evil")*, produced by Tonya Allen, Julie Barkley, Juliet Sutherland, Charles Franks, and the Online Distributed Proofreading Team, Project Gutenberg, September 11, 2012, http://www.gutenberg.org/files/6099/6099-h/6099-h.htm. I thank Kerry Keen for his translation of this phrase from French to English.

GLOSSARY

229   *The geological period from 2.6 million years ago*: "Pleistocene," *Wikipedia*, last modified on March 13, 2017, https://en.wikipedia.org/wiki/Pleistocene.

BIBLIOGRAPHY

Allen, Richard K., and George F. Edmunds Jr. "A revision of the Genus *Ephemerella* (Ephemeroptera: Ephemerellidae) VIII. The Subgenus *Ephemerella* in North America." *Miscellaneous Publications of the Entomological Society of America* 4 (1965): 244-282.

Arbona, Fred L., Jr. *Mayflies, the Angler, and the Trout.* Tulsa: Winchester Press, 1980.

Baker, Robert W. "Pleistocene History of West-Central Wisconsin." *31st Annual Midwest Friends of the Pleistocene Field Conference, Friends of the Pleistocene Field Trip Guide Book* 11, 1984.

Baker, Robert W. "Evidence for Glacial Lake River Falls, Paul Cudd and Sons Incorporated Gravel Quarry." In *Paleogeography and Structure of the St. Croix River Valley*, edited by Ian Williams, 53rd Annual Tri-State Geological Conference, 1989.

Baker, Robert W., J. F. Diehl, T. W. Simpson, L. W. Zelazny, and S. Beske-Diehl. "Pre-Wisconsinan glacial stratigraphy, chronology, and paleomagnetics of west-central Wisconsin." *Geological Society of America Bulletin* 94 (1983): 1442-1449.

Baudelaire, Charles. "VIII." In *"Les Fleurs du Mal" ("The Flowers of Evil")*, produced by Tonya Allen, Julie Barkley, Juliet Sutherland, Charles Franks, and the Online Distributed Proofreading Team. Project Gutenberg, September 11, 2012. http://www.gutenberg.org/files/6099/6099-h/6099-h.htm.

Bell, John M. *The Assessment of Thermal Impacts on Habitat Selection, Growth, Reproduction, and Mortality in Brown Trout* (Salmo trutta *L.*): A Review of the Literature. Applied Ecological Services Project 05-0206, Vermillion River EPA Grant #WS 97512701-0, (2006): 1-23.

Borger, Gary A. *Naturals: A Guide to Food Organisms of the Trout.* Harrisburg: Stackpole Books, 1980.

Borror, Donald J., Charles A. Triplehorn, and Norman F. Johnson. *An Introduction to the Study of Insects.* 6th ed. Philadelphia: Saunders College Publishing, 1989.

Bouchard, R. William, Jr. *Guide to Aquatic Invertebrates of the Upper Midwest: Identification Manual for Students, Citizen Monitors, and Aquatic Resource Professionals.* St. Paul: University of Minnesota, 2004. *Printed copies of this guide are available from Dr. Leonard C. Ferrington Jr., University of Minnesota, ferri016@umn.edu. They are $39.95 each plus $1.50/copy handling for single orders. More information is available at: http://www.entomology.umn.edu/faculty-staff/leonard-ferrington.*

Bousfield, E. L. "Fresh-water amphipod crustaceans of glaciated North America." *Canadian Field-Naturalist* 72 (1958): 55-113.

Byers, George W. "Tipulidae." In *An Introduction to the Aquatic Insects of North America*, edited by Richard W. Merritt and Kenneth W. Cummins, 549-570. Dubuque: Kendall/Hunt Publishing Company, 1996.

City of River Falls. "2002 Storm Water Management Ordinance." http://www.rfcity.org/index.aspx?NID=262.

City of River Falls. "Kinni River Monitoring." http://www.rfcity.org/index.aspx?NID=254.

City of River Falls. "North Kinnickinnic River Monitoring Project, 2014 Report." http://wi-riverfalls.civicplus.com/ArchiveCenter/ViewFile/Item/147.

Coffman, William P., and Leonard C. Ferrington Jr. "Chironomidae." In *An Introduction to the Aquatic Insects of North America*, edited by Richard W. Merritt and Kenneth W. Cummins, 635-754. Dubuque: Kendall/Hunt Publishing Company, 1996.

Cummins, Kenneth W. "Trophic relations of aquatic insects." *Annual Review of Entomology* 18 (1973): 183-206.

Cunningham, Paul, Matt Diebel, Joanna Griffin, John Lyons, Matt Mitro, and John Pohlman. "Adaptation Strategies for Brook Trout Management in the Face of Climate Change." 7th Annual Driftless Area Symposium, LaCrosse, Wisconsin, February, 2014.

Darwin, Charles. *On the Origin of Species.* London: John Murray, 1859.

Dermott, R. "Ingestion rate of the burrowing mayfly *Hexagenia limbata* as determined with ^{14}C." *Hydrobiologia* 83 (1981): 499-503.

DuBois, Robert B. "Aquatic insects of the Bois Brule River System, Wisconsin." *Wisconsin Department of Natural Resources Technical Bulletin* 185 (1993): 1-35.

Edmunds, George F., Jr., Steven L. Jensen, and Lewis Berner. *The Mayflies of North and Central America.* Minneapolis: University of Minnesota Press, 1976.

Edmunds, G. F., Jr., and R. D. Waltz. "Ephemeroptera." In *An Introduction to the Aquatic Insects of North America*, edited by Richard W. Merritt and Kenneth W. Cummins, 126-163. Dubuque: Kendall/Hunt Publishing Company, 1996.

Finley, R. W. "Map of the Original Vegetation Cover of Wisconsin." St. Paul: North Central Forest Experiment Station, USFS-USDA, 1976. Wisconsin Geological and Natural History Survey. University of Wisconsin-Extension. https://wgnhs.uwex.edu/pubs/000386/.

Flint, Oliver S., Jr. "The Genus *Brachycentrus* in North America, with a Proposed Phylogeny of the Genera of Brachycentridae (Trichoptera)." *Smithsonian Contributions to Zoology* 398 (1984): 1-58.

Fremling, Calvin R. "Methods for mass-rearing *Hexagenia* mayflies (Ephemeroptera:Ephemeridae)." *Transactions of the American Fisheries Society* 96 (1967): 407-410.

Galli, John. *Thermal Impacts Associated with Urbanization and Storm Water Management Best Management Practices.* Prepared for the Sediment and Stormwater Administration of the Maryland Department of the Environment, Baltimore, MD, 1990.

Gullan, P. J., and P. S. Cranston. *The Insects: An Outline of Entomology.* 2nd ed. Oxford: Blackwell Science, 2000.

Gunderson, Jeff. "Rusty Crayfish: A Nasty Invader." Minnesota Sea Grant, Last modified December, 2008. http://www.seagrant.umn.edu/ais/rustycrayfish_invader.

Hafele, Rick, and Scott Roederer. *An Angler's Guide to Aquatic Insects and Their Imitations.* Boulder: Johnson Books, 1995.

Hall, Ronald J., Lewis Berner, and Edwin F. Cook. "Observations on the biology of *Tricorythodes atratus* McDunnough (Ephemeroptera: Tricorythidae)." *Proceedings of the Entomological Society of Washington* 77 (1975): 34-49.

Harden, Phillip H. *The Stoneflies (Plecoptera) of Minnesota.* PhD diss., University of Minnesota, 1949.

Harden, Phillip H., and Clarence E. Mickel. "The stoneflies of Minnesota (Plecoptera)." *University of Minnesota Agricultural Experiment Station Technical Bulletin* 201 (1952): 1-84.

Hickman, Cleveland, Jr., Larry S. Roberts, Allan Larson, and Helen I'Anson. *Integrated Principles of Zoology.* 12th ed. New York: McGraw-Hill, 2004.

Hilsenhoff, William L. "Use of arthropods to evaluate water quality of streams." *Wisconsin Department of Natural Resources Technical Bulletin* 100 (1977): 1-15.

Hilsenhoff, William L. "Using a biotic index to evaluate water quality in streams." *Wisconsin Department of Natural Resources Technical Bulletin* 132 (1982): 1-22.

Hilsenhoff, William L. "The Brachycentridae (Trichoptera) of Wisconsin." *Great Lakes Entomologist* 18 (1985): 149-154.

Hilsenhoff, William L. "An improved biotic index of organic stream pollution." *Great Lakes Entomologist* 20 (1987): 31-39.

Hilsenhoff, William L. "Rapid field assessment of organic pollution with a family-level biotic index." *Journal of the North American Benthological Society* 7 (1988): 65-68.

Hilsenhoff, William L. "Aquatic insects of Wisconsin, keys to Wisconsin genera and notes on biology, habitat, distribution and species." *University of Wisconsin-Madison Natural History Museums Council Publication* 3, G3648 (1995): 1-79.

Hilsenhoff, William L. "Effects of a catastrophic flood on the insect fauna of Otter Creek, Sauk County, Wisconsin." *Transactions of the Wisconsin Academy of Sciences, Arts and Letters* 84 (1996): 103-110.

Hilsenhoff, William L., Jerry L. Longridge, Richard P. Narf, Kenneth J. Tennessen, and Craig P. Walton. "Aquatic insects of the Pine-Popple River, Wisconsin." *Wisconsin Department of Natural Resources Technical Bulletin* 54 (1972): 1-42.

Hilsenhoff, William L., and Steven J. Billmyer. "Perlodidae (Plecoptera) of Wisconsin." *Great Lakes Entomologist* 6 (1973): 1-14.

Hilsenhoff, William L., and Kurt L. Schmude. "Riffle beetles of Wisconsin (Coleoptera: Dryopidae, Elmidae, Lutrochidae, Psephenidae) with notes on distribution, habitat, and identification." *Great Lakes Entomologist* 25 (1992): 191-213.

Hobbs, H. H., III, and Joan P. Jass. *The Crayfishes & Shrimp of Wisconsin (Cambaridae, Palaemonidae).* Milwaukee: Milwaukee Public Museum, 1988.

Holdsworth, R. P., Jr. "The life history and growth of *Pteronarcys proteus* Newman." *Annals of the Entomological Society of America* 34 (1941): 495-502.

Holzenthal, Ralph W., Roger J. Blahnik, Aysha Prather, and Karl Kjer. "Trichoptera. Caddisflies." Last modified July 20, 2010. http://tolweb.org/Trichoptera/8230/2010.07.20.

Houghton, David C., Jeffrey J. Dimick, and Richard V. Frie. "Probable displacement of riffle-dwelling invertebrates by the introduced rusty crayfish, *Orconectes rusticus* (Decapoda: Cambaridae), in a north-central Wisconsin stream." *Great Lakes Entomologist* 31 (1998): 13-24.

Hughes, Dave. *American Fly Tying Manual.* Portland: Frank Amato Publications, 1986.

Humphrey, J. R. "The Kinnie." *Fly Fisherman Magazine*, July, 1989, 32-35.

Humphrey, Jim, and Bill Shogren. *Trout Streams of Wisconsin and Minnesota.* 2nd ed. Woodstock: Backcountry Guides, 2001.

Hunt, Toby, Johannes Bergsten, Zuzana Levkanicova, Anna Papadopoulou, Oliver St. John, Ruth Wild, Peter M. Hammond, Dirk Ahrens, Michael Balke, Michael S. Caterino, Jesús Gómez-Zurita, Ignacio Ribera, Timothy G. Barraclough, Milada Bocakova, Ladislav Bocak, and Alfried P. Vogler. "A comprehensive phylogeny of beetles reveals the evolutionary origins of a superradiation." *Science* 318 (2007): 1913-1916.

Hyman, Libbie H. *The Invertebrates.* 6 vols. New York: McGraw-Hill, 1940-1967.

International Commission on Zoological Nomenclature (ICZN). "What's in a name? Scientific names for animals in popular writing." http://iczn.org/content/what%E2%80%99s-name-scientific-names-animals-popular-writing#.

Jacobus, Luke M., and W. P. McCafferty. "Revisionary contributions to North American *Ephemerella* and *Serratella* (Ephemeroptera: Ephemerellidae)." *Journal of the New York Entomological Society* 111 (2003): 174-193.

Johnson, Kent. "Urban Storm Water Impacts on a Coldwater Resource." The Second World Congress of the Society of Environmental Toxicology and Chemistry (SETAC), Vancouver, BC, Canada, 1995. http://www.rfcity.org/DocumentCenter/View/97.

Johnson, Kent. *Evaluating the Thermal and Hydrological Impacts of Kinnickinnic River Hydropower Impoundments in River Falls, WI, Summary of Monitoring Results.* Kiap-TU-Wish Chapter, Trout Unlimited, 2014.

Johnson, Kent, and Andy Lamberson. "A Storm on the Horizon." Kiap-TU-Wish Chapter, Trout Unlimited video. Uploaded on February 22, 2011. https://www.youtube.com/watch?v=d2qVo5fRcT4.

Kingsley, Charles. "Chalk-Stream Studies." In *Prose Idylls, New and Old*, transcribed from the 1882 Macmillan and Co. edition by David Price. Project Gutenberg, November 5, 2014. http://www.gutenberg.org/files/7032/7032-h/7032-h.htm.

Kinnickinnic River Land Trust. "Ecology." http://kinniriver.org/kinnickinnic-river/ecology/.

Kucharik, Christopher J., and Shawn P. Serbin. "Impacts of recent climate change on Wisconsin corn and soybean yield trends." *Environmental Research Letters* 3 (2008): 1-10. http://iopscience.iop.org/article/10.1088/1748-9326/3/3/034003/pdf.

LaFontaine, Gary. *Caddisflies.* Guilford: The Lyons Press, 1981.

Lamarck, Jean-Baptiste Pierre Antoine de Monet, Chevalier de. *Natural History of Invertebrates.* 7 vols. 1815-1822.

Lee, Richard E., Jr. "Insect cold-hardiness: To freeze or not to freeze." *Bioscience* 39 (1989): 308-313.

Lenat, David R. "Water quality assessment of streams using a qualitative collection method for benthic invertebrates." *Journal of the North American Benthological Society* 7 (1988): 222-233.

Leonard, Justin W. "The nymph of *Ephemerella excrucians* Walsh." *Canadian Entomologist* 81 (1949): 158-160.

Leonard, Justin W., and Fannie A. Leonard. *Mayflies of Michigan Trout Streams.* Bloomfield Hills: Cranbrook Institute of Science, 1962.

Leonard, Justin W., and Fannie A. Leonard. "An Annotated List of Michigan Trichoptera." *Occasional Papers of the Museum of Zoology, University of Michigan* 522 (1949): 1-35.

Lillie, Richard A., Stanley W. Szczytko, and Michael A. Miller. *Macroinvertebrate Data Interpretation Guidance Manual.* Wisconsin Department of Natural Resources PUB-SS-965 (2003): 1-57.

Lopez, Barry. "Children in the Woods." In *Crossing Open Ground*, 147-151. New York: Vintage Books, 1989.

Lopez, Barry. "Learning to See." In *About This Life*, 223-239. New York: Vintage Books, 1998.

Macfarlane, Robert. *The Wild Places.* New York: Penguin Books, 2007.

Marsh, James M. "Field Notebook 151 (Exterior Boundary Surveys)." In *Wisconsin, Commissioners of Public Lands, Surveyors' Field Notes, 1832-1865.* (microfilm for 1847 notes accessed through University Archives and Area Research Center, University of Wisconsin-River Falls).

Martin, Martin. *A Voyage to St. Kilda, 1697.* London: Dan Browne, 1698. Grian Press, 2011, http://www.grianpress.com/SKW/Martin/Voyage_to_St_Kilda.html.

McCafferty, W. Patrick. *Aquatic Entomology: The Fishermen's and Ecologists' Illustrated Guide to Insects and Their Relatives.* Boston: Jones and Bartlett Publishers, 1981.

McFadden, James T., and Edwin L. Cooper. "An ecological comparison of six populations of Brown Trout (*Salmo trutta*)." *Transactions of the American Fisheries Society* 91 (1962): 53-62.

Minnesota Department of Natural Resources Climate Journal. "Heavy Rains Fall on Southeastern Minnesota: August 18-20, 2007." http://www.dnr.state.mn.us/climate/journal/ff070820.html.

Minnesota Department of Natural Resources Climate Journal. "24-hour Minnesota Rainfall Record Broken August 19, 2007." http://www.dnr.state.mn.us/climate/journal/24hour_rain_record.html.

Mitro, Matthew, John Lyons, and Sapna Sharma. "Coldwater Fish and Fisheries Working Group Report." *Wisconsin Initiative on Climate Change Impacts*, 2011, http://www.wicci.wisc.edu/report/coldwater-fish-and-fisheries.pdf.

Muir, John. *My First Summer in the Sierra.* Project Gutenberg, May 26, 2010. http://www.gutenberg.org/files/32540/32540-h/32540-h.htm.

Mundahl, Neal D., and Michael J. Benton. "Aspects of the thermal ecology of the rusty crayfish *Orconectes rusticus* (Girard)." *Oecologia* 82 (1990): 210-216.

National Aeronautics and Space Administration. "Climate change: How do we know?" 2017. https://climate.nasa.gov/evidence/.

National Geographic. *The Climate Issue.* November 2015.

National Oceanic and Atmospheric Administration. "Climate Change & Global Warming." 2017. https://www.climate.gov/news-features/category/96/all.

Nebeker, Alan V., and Armond E. Lemke. "Preliminary studies on the tolerance of aquatic insects to heated waters." *Journal of the Kansas Entomological Society* 41 (1968): 413-418.

Neill, Edward D., and J. Fletcher Williams. *History of Washington County and the St. Croix Valley, including the Explorers and Pioneers of Minnesota, and Outlines of the History of Minnesota*. Minneapolis: North Star Publishing Company, 1881.

Pennak, Robert W. *Fresh-water Invertebrates of the United States*. New York: John Wiley & Sons, 1978.

Prucha, John J., and Norman A. Foss. *Kinnickinnic Years*. Syracuse: Arrow Printing, 1993.

Purves, William K., David Sadava, Gordon H. Orions, and H. Craig Heller. *Life, The Science of Biology*. 7th ed. Sunderland: Sinauer Associates, Inc., 2004.

Raleigh, Robert F. *Habitat suitability index models: Brook trout*. U. S. Department of Interior, Fish and Wildlife Service, FWS/OBS-82/10.24 (1982): 1-42.

Randolph, R. Patrick, and W. Patrick McCafferty. "Diversity and distribution of the mayflies (Ephemeroptera) of Illinois, Indiana, Kentucky, Michigan, Ohio, and Wisconsin." *Bulletin of the Ohio Biological Survey* 13 (1998): 1-188.

River Falls Journal. "Izaak Walton League to the Rescue," July 31, 1930. Permission to reprint excerpt granted by publisher Steve Dzubay, June 15, 2015.

Ross, Herbert H. "The Caddis Flies, or Trichoptera, of Illinois." *Bulletin of the Illinois Natural History Survey* 23 (1944): 1-326.

Rufer, Moriya M., and Leonard Ferrington Jr. "Volunteer Stream Monitoring Interactive Verification Program (VSM-IVP), Version 1." September, 2006. http://midge.cfans.umn.edu/vsmivp/.

Runkel, A. C. "Minnesota at a Glance Ancient Tropical Seas - Paleozoic History of Southeastern Minnesota." Minnesota Geological Survey. Last modified June, 2002. http://conservancy.umn.edu/bitstream/handle/11299/59447/Paleozoic_bdrk.pdf?sequence=27&isAllowed=y.

Schreiber, Ken. *Kinnickinnic River Priority Watershed Surface Water Resource Appraisal Report*. Wisconsin Department of Natural Resources, West Central Region, 1998.

Schreiber, Ken. *The Parker Creek fish kill: A consequence of current manure management practices in Wisconsin*. Wisconsin Department of Natural Resources, West Central Region, 1999.

Scripps Institution of Oceanography, University of California San Diego. "The Keeling Curve." 2017. https://scripps.ucsd.edu/programs/keelingcurve/.

Shear, William A., and Jarmila Kukalova-Peck. "The ecology of Paleozoic terrestrial arthropods: the fossil evidence." *Canadian Journal of Zoology* 68 (1990): 1807-1834.

Seitz, Greg. "Dragonfly Paradise." *Minnesota Conservation Volunteer*, July-August, 2016, 12-13.

Stewart, K. W., and P. P. Harper. "Plecoptera." In *An Introduction to the Aquatic Insects of North America*, edited by Richard W. Merritt and Kenneth W. Cummins, 217-266. Dubuque: Kendall/Hunt Publishing Company, 1996.

Stewart, Kenneth W., and Bill P. Stark. *Nymphs of North American Stonefly Genera (Plecoptera)*. Denton: University of North Texas Press, 1993.

University of California Museum of Paleontology. "The Carboniferous Period." Last modified June 30, 2011.
http://www.ucmp.berkeley.edu/carboniferous/carboniferous.php.

United States Geological Survey. "USGS 05342000 KINNICKINNIC RIVER NEAR RIVER FALLS, WI."
http://waterdata.usgs.gov/wi/nwis/uv/?site_no=05342000.

Voss, Karen, ed. *Nonpoint Source Control Plan for the Kinnickinnic River Priority Watershed Project*. Wisconsin Department of Natural Resources Publication WT-522, 1999.
http://dnr.wi.gov/topic/nonpoint/documents/9kep/Kinnickinnic_River-St_Croix_Co.pdf.

Wallace, J. Bruce, and N. H. Anderson. "Habitat, life history, and behavioral adaptations of aquatic insects." In *An Introduction to the Aquatic Insects of North America*, edited by Richard W. Merritt and Kenneth W. Cummins, 41-73. Dubuque: Kendall/Hunt Publishing Company, 1996.

Waters, Thomas F. "Diurnal periodicity in the drift of stream invertebrates." *Ecology* 43 (1962): 316-320.

Waters, Thomas F. "The drift of stream insects." *Annual Review of Entomology* 17 (1972): 253-272.

Waters, Thomas F., and Jay C. Hokenstrom. "Annual production and drift of the stream amphipod *Gammarus pseudolimnaeus* in Valley Creek, Minnesota." *Limnology and Oceanography* 25 (1980): 700-710.

Waters, Thomas F., ed. *Sediment in Streams: Sources, Biological Effects, and Control*. Monograph 7. Bethesda: American Fisheries Society, 1995.

Wehrly, Kevin E., Lizhu Wang, and Matthew G. Mitro. "Field-based estimates of thermal tolerance limits for trout: incorporating exposure time and temperature fluctuation." *Transactions of the American Fisheries Society* 136 (2007): 365-374.

Wiggins, Glenn B. *Larvae of the North American Caddisfly Genera (Trichoptera)*. 2nd ed. Toronto: University of Toronto Press, 1996.

Wikipedia, "Pleistocene." Last modified March 13, 2017,
https://en.wikipedia.org/wiki/Pleistocene.

Williams, D. D., and H. B. N. Hynes. "The recolonization mechanisms of stream benthos." *Oikos* 27 (1976): 265-272.

Wilson, E. O. *The Diversity of Life*. Cambridge: Harvard University Press, 1992.

Wisconsin Department of Natural Resources. *Guidelines for Evaluating Habitat of Wadable Streams*. Bureau of Fisheries Management and Habitat Protection, Monitoring and Data Assessment Section, July, 2000.

Wisconsin Department of Natural Resources. "Wisconsin State Natural Areas Program Kinnickinnic Wet Prairie (No. 383)." http://dnr.wi.gov/topic/Lands/naturalareas/index.asp?SNA=583.

Wisconsin Initiative on Climate Change Impacts. "Wisconsin's Changing Climate: Impacts and Adaptations." Nelson Institute for Environmental Studies, University of Wisconsin-Madison and the Wisconsin Department of Natural Resources, Madison, Wisconsin, 2011. http://www.wicci.wisc.edu/publications.php.

Wisconsin, State of. Circuit Court Document, St. Croix County, Case No. 98 FO 779, 14 January 1999.

Wulf, Andrea. *The Invention of Nature: Alexander von Humboldt's New World.* New York: Alfred A. Knopf, 2015.

Zimmerman, Melvin C., and Thomas E. Wissing. "Effects of temperature on gut-loading and gut-clearing times of the burrowing mayfly, *Hexagenia limbata.*" *Freshwater Biology* 8 (1978): 269-277.

TABLES

TABLE 1. KINNICKINNIC RIVER INSECT STUDY SAMPLE SITES

Collection Site Number*	Collection Site Name	River mile(s) from St. Croix River
1	Kinnickinnic River State Park	0.5
1B	Kinnickinnic River State Park (alternate collection site**)	1.6
2	County Highway F	2.1
3	Lower Kinni 3†	3.8
4	Lower Kinni 4†	5.4
5	Lower Kinni 5†	6.5
6	Confluence with Rocky Branch	8.4
7	Division Street, City of River Falls	10.0
8	State Highway 35	10.8
9	Quarry Road	12.8
10	Liberty Road	14.6
11	North River Road	16.0
12	County Highway JJ	17.4
13	County Highway J	18.0
14	Steeple Drive	18.9
15	County Highway N	20.6
16	Interstate 94	21.4
17	140th Street	22.4

*Site numbers, site locations, and river miles are based on WDNR habitat evaluation data collected in 1996 (M. Engel, personal communication, 1998).

**Collection site utilized during high water at Site 1.

†Sites designated Lower Kinni with site numbers were accessed by water, or overland by permission of landowner.

TABLE 2. COMMONLY COLLECTED INSECTS AND CRUSTACEANS
OF THE KINNICKINNIC RIVER, 2001

Order	Family	Genus/species
Ephemeroptera		
	Ephemerellidae	*Ephemerella excrucians*
		Ephemerella needhami
	Leptohyphidae	*Tricorythodes allectus*
	Heptageniidae	*Stenonema vicarium*
	Baetidae	*Baetis brunneicolor*
		Baetis tricaudatus
Plecoptera		
	Taeniopterygidae	*Taeniopteryx nivalis*
	Perlodidae	*Isoperla slossonae*
Trichoptera		
	Hydropsychidae	*Ceratopsyche alhedra*
		Ceratopsyche alternans
		Ceratopsyche slossonae
		Cheumatopsyche sp.
	Brachycentridae	*Brachycentrus occidentalis*
Megaloptera		
	Sialidae	*Sialis sp.*
Coleoptera		
	Elmidae	*Optioservus fastiditus* (l+a)†
Diptera*		
	Tipulidae	*Antocha* sp.
		Dicranota sp.
Amphipoda		
	Gammaridae	*Gammarus pseudolimnaeus* (l+a)†
Isopoda		
	Asellidae	*Caecidotea racovitzai*

*excepting Chironomidae

†Both larvae and adults of riffle beetles (Elmidae) and scuds (Gammaridae) were collected and counted.

TABLE 3. LARVAL MAYFLY COLLECTIONS FROM THE KINNICKINNIC RIVER BY SITE

Genus/species	|	Collection site number															
	1	2	3	4	5	6	7	8	9	10	11	12	13	14	15	16	17
Ephemerella needhami	□	●	●	●	●	●	●	●	●	●	●	●	●	●	●	●	●
Ephemerella excrucians	●	●	●	●	●	●	●	●	●	●	●	●	●	●	●	●	
Timpanoga (Dannella) simplex									●		●	●	●				
Hexagenia sp.	●																
Tricorythodes allectus	●	●	●	●	●	●	■	●		■				●			
Stenonema mediopunctatum	●	●	●	●	●	●											
Stenonema vicarium	●	●	●	●	●	●	●	●	●	●							
Stenacron interpunctatum	●	●		●	●	●		●									
Isonychia sp.	■	●		●													
Acentrella sp.	●	●	●	●	●	●	●	■		●							
Baetis brunneicolor	●	●	●	●	●	●	●	●	●	●	●	●	●	●	●	●	●
Baetis flavistriga	●	●	●	●	●	●	●	●	●	●	■	●	●	●			●
Baetis tricaudatus	●	●	●	●	●	●	●	●	●	●	●	●	●	●	●	●	●
Plauditis punctiventris	●	●	●	●	●	●	●	●	●	●	■	●	■				

● = 2001 site collection; □ = 2001 alternate site (1B) collection;

■ = site collection during 1999 pilot study not repeated in 2001

TABLE 4. LARVAL STONEFLY COLLECTIONS FROM THE KINNICKINNIC RIVER BY SITE

Genus/species	Collection site number																
	1	2	3	4	5	6	7	8	9	10	11	12	13	14	15	16	17
Taeniopteryx sp.	●	●	●	●	●	●	●	●	●	●	●	●	●	●	●	●	●
Paragnetina media	●	●	●	●	●	●	●	●									
Perlesta decipiens	●	■	●	●	●	●											
Isoperla bilineata	●	●	●	●													
Isoperla transmarina	●	●	●	●	●	■	●		■								
Isoperla slossonae	●	●	●	●	●	●	●	●	●	●		●	●	●			
Isoperla dicala	●	●	●	●	■	●		●	■								
Pteronarcys pictetii	●	●	●	●	●	●		■	■	●							

● = 2001 site collection; □ = 2001 alternate site (1B) collection;
■ = site collection during 1999 pilot study not repeated in 2001

TABLE 5. LARVAL CADDISFLY COLLECTIONS FROM THE KINNICKINNIC RIVER BY SITE

Genus/species	1	2	3	4	5	6	7	8	9	10	11	12	13	14	15	16	17
Ceratopsyche alhedra	●	●	●	●	●	●	●	●	●								
Ceratopsyche alternans	●	●	●	●	●	●		■	●								
Ceratopsyche slossonae	●	●	●	●	●	●	●	●	●	●	●	●	●	●	●	●	■
Cheumatopsyche sp.	●	●	●	●	●	●	●	●		●	●	●	●		●		
Hydropsyche betteni	●	●	●	●		●	●				●	●	●		●		
Glossosoma sp.	●	●	■	●	●	●	●	●	●		●			●	●	●	●
Protoptila sp.	■	●	●	●	●	■	●		●								
Brachycentrus occidentalis	●	●	●	●	●	●	●	●	●	●	●	●	●	●	●	●	●

Collection site number

● = 2001 site collection; □ = 2001 alternate site (1B) collection;
■ = site collection during 1999 pilot study not repeated in 2001

TABLE 6. ALDERFLY, BEETLE, TRUE FLY, SCUD, AND ISOPOD COLLECTIONS FROM THE KINNICKINNIC RIVER BY SITE

ORDER — Family/genus/species	1	2	3	4	5	6	7	8	9	10	11	12	13	14	15	16	17
MEGALOPTERA																	
Sialidae, Sialis sp.		■			●		●	●	●	●	●	●	●	●	●	●	●
COLEOPTERA*																	
Dryopidae, Helichus striatus	●	●	■	●	●	●	●	■	●	●	●	■	●				●
Elmidae, Optioservus fastiditus	●	●	●	●	●	●	●	●	●	●	●	●	●	●	●	●	●
DIPTERA																	
Tiptulidae, Antocha sp.	●	●	●	●	●	●	●	●	●	●	●	●	●	●	●	●	●
Tipulidae, Dicranota sp.	●	●	●	●	●	■	●	●	●	●	●	●	●	●	●		■
Tipulidae, Tipula sp.	●	●	●	●	●	●	●	●	●	●	●	●	●	●	●	●	●
Tipulidae, Pilaria sp.			●														
Athericidae, Atherix variegata	●	●	●	●	●	●	■										
AMPHIPODA*																	
Gammaridae, Gammarus pseudolimnaeus	●	●	●	●	●	●	●	●	●	●	●	●	●	●	●	●	●
ISOPODA*																	
Asellidae, Caecidotea racovitzai	●	●	●	●	●	●	●	●	●		●	●	●	●	●	●	●

Collection site number

● = 2001 site collection; □ = 2001 alternate site (1B) collection;
■ = site collection during 1999 pilot study not repeated in 2001

*Both larvae and adults of riffle beetles (Dryopidae and Elmidae), scuds, and isopods (Gammaridae and Asellidae) were collected and counted.

ILLUSTRATION SOURCES

All photographs accompanying the essays were acquired by the author with the exceptions of those prefacing *Looking and Learning*, created by Charlie Rader (used with permission) and *Postscript*, taken by an unknown photographer (provided by UWRF Archives and Area Research Center). Drawn illustrations were generated from Kinnickinnic River specimen photos or redrawn from the literature references acknowledged in the following summary list.

Drawing acknowledgments by pages and figure numbers:

> *Hexagenia* - Edmunds, Jensen, Berner 1976, p. 285, Fig. 427
> *Tricorythodes* - Burks 1953, p. 45, Fig. 96
> *Baetis* - Burks 1953, p. 131, Fig. 298
> *Taeniopteryx* - Fullington and Stewart 1980, p. 247, Fig. 5
> Common net-spinner - Wiggins 1996, p. 139, Fig. 7.5
> *Glossosoma* excluding case - Wiggins 1996, p. 61, Fig. 1.4A
> *Stenelmis* - Pennak 1978, p. 652, Fig. 447G
> *Chironomus* - Pennak 1978, p. 693, Fig. 472(H) and p. 696, Fig. 474(J)
> Crayfish - Pennak 1978, p. 467, Fig. 322

Drawing sources:

Burks, B. D. "The Mayflies, or Ephemeroptera, of Illinois." *Illinois Natural History Survey Bulletin* 26 (1953): 1-216.

Edmunds, George F., Jr., Steven L. Jensen, and Lewis Berner. *The Mayflies of North and Central America*. Minneapolis: University of Minnesota Press, 1976.

Fullington, Kate E., and K. W. Stewart. "Nymphs of the stonefly genus *Taeniopteryx* (Plecoptera: Taeniopterygidae) of North America." *Journal of the Kansas Entomological Society* 53 (1980): 237-259.

Pennak, Robert W. *Fresh-water Invertebrates of the United States*. New York: John Wiley & Sons, 1978.

Wiggins, Glenn B. *Larvae of the North American Caddisfly Genera (Trichoptera)*. 2nd ed. Toronto: University of Toronto Press, 1996.

ORGANIZATIONS

Organizations dedicated to the health and preservation of the Kinnickinnic River

City of River Falls
   http://www.rfcity.org/index.aspx?nid=251 (Storm Water)
   Engineering Department
   River Falls, WI 54022
   715-426-3409

Friends of the Kinni
   http://www.friendsofthekinni.org/
   friendsofthekinni@gmail.com

Kiap-TU-Wish Chapter of Trout Unlimited
   http://www.kiaptuwish.org/
   kiaptuwish@hotmail.com
   P.O. Box 483
   Hudson, WI 54016

Kinnickinnic River Land Trust
   http://kinniriver.org/
   info@kinniriver.org
   265 Mound View Road, Suite C
   P.O. Box 87
   River Falls, WI 54022
   715-425-5738
   715-425-5771 fax

Kinni Consortium
   http://kinniconsortium.org/index.html
   324 Agricultural Science Building
   University of Wisconsin-River Falls
   611 South 3rd Street
   River Falls, WI 54022

Pierce County Land Conservation Department
   http://www.co.pierce.wi.us/Land%20Conservation/Land_Conservation_Main.php
   Pierce County Office Building, Room 12
   412 West Kinne Street
   P.O. Box 67
   Ellsworth, WI 54011
   715-273-6763
   715-273-1123 fax

St. Croix County Land Conservation Department
http://www.co.saint-croix.wi.us/resourcemgt
Community Development, Resource Management Division
1960 8th Avenue, Suite 140
Baldwin, WI 54002
715-531-1930

United States Geological Survey
https://waterdata.usgs.gov/usa/nwis/uv?05342000
National Water Information System
USGS Water Resources
U.S. Department of the Interior
1-888-ASK-USGS (1-888-275-8747)

Wisconsin Department of Natural Resources
http://dnr.wi.gov
DNR Satellite Center
890 Spruce Street
Baldwin, WI 54002
715-684-2914
715-684-5940 fax

ACKNOWLEDGMENTS

For unwavering support during the writing and compilation of these essays, I express heartfelt appreciation to my wife, Susan, and my daughter, Dana.

I began writing about river insects and crustaceans with a piece on the biology of scuds prepared for *RipRap*, the newsletter of the Kiap-TU-Wish Chapter of Trout Unlimited. Jonathan Jacobs, then editor, published the story, suggesting it could become the first of a regular series of articles on entomology and ecology. I thank Jonathan for identifying potential interest and providing the stimulus to write more.

After several years of sharing stories through *RipRap*, I began submitting for the entomology column of *Midwest Fly Fishing*, thanks to Tom Helgeson, editor and publisher of the magazine. I remain indebted to Tom for the opportunity he gave me to write about stream creatures and his long-term commitment to accounts of my river work and its outcomes.

With positive feedback generated by these earlier experiences, I embarked on creation of a sequence of new narratives, reworked earlier ones at length, and ultimately shared several with colleague, friend, and fly fisher Ken Olson. Ken's positive comments were an inspiration to record further accounts of invertebrate river life, and in some way make them available to potential readers. I am grateful to Ken for his hearty, and timely, encouragement.

For review of the essay compilation following its initial assembly I thank my friend and river-minded colleague Kent Johnson. Kent's background in aquatic entomology and years of dedicated work on the health of the Kinnickinnic River made him an ideal reviewer. With his notable perspective on coldwater streams and knowledge of conditions that allow cold-adapted life to thrive the entire collection improved significantly. Beyond the reviewing process, Kent generously contributed concepts and content on thermal issues as these topics arose in specific essays.

I am very grateful to Kay Keller for taking on the job of editing the essays. Kay provided expertise from the perspective of an accomplished writer with strong language skills and as a general reader. Kay promised to be tough, and followed through in due order. Her consistent and tireless suggestions throughout the process were a significant contribution to the narratives.

For proofreading the essays I am appreciative of the meticulous work of Jonathan Jacobs. Jonathan added the expertise of writer, editor, fly fisher, and fly fishing instructor to the job of proofreading. His willingness to work beyond the basics of proofreading, including providing valuable phraseology suggestions, greatly increased readability of the stories.

It was a pleasure working with Sally Shepherd and Steve Delmont of Romeii, LLC, on presentation of the collection. Sally moved the project from manuscript to book format with efficiency and creativity. I thank her for her methodical approach and thoughtful suggestions as layout progressed. I also appreciate Sally's continued patience through the process.

I also want to thank former publisher of the *River Falls Journal*, Steve Dzubay, for permission to reprint the 1930 article excerpt.

~⁄ι∖~

For support of the macroinvertebrate survey work on which much of the assemblage is based I thank these organizations and institutions: Kiap-TU-Wish Chapter of Trout Unlimited; Wisconsin Department of Natural Resources; Wisconsin Academy of Sciences, Arts, and Letters (Lois Almon Small Grants Program); Department of Biology, University of Wisconsin-River Falls; and UWRF Foundation (1998-99 Kettelkamp-Lieneman Professorship funded by A. Duane and Phyllis Anderson).

I am grateful to the following for assistance on my Kinnickinnic insect projects and this compilation in various ways: Michael Alwin, Bob Baker, Raymond Bouchard, Eve Day, Jeffrey Dimick, Marty Engel, David Etnier, Roger Fairbanks, Len Ferrington Jr., Brad Gee, Kevin Greaser, Jennifer Hermey, William Hilsenhoff, Ralph Holzenthal, Jim Humphrey, Luke Jacobus, Kerry Keen, Bob Kinderman, Karen Klyczek, Bob Loch, Michelle Marko, R. Pat McCafferty, Zane McCallister, Heather McElwain, Dave McKinney, Rick McMonagle, Mike Middleton, Darby Nelson, Dave Norling, Northwoods Friends of the Arts Writers Group (Ellie Larmouth, leader), Kathryn Otto, In-grid Peterson, Tim Popple, Charlie Rader, W. Pat Randolph, Andy Roth, Kurt Schmude, Ken Schreiber, Guenter Schuster, Eric Secrist, Stan Szczytko, Tom Waters, and John Wheeler. I appreciate, too, the consideration of landowners along the Kinnickinnic who granted permission to access river sites through their properties.

In spite of considerable help from all of these generous people, I alone am responsible for any inaccuracies.

〜ﾉ\〜

Lastly, I want to pay homage to the Kinnickinnic, this river that summoned me for a closer look, captured my attention, and wouldn't let go. May it always be a source of curiosity, inspiration, and reflection. May it forever flow clear, cold, and free.

MACROINVERTEBRATE INVENTORY DATA SHEET

Macroinvertebrate Inventory Data Sheet	
Stream name , DNR waterbody code	Kinnickinnic River, 2601800
DNR subwatershed name	LKS RFS SFS MKS UKS
DNR station number and river mile	Station number: River mile:
Township and range	Township N: 27 28 29 30 Range W: 17 18 19 20
Section and quarter	Section: Quarter: NW NE SW SE
GPS (UTM) position	15 05 ___ ____ E 49 ___ ____ N
GPS waypoint name	
Collector's name	Clarke Garry
Sampling date (YYYY-MM-DD)	2001- ____ - ____
Stream status relative to normal	N (circle N if normal)
Meteorological conditions	
Collection time (start and end)	Start: End:
Temperatures: air, water	Air (°C): Water (°C):
Habitat photo(s)	Roll #: Frame #:
Other photo documentation	
Ten samples taken to be representative of the habitat diversity of the 100m macroinvertebrate station *Note number of each sample to take; check mark when each is taken.* *Rock categories:* *bedrock* *boulder = >25 cm* *rubble/cobble = 6.5-24 cm* *gravel = 2.0 mm-6.4 cm* *sand = < 01.9 mm* *silt = < 0.06 mm*	☐ riffle (rock based) ☐ riffle (mixed substr) ☐ cobble ☐ cobble + gravel ☐ gravel ☐ gravel + sand ☐ sand ☐ sand + silt ☐ silt ☐ silt + detritus ☐ submerged vegetation ☐ snag + detritus ☐ overhanging bank veg ☐ gravel + sand + silt ☐ detritus (leaves, etc.)
Assigned sample number:	

ABOUT THE AUTHOR

Clarke Garry earned his bachelor's degree in zoology from the University of Missouri and master's and PhD degrees in entomology from the University of Missouri and University of Wisconsin-Madison. He retired after thirty years as professor of biology at the University of Wisconsin-River Falls where he taught General Zoology and Entomology for undergraduates.

While teaching at UWRF, Garry received the *Outstanding Faculty Member* and *Outstanding Faculty Scholarship* awards in the Science and Mathematics Division, College of Arts and Sciences. The Kiap-TU-Wish Chapter of Trout Unlimited presented him with their *Recognition Award* for a "critical project documenting the insects of the Kinnickinnic River that will be invaluable in monitoring the overall health of the river in years to come."

Insect studies have taken Garry to the North Slope of Alaska, the northern Yukon Territory, inland landscapes east and west of Hudson Bay, and foothills of the Andes in Colombia, South America. He received a grant from the National Geographic Society to study ground beetles of the tundra-boreal forest transition zone of northern Manitoba.

Made in the USA
Columbia, SC
15 July 2017